THE UNITED STATES AND MEXICO: FACE TO FACE WITH NEW TECHNOLOGY

Cathryn L. Thorup and contributors:

Alan Madian
Mauricio de Maria y Campos
James K. Galbraith
James P. Womack
Susan Walsh Sanderson
M. Patricia Fernández Kelly
Cassio Luiselli Fernández
Joan Brodovsky

Series editors:
Richard E. Feinberg
Valeriana Kallab

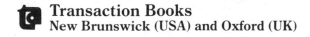
Transaction Books
New Brunswick (USA) and Oxford (UK)

Library of Congress Catalog Number: 86-50514
ISBN: 0-88738-120-0 (cloth)
ISBN: 0-88738-663-6 (paper)
Printed in the United States of America

Library of Congress Cataloging-in-Publication Data

The United States and Mexico

(U.S.-Third World policy perspectives; no. 8)
1. United States—Foreign relations—Mexico. 2. Mexico—Foreign relations—United States. 3. United States—Foreign economic relations—Mexico. 4. Mexico—Foreign economic relations—United States. 5. Technology — Social aspects—Mexico. 6. Technology—Social aspects—United States.
I. Thorup, Cathryn. II. Madian, Alan. III. Series.
E183.8.M6U582 1985   327.73072   86-50514
ISBN 0-88738-120-0
ISBN 0-88738-663-6 (pbk.)

The views expressed in this volume are those of the authors and do not necessarily represent those of the Overseas Development Council as an organization or of its individual officers or Board, Council, Program Advisory Committee, and staff members.

The United States and Mexico: Face to Face with New Technology

Acknowledgments

U.S.-Mexico Project Director and Guest Editor:
Cathryn L. Thorup

Series Editors, U.S.-Third World Policy Perspectives:
Richard E. Feinberg
Valeriana Kallab

Assistant Editor
Melissa Vaughn

The Overseas Development Council gratefully acknowledges the assistance of the Ford, William and Flora Hewlett, and Rockefeller Foundations, whose financial support contributes to the preparation and dissemination of the policy analysis presented in ODC's U.S.-Third World Policy Perspectives series.

On behalf of the ODC and the authors contributing to this policy study, the editors wish to express special thanks to members of the U.S.-Mexico Policy Committee of ODC's U.S.-Mexico Project, especially Guy F. Erb, the Committee's chairman, for their contributions to the evolution of this study; and to the experts and policymakers who participated in a ODC's major binational meeting on the impact of technological change on U.S.-Mexican relations—co-sponsored by the Johnson Foundation at Wingspread in November 1985—and whose discussions contributed greatly to the preparation of this book. Special thanks for comments on early drafts of several of the chapters in this volume are due John P. Lewis, chairman of ODC's Program Advisory Committee, and to James K. Galbraith and Henry R. Nau, members of that Committee; and to Eugene Skolnikoff, member of ODC's Council.

Special thanks for translation and bilingual administrative assistance in the preparation of the manuscript go to Kathryn Carovano and Vanessa Cano, and for editorial and production assistance to Valerie Mims.

Contents

Foreword, by John W. Sewell xi

Overview:
The United States and Mexico:
Face to Face with New Technology
Cathryn L. Thorup 1

    The New Technologies 2
    Created Comparative Advantage 4
    Economic Obstacles 7
    Political Constraints 10
    Policy Implications 16
    Channeling Technology 22

Summaries of Recommendations 27

1. **Technology and the Changing Industrial Balance**
   Alan L. Madian 41

    The Limits of Prophecy 42
    Created Comparative Advantage: Theoretical Origins 44
    Relations Between Advanced Developing and Developed
      Countries 46
    Developed-Country Industrial Decline: A Closer Look at the
      Causes 52
    Policy Choices 56
    Implications for the United States and Mexico 63

2. **Mexico's New Industrial Development Strategy**
   Mauricio de Maria y Campos 67

    The Policy Background 68
    Mexico's New Development Strategy 70
    Trade Policy 72
    Structural Change: Policy Implementation and Some Results.... 73
    The Mexican Automobile Industry 74
    The Mexican Chemical-Pharmaceutical Industry 76
    The Development of the Mexican Electronics Industry 77
    The Role of Technological Change in Mexico's Development
      Strategy 79

3. **U.S. Macroeconomic Strategy and the**
   Advanced Developing Countries
   James K. Galbraith 83

    U.S. Macroeconomic Strategy 83
    The Structure of U.S. Production, Trade, and Protection 87
    Implications for Advanced Developing Countries 91
    The Supply of Finance 95
    Conclusions 97

4. **Prospects for the U.S.-Mexican Relationship in the Motor Vehicle Sector**
   James P. Womack   101

   The Trajectory of the World Motor Vehicle Industry   102
   The Evolution of the U.S.-Mexican Relationship
      in the Motor Vehicle Industry   110
   Technological and Organizational Factors in the Fourth
      Phase of the U.S.-Mexican Relationship   117
   Proposals for Advancing the Relationship   119

5. **Automated Manufacturing and Offshore Assembly in Mexico**
   Susan Walsh Sanderson   127

   Trends in Offshore Electrical and Electronics Assembly   129
   Trends in Automation   132
   Technological Projections   134
   Impact on Offshore Assembly in Mexico   134
   The Role of Technological and Economic Factors in the
      Diffusion of New Technologies   136
   Policy Implications   140
   Conclusions   147

6. **Technology and Employment Along the U.S.-Mexican Border**
   M. Patricia Fernández Kelly   149

   Advanced Technology and Industrial Development
      Along the U.S.-Mexican Border   150
   Maquila Employment, Technology, and Women   156
   Future Policy   162

7. **Biotechnology and Food: The Scope for Cooperation**
   Cassio Luiselli Fernández   167

   Current State of the Industry   168
   Obstacles to the Industry's Development   170
   Demand Prospects   171
   Mexico: A Base for Biotechnology?   172
   Potential Applications of Biotechnology in Mexico   175
   The Policy Dimensions of Biotechnology   180
   Conclusion: Biotechnology and the U.S.-Mexican Relationship . . .   181

8. **The Mexican Pharmochemical and Pharmaceutical Industries**
   Joan Brodovsky   187

   Global Technological Change in the Pharmaceutical
      and Pharmochemical Industries   189
   Mexico's Pharmaceutical Industry   191
   Mexico's Pharmochemical Industry   198
   Relations Between the Mexican Government and the Industries .   203
   U.S.-Mexican Relations and
      the Mexican Pharmaceutical Industry   210

The United States and Mexico: Face to Face with New Technology

Foreword

Since 1979, the U.S.-Mexico Project of the Overseas Development Council has involved representatives of the academic, public, and private sectors of the United States and Mexico in an ongoing process of policy research and dialogue to improve communication and policymaking in the bilateral relationship. Since its founding, the Project has held eight major binational meetings; established an informal network of contacts among decision-makers in Mexico and the United States; created three different types of seminar programs in Washington, D.C. for the discussion of key mutual concerns; and disseminated the results of its policy-related research through publications, meetings, and press briefings. The Project's diverse activities have been made possible by the generous contributions of the Ashland Oil Foundation, Inc., the Atlantic Richfield Foundation, Avon Products, Inc., Bank of America, the Javier Barros Sierra Foundation, The Ford Foundation, the General Electric Foundation, the William and Flora Hewlett Foundation, the Johnson Foundation, and the Xerox Foundation.

As a part of this process, the U.S.-Mexico Policy Committee, chaired by Guy F. Erb, was established to bring together leaders from diverse sectors of both societies to discuss the key issues of the bilateral agenda and to guide the research agenda of the U.S.-Mexico Project. In March 1984, the U.S.-Mexico Policy Committee met at the Johnson Foundation's center at Wingspread in Racine, Wisconsin, to discuss the issues ahead in U.S.-Mexican relations. At this meeting, forty-five prominent Mexican and U.S. government, business, and academic leaders discussed the issues of regional security, trade, capital formation, and the "social border" and identified the impact of technological development on the relationship between the United States and Mexico as a critical area needing attention in the period immediately ahead.

The vulnerability of Mexico to the vicissitudes of the U.S. economy has long been recognized. But recently it has also become apparent that the health of a good portion of the U.S. economy is inextricably linked to that of Mexico. The financial crisis and recession in Mexico that began in 1982 translated into depressed earnings for many U.S. corporations with investments in Mexico, a sharp fall in U.S. exports, a slump in the U.S. border economy, a need to reschedule debt repayments to U.S. banks, an increase in border crossings by undocumented Mexican workers into the United States, and a loss of U.S. jobs.

While the two countries face some similar dilemmas—both are among the world's largest debtors and both are struggling to come to terms with an increasingly competitive international environment—they do so with very different resources and skill levels. Very little systematic research exists, however, on the general topic of the links between technology and trade, investment, and labor flows in the bilateral relationship or their policy implications.

Following the recommendations of the U.S.-Mexico Policy Committee, two meetings were organized by ODC's U.S.-Mexico Project in late 1984 and early 1985—one in Washington, D.C and one in Mexico City. These meetings brought together government, business, and labor representatives to discuss the design of this binational research project. Additionally, extensive consultations were carried out with individuals in both countries in preparation for a major binational meeting to be convened in November 1985 at Wingspread. Eight papers were commissioned for this meeting highlighting the linkages between development issues and global technological change, the impact of alternative policy trade-offs, both within and between the two countries, and the options available to public and private sector policymakers. Mauricio de Maria y Campos, Mexico's Under Secretary of Commerce for Industrial Development, and Charles W. Robinson, President of the Energy Transition Corporation and former U.S. Under Secretary of State for Economic Affairs, served as co-chairs of the meeting.

The authors of this volume—government, business, and academic specialists from the two countries—benefited from comments on their papers at Wingspread and, on an individual basis, from an international field of experts. They have analyzed technological change from the perspectives of both the United States and Mexico. They underscore the complexity of the linkages between these two asymmetrical powers, exploring options for mutually constructive policies and pinpointing areas of conflict, without assuming that either country is more responsible than the other for resolving bilateral problems. The study takes an integrated approach toward the interplay of political, economic, cultural, and social forces in the process of technological change, exploring the relationships between technological advance and unemployment, immigration, protectionism, and debt. The authors examine the impact that each country's policy choices—based on its own national economic and political objectives—have upon the dynamics of the bilateral relationship; and they suggest how U.S.-Mexican policy complementarity can be enhanced. Individual chapters present many different perceptions and expectations of technological change and offer valuable assessments of the policy constraints faced in each country, the limits to political will, and the role of domestic interest groups.

We hope that the analyses in this volume will make a constructive contribution to the ongoing debate on relations between the United States and Mexico.

John W. Sewell, *President*
July 1987   *Overseas Development Council*

The United States and Mexico:
Face to Face with New Technology

Overview

The United States and Mexico: Face to Face with New Technology

Cathryn L. Thorup

Industrial competitiveness has emerged as a key political and economic issue in the United States. It is a topic that means many things to many people, yet reflects a consensus of concern about the deterioration of the U.S. trade position at a time of greater foreign economic competition from Japan and Europe and growing economic strength on the part of the newly industrializing countries (NICs). Competitiveness is affected by a number of factors, including wage rates, exchange rate policy, trade policy, education, capital formation, and technology. This book explores the dynamic effect of technological innovation on the economic development strategies pursued by the United States and by Mexico and on the economic and political relationship between the two countries.

A common U.S. response to this relative decline in its international trade position has been to blame foreign governments for "unfair trade practices." Frequently, protectionism lies hidden under the new guise of promoting competitiveness. Congressional, business, and labor debates often focus on using U.S. trade policy to prevent other countries from eroding the U.S. position, rather than on measures to make the United States more competitive. In the same way, in Mexico, it is sometimes easier to argue that economic problems are a consequence of

Note: While taking responsibility for the views reflected here, the author wishes to give special thanks for their comments, assistance, and encouragement in the preparation of this overview essay to: Emily Alejos, Robert L. Ayres, Lynne J. Brown, Kathryn Carovano, Guy F. Erb, Dieter Ernst, James K. Galbraith, Stephan Haggard, Miguel Leaman, John P. Lewis, Enrique Martin del Campo, Henry R. Nau, Richard Newfarmer, Susan Sanderson, Eugene Skolnikoff, and Mary L. Williamson.

1

exploitation by the North that threatens ultimately to lead to a more dependent and technologically subservient South, than it is to make the necessary hard choices among fiercely competing domestic interests.

Looking at these issues through the prism of U.S. long-term economic and political interests, this volume examines the technological dimensions of what is perhaps this country's most demanding and complex bilateral relationship. The authors explore the impact of technological change upon the economic and political structures of Mexico and the United States and ways in which the coordination of national policies might be maximized. Attention is paid to the policy constraints faced by each country, to asymmetries of power and perception between the United States and Mexico as they come face to face with technological change, to the manner in which the costs and benefits of technological advance are distributed both between and within the two countries, and to the role of domestic interest groups in preventing or promoting the adoption of specific development strategies. The authors offer recommendations for improving bilateral economic interaction, reducing the adjustment costs of technological change, and avoiding diplomatic tensions between the two nations.

The New Technologies

Concern about the effects of technological change has been a constant in the history of industrial development. Current attention to the impact of technology on jobs, wages, skill levels, and foreign exchange earnings has been heightened by the appearance of a wide array of new technologies.

The term "new technologies" encompasses a variety of new materials, new techniques for production, and new forms of social organization in industry. These advances in materials substitution, automation and robotization, communications and information technology, and social organization are already having a marked effect on international commodity markets and on the manufacturing and service sectors, but the long-term ramifications of these advances are not easily discernible. This study explores the possibilities.

Materials substitution is made possible by the improvement of traditional materials and the development of new ones. The new materials may reduce energy costs, improve the quality of the locally produced product and/or lower its cost. New developments in fiber optics, for example, have improved data transmission; 50-100 pounds of fiberglass cable can send as many telephone messages as one ton of copper wire, using less energy in the process. Advanced ceramics, given their lighter weight and greater heat tolerance, are beginning to re-place metal parts in automobile engines. Polymers, plastics, and fiber-reinforced composite materials—with greater flexibility, strength, and resistance to corrosion—increasingly are utilized in autos and aircraft. A most promising development has been in the area of superconduc-tors—new ceramic materials that conduct electricity without energy-wasting resistance, at higher temperatures than previously believed possible. One potential application is in the production of much faster and more powerful computers.

Advances in biotechnology make it possible to use live organisms, or their components, in the production of goods and services. As Cassio Luiselli points out in this volume, this opens up the possibility of further vast improvements in the quality, cost, and quantity of agri-cultural production. Developments in genetic engineering make it possible to produce cells with characteristics different from those of the parent cell. Recombinant genetic techniques for modifying bacterial metabolism (or "gene splicing") have opened possibilities for the man-ufacture by fermentation of many substances previously obtained from natural—and therefore finite—sources. Medical research on AIDS, among other diseases, has gained from these developments. Currently the most promising work toward discovery of a safe, affordable AIDS vaccine is based on gene splicing, while efforts to develop a more accurate, less expensive screening test for AIDS uses viral proteins cloned through genetic engineering.

New developments in *automation and robotization* are having a powerful effect on the way in which a wide variety of products are manufactured. Robotization refers to a range of technologies (including robot arms, mobility, sensing, and decision-making) that allow comput-ers to interact with the physical world. The introduction in automated factories of computer-aided design and computer-aided manufacturing (CAD/CAM)—in particular, numerically controlled machine tools—unites management and control functions with the physical side of the manufacturing process, so that all auxiliary functions are merged into an integrated system. The goal is to improve product quality, efficiency, and reliability while reducing production costs.

New materials require refined processing techniques and, often, less labor, as Alan Madian discusses in his chapter. As a result of advances in microelectronics—including miniaturization, more inte-grated circuits, faster speed, greater memory—techniques that pre-viously required years of training are now embodied in machines. Some manufactured components can in fact now be made only by machines.

Advances in microelectronics and the computer industry have also affected *communications and information technology*, producing extraordinarily complex and efficient mechanisms for information analysis, storage, and communications, thus making feasible the sharing of research and development (R & D) efforts and breakthroughs around the world. Sophisticated communications networks linking worldwide information flows and services have given added impetus to the de-centralization of production and to the highly centralized control that have been characteristic of multinational operations. A case in point is the new Ford plant in Mexico that employs Mexican workers using Japanese, Mexican, and U.S. components to build a Japanese-designed car for the U.S. market.

Economies of scale are also altered through the automated linkage of global information and production. In some industries, the combination of computers, reprogrammable machines, and robots has made significant economies of scale possible through small production runs of a wide variety of products (as opposed to a high volume of a homogeneous product). The product design is also easily reprogrammed, making it possible, with a lower inventory, to produce high-quality goods catering to a variety of tastes.

Along with new materials and new techniques of production have come new patterns of *social organization*. Simplified product design has led to innovative approaches in production management and production philosophy, based on group cooperation and skill-sharing. Suppliers, assemblers, and manufacturers are all more closely involved in the production process, lessening duplication, making planning more flexible, enhancing feedback information on system needs, and promoting a sharing of resources. Quality, near-zero inventories, and in most cases production near the final market are all emphasized. The last of these points is particularly relevant to U.S.-Mexican relations because of the geographic proximity of the two countries.

While the difficulty of altering well-entrenched patterns of social organization should not be underestimated, a developing country such as Mexico could, as James Womack discusses, gain a substantial advantage through the application of these new forms of organization, which are relatively inexpensive compared to the expensive, high-risk breakthrough innovations in machinery.

Created Comparative Advantage

Technology affects a wide variety of political, economic, and societal structures. The advances described above will create new products, jobs, and investment opportunities. But they will also displace other firms and workers, and they will have a disruptive impact on entire communities. The task of dealing with the resultant dislocations—some temporary, some permanent—will create serious social and political problems in the United States, particularly at the local and state level. For a developing country like Mexico, such disruptions could be overwhelming.

The key to improved competitiveness will lie in a relatively more flexible industrial structure and social organization capable of quickly taking advantage of new technological advances. This raises both old and new questions regarding technology transfer and domestic R & D, as well as issues regarding the feasibility—or desirability—of socio-cultural change where social groups are relatively less flexible.

New techniques render old views on comparative advantage obsolete, as geographic location and relative wage rates become less important and as new materials replace natural materials, contributing to a sharp drop in commodity prices in the 1980s. One bright spot for a major oil producer like Mexico is that petroleum-based synthetic products may, over time, help push oil prices back up.

What really matters at the macro level are new forms of global competition and the internationalization of trade, production, and finance. At the firm level, decisions regarding when and where to invest in automation are affected by, among other variables, the nature and rate of technological change in each specific industrial sector, comparative cost factors, government policies, macroeconomic variables, and firm size. Additionally, technology engenders a bias toward certain factors of production (for example, robotization toward capital, or software technology toward highly skilled labor), thus influencing a firm's decision regarding geographic location. Currently, automated factories tend to be located close to major sources of raw materials and/or consumers that also offer an adequate supply of skilled engineering personnel rather than of low-cost labor.

These requirements—and the fact that automation reduces shop floor personnel—have tended to slow the development and acceptance of automated manufacturing techniques. Whether worldwide sourcing of production will be replaced by a return to centralized production is as yet unclear.[1] In any event, it seems unlikely that there will be a mass return of U.S. offshore production facilities in Mexico to the United States. As Patricia Fernández Kelly and James Galbraith argue in this volume, Mexico's proximity to the United States and the size of its domestic market make it an especially attractive site for offshore production. Growing U.S. and Japanese investment in Mexican in-bond industries underscores the vitality of Mexican offshore production, at least for the medium run.

It is in the interests of the developing countries that automated systems become easier to operate and maintain. In this way, developing countries that have substantial markets but lack a sizable *skilled* labor force could still be chosen as manufacturing sites. The end result would be domestic production of highly complex products for the local and international market, using local energy and raw materials. Patricia Fernández Kelly and Susan Sanderson examine the costs and benefits of offshore production in terms of both revenue and social welfare. Fernández Kelly concludes that the *maquila* industry is a vital source of earnings for Mexico, but that steps must be taken to increase the benefits it provides to Mexico.[2] Sanderson and James Womack are less optimistic about the long-term prospects for the maquila industry, given its vulnerability to changes in U.S. manufacturing strategies due, in particular, to advances in automation.

In the past, the prior economic development of some nations made it relatively more difficult for latecomers to develop. Today, the new technologies are altering barriers to entry and market access. As "created" comparative advantage resulting from dynamic private and public sector interventions begins to take precedence over "natural" comparative advantage linked to a static set of natural endowments, it may matter more who invested last than first. In some instances, as Alan Madian discusses, technological leapfrogging allows new entrants—at least those with the resources to take advantage of late-start strategies—to speed past traditional economic powers by building on the latter's technological know-how to skip ahead. Organizational innovation is particularly important to the success of these "fast followers."

Yet the barriers to entry that do still exist—particularly in the electronics sector—should not be underestimated. It is generally still easier for a developing country to compete in those sectors where technology is changing relatively more slowly. Furthermore, a country that is interested in being internationally competitive cannot rely on "being second" as a viable, long-term technology policy; technological innovation is a critical component of international competitiveness. As innovation becomes faster and the learning curve shorter, and as development time and the product life cycle are reduced, it may become increasingly difficult to keep up with new developments if the producer has not been involved early on in the process.

Thus for Mexico one of the key questions raised by the new technological possibilities is whether to spend scarce domestic resources to strengthen domestic R & D or to rely on the acquisition and assimilation of foreign technology. The extent of foreign involvement in the economy has long been the subject of heated political debate in Mexico, and this carries over into the field of technology.[3] Mexico relies on the United States for two-thirds of its technology contracts and is concerned about being so reliant on one provider. The asymmetries of political and economic power between the two countries have produced in Mexico a cautious approach to policy measures that would draw the two countries closer together. Some Mexicans fear that closer links with the United States will further reduce national autonomy.

For that reason—and because international competitiveness requires it—increasing attention is being paid by policymakers in Mexico to the need to develop the capacity for indigenous R & D without abandoning attempts to secure the transfer of technology through foreign investment or "unbundled" licensing agreements. The dilemma for Mexico, as both Galbraith and Womack point out in their chapters, is that the financial constraints imposed by Mexico's debt burden make direct foreign investment and joint production activities more feasible than Mexican investment in domestic R & D. In select areas, Mexico may be able to design new technology. In most fields, however, it can only reduce its external overdependence by training Mexican engineers to assimilate, operate, and repair imported technology.

One of the issues traditional to discussions of technology transfer is that of the "appropriateness" of a given technology to the local conditions and objectives of a developing country. Critics have alleged that the technology transferred by the advanced countries to Mexico—and to other developing countries—often is costly, obsolete, and more suited to a country with a shortage of labor than to one with a huge labor surplus. Yet one alternative for Mexico—banning imports of foreign technology—would mean falling even further behind in a chimeric pursuit of technological autarky. Inside Mexico, the debate has progressed now to a point where it is generally agreed that Mexican policymakers will simultaneously pursue three objectives: first, stimulate indigenous R & D; second, encourage technology transfer to ensure that the country is not left isolated from global economic trends, but instead establishes future economic niches for itself; and third, take care that technology—both imported and home-grown—is, to the degree possible, well suited to the country's development objectives and real possibilities.

Technological choices—whether made by governments or by firms—are increasingly complex. Automation and robotization may lead to a temporary loss of jobs but eventually provide a country the competitive edge it needs to create more jobs. As James Womack suggests in his chapter, the answer may be to look for "best practice" plants, seeking employment gains by increasing the volume of production rather than by increasing the number of worker hours per unit of output.

Economic Obstacles

In both nations, rapid technological change is coming at a time of severe macroeconomic constraints, inadequate levels and patterns of investment, heated debate over the proper role of the public sector, and domestic pressures for protection against externally induced change. How each nation copes with these pressures will affect the economy of the other—as will the technology choices each country pursues.

Mexico

Until the economic crisis of 1976, Mexico relied successfully on rapid overall growth and price stability to provide the economic foundation for political stability. Announcement of the discovery of vast oil reserves in 1977 permitted the country to once again achieve very high growth rates and to avoid the oil-based price shocks of the late 1970s. But the disadvantages of oil-based development became painfully clear in 1981, when the price of oil began to drop; in 1982, Mexico faced many of the same economic problems it had successfully ignored in the late 1970s.

Today Mexico is confronted with a huge foreign debt, with 60 per cent of its export earnings currently going to debt service. It is also experiencing erratic oil prices (in 1986 they dropped approximately 60 per cent), a stagnant domestic market, a 40-per-cent real decline in minimum wages since 1982, and explosive inflation (100 per cent in 1986). Other major problems include the lack of a strong domestic entrepreneurial class and a generalized crisis of confidence in the Mexican economy. With one million new entrants into the work force every year and combined unemployment and underemployment totaling about 40 per cent, employment is a serious concern.[4] Together, these factors have created economic and political constraints that substantially reduce the Mexican government's margin of maneuver in the elaboration of economic development plans—while the private sector is not yet strong enough to pick up the slack. Thus Mexico is undertaking industrial restructuring and opening up its economy to more market competition at a moment of great economic vulnerability.

In these circumstances, both the threat and the promise inherent in technological change take on added significance. As Mauricio de Maria y Campos points out in a chapter in this volume, Mexico is highly dependent on foreign technology due to a long period of excessive protection from external competition, the absence of a climate conducive to risk-taking and innovation, and low spending on R & D. One problem faced by Mexican policymakers is how to find sources of capital—both financial and human—to fuel technological transformation when both domestic and foreign savings and investment are down. Technology transfer is less likely in an atmosphere of economic stagnation, yet without it, the business climate is condemned to further deterioration.

Mexico has taken dramatic steps to turn its economy around in spite of—and because of—these tremendous international and domestic economic constraints. The issue is no longer *whether* Mexico will open up its economy, but rather *how* it will do so—how far, how fast, and for how long. Economic "opening" has been pursued through a variety of measures, including Mexico's entry into the General Agreement on Tariffs and Trade (GATT), the sale or closure of many state-owned enterprises, an offering to the private sector of 34 per cent of the stock of two of the major Mexican banks, relaxation of foreign investment restrictions, reduction of the government deficit, and various measures of deregulation. In addition, the Mexican government increased the protection of intellectual property rights in January 1987.[5] None of this takes Mexico as far as many in the United States would like to see it go, but it does constitute a tremendous shift in the way Mexico has run its economy over the past four decades.

The Mexican government, in close consultation with labor and business interests, will continue to play a key role in the economy, engaging in intense bargaining with foreign governments and firms to maximize the benefits to be derived from foreign technology transfer.[6] As multinational corporations vie for new markets in an increasingly competitive international market for technology, Mexico will attempt to play off the various firms using access to its home market and its proximity to the U.S. market as bargaining chips. In contrast to the case in the extractive industries, when it comes to the manufacturing industries, public and private sector bargaining power in Mexico is strongest at the initial point of investment. It is then that the government is most able to set rules of the game that will bring to Mexico the type of technology most closely in line with its development objectives.[7]

To bring about and sustain economic recovery, Mexico will have to gradually but fundamentally alter its political structures and the decision-making processes whereby it allocates resources. It will also have to strengthen its willingness to engage with the rest of the world. The transformation of Mexico into a technologically competitive society requires nothing less. A recovery based on such solid foundations could in turn bring fresh investment by both foreign and domestic investors. A return to growth in Mexico would go far to extend the country's technological frontiers.

United States

Despite rhetoric and perceptions to the contrary, the U.S. government is also highly involved in the economy—through regulations, exchange-rate and trade policy, interest rates, and subsidies for certain sectors—in addition to active support of the interests of U.S.-based multinational corporations abroad and U.S. global trade and financial interests. Even so, the role of the public sector is more indirect in the United States than it is in Mexico, and there is less long-range planning. There is no federal mechanism to identify sectors where opportunity lies or where the United States can be particularly competitive.

Nor is there any agreement that any such mechanism *should* exist.[8] At the same time, growing foreign investment in production facilities in the United States and investment by U.S. companies in offshore production are making it increasingly difficult for U.S. public policymakers to implement national economic strategies directly.[9]

Moreover, the process of adjustment is made more difficult in the United States as the country comes to terms with its transition from an industrial economy to one where close to 70 per cent of the employed, civilian labor force already works in the services sector.[10] Since 1980, over one million manufacturing jobs have been lost in the United States.[11] As James Galbraith argues in his chapter, this is a relentless process that is precipitated by cyclical contractions in the U.S. economy.

Since 1982, the United States has increased its overall R & D expenditures, which are divided roughly evenly between the public and private sector. This is largely the result of increases in defense-related expenditures, which account for approximately three-fourths of U.S. federal government expenditures on R & D. If defense-related R & D expenditures are excluded, the estimated U.S. R & D/GNP ratio (1.9 per cent) is well below that of West Germany (2.5 per cent in 1985) and Japan (2.6 per cent in 1984). The speed with which innovations are adapted to commercial purposes is a critical factor in achieving international competitiveness, and here the United States is generally relatively slower than Japan in developing marketable products despite frequent leads in basic research.

Future industrial strategies must have a large technological component. For the United States and Mexico, however, the need for creative technology strategies of the sort Galbraith and Womack discuss unfortunately has come when the constraints are high. Moreover, because of the linkages between the two economies, national technology policy options correlate directly with the health of *both* economies, increasing when the economies are growing and shrinking with their decline. Although Mexico's economic recovery must be based on actions by its domestic public and private sectors, economic trends in the United States will greatly influence Mexico's ability to return to and sustain strong economic growth. By the same token, a healthier Mexican economy would make a positive contribution to the expansion of U.S. jobs and export sales.[12]

Political Constraints

A country's technology choices of course depend not only on the availability of economic resources and a careful assessment of the expected economic and social effects of change, but also on the political feasibility of implementation. Which are the key constituencies in the debate over specific technology choices? What economic and political resources do the different potentially affected groups hold? How will the structural dislocation occasioned by a given technological innovation vary by region, by sector, and by social class and gender? Where will the short-run burden of adjustment fall? And who will lose and benefit in the long run?

Who Benefits?

Technological advance clearly opens options for a society—but for which members and sectors of that society? Enthusiasm to be "modern" must be tempered by a realistic assessment of the social and sectoral trade-offs. How and by whom decisions are made concerning technological choices that will have major social as well as economic impact is significant for both the short and long run. Once a technology is adopted, vested interests develop that make it harder to shift the direction of technological development further down the road. In this context, the strength of organized labor is of course critical to any analysis of the politics of technological change. Stronger organization may mean that a country is relatively less permeable to technological advance if that change is associated with job loss or other job-related dislocation.

Patricia Fernández Kelly examines one aspect of the equity issue: the class and gender impact of technology as it relates to the maquila industry, concluding that, currently, hiring practices distort local patterns of employment and provide insufficient avenues for advancement in either skills or the standard of living for the predominantly female labor force.

In elaborating technology strategies, policymakers must anticipate public reaction to the negative effects of technological change, particularly to the loss of jobs. Without public debate of these questions and sufficient consensus about the direction being followed, it is likely that multiple, short-term, adverse effects and postponed benefits will tend to produce increased opposition to a policy. On the other hand, knowledge that the costs of adjustment to a new technology are being borne equitably within the society will help to promote it.

A successful transition will require compensation to the losers (through retraining or relocation, for example), effective channels for communication of dissent, and a clear articulation of the benefits to be obtained through the adoption of new technologies.

Political Change and Economic Liberalization in Mexico

Mexico's most serious economic crisis since the 1930s has provoked domestic debate, but as of yet no consensus on the future direction of national development policy. There is a direct link between economic development and political "opening" or reform in Mexico; economic crisis creates pressures for political reform, but the implementation of reform requires an environment of confidence and growth. In Mexico today, a more articulated network of domestic interest groups and calls for political pluralism add new complexity to the decision-making process. The introduction of new technologies will alter the current industrial structure and further contribute to the consolidation of new political groups and labor organizations with varying ideas on how best to capture and develop technology and how to deal with its impact on jobs, wages, and competitiveness.

Signs of movement toward an internal reallocation of power can be seen in the gradual strengthening of the Mexican Congress vis-à-vis executive power, the growing diversity of Mexican society, greater regional and local autonomy, and more open public policy debates. One example of these shifts was the 1986 debate in Mexico over intellectual property rights, in which both international companies and Mexican domestic interest groups assumed an unusually active public role by presenting their cases to the Mexican Congress.

Any decisions on technology development in Mexico will have to take into account the domestic political pressures currently confronted by the Mexican public sector. Policy implementation is more difficult the weaker the government and the more fragile the economy. The government's room for maneuver has declined alongside the Mexican economy, while U.S. pressure for a series of economic and political reforms has increased. Mexican politicians and officials must always be wary of anti-U.S. sentiment among their constituents and U.S. rewards for "good behavior" on economic issues often pale beside the domestic political costs of appearing to comply with U.S. pressure.

Most U.S. policymakers perceive a stronger Mexican private sector to be in the U.S. interest. Yet in Mexico, even the suggestion of greater private sector participation in Mexico's economy or political system can provoke sharply negative reactions. Nevertheless, as already mentioned, the de la Madrid administration has taken a number of difficult steps to reduce the role of the state in the Mexican economy and to offset to some extent the effect of the 1982 nationalization of Mexican commercial banks.

Interest Group Politics in the United States

The United States has a long tradition of bargaining and negotiation involving various domestic interest groups, the U.S. government, business, and labor. Consequently, the elaboration of any public approach to technology policy is even more complicated in the United States than in Mexico, as many more domestic actors are able to make themselves heard.[13]

Organized labor has been especially vocal in articulating its concerns. Having already made numerous wage and benefit concessions, labor leaders are not well disposed to accept what they view as "unfair" competition from abroad. Yet despite U.S. labor's strength—and its greater degree of autonomy vis-à-vis the government than exists in the case of Mexico—its position has been hurt both by the offshore production option offered by Mexico and other developing countries and by the lack of union organization in the service sector, where many new jobs have been created. As James Galbraith points out, the former has particularly weakened labor's position in wage negotiations

Although the loss of jobs is currently perceived to constitute the biggest threat of all, this situation may change. Over the next fifteen years, the U.S. population and work force will grow more slowly than at any time since the 1930s.[14] Changes in labor force participation notwithstanding, tighter labor markets may reduce labor's concern regarding offshore production and, in a related development, increase U.S. demand for immigrant labor from Mexico.

Regional Politics Within Mexico and the United States

In both countries, technological advance has strengthened the border regions. In Mexico—where the maquila industry was first endorsed to encourage the development of a remote and underpopulated region— the economic strength of the northern border has translated into growing political power for that area. In the United States, the growth of the Southwest was, until very recently, in sharp contrast with declining economic strength in parts of the Midwest and Northeast. In both countries, there is considerable concern that federal control of the border regions has diminished. Despite its desire to decentralize, the Mexican government is particularly concerned about the costs of border development in terms of a loss of national control and national unity.

Discussions in both the United States and Mexico on the impact of the maquila industry provide one concrete example of the regional implications of certain technology strategies. The plants are today Mexico's second largest earner of foreign exchange, with over 1,000 plants employing close to 300,000 Mexican workers in 1987. The plants are concentrated on Mexico's northern border, but a growing number of companies are moving south in Mexico, where there is a greater abundance of labor.

Opponents of the plants believe that U.S. jobs are being shipped abroad, and that the benefits to Mexico are superficial. They argue further that the recent surge in maquila operations is a temporary phenomenon linked to the Mexican economic crisis, which has pushed wages down even further relative to the United States, and therefore does not represent a permanent contribution to the Mexican economy. Proponents stress that proximity makes offshore production in Mexico a special case, since the move to Mexico has allowed a wide variety of satellite support activities to remain in the United States, thus actually benefitting U.S. labor. They argue that in the absence of the offshore option in Mexico, some multinational firms would have moved their entire operations to Southeast Asia and these satellite U.S. jobs would not have been created.

In 1985, over 5,000 U.S. suppliers, located in forty-four U.S. states, provided raw materials and/or equipment and services to the *maquiladora* plants in Mexico.[15] In El Paso, Texas, for example, one out of five jobs is tied in to maquila production.[16] Of course it is small consolation for a displaced worker in Buffalo, New York, to know that, because of the offshore option in Mexico, new jobs are now available for workers in other parts of the United States.

For policymakers in the United States, the key question is how to conserve the benefits of maquila production at the macro level—in terms of the improved competitiveness of U.S. products, for example—while still compensating losers at the regional and local levels. And, Mexican policymakers, as Patricia Fernández Kelly concludes, must redouble their efforts to integrate maquila production into the larger process of national development through backward linkages—to absorb significant proportions of domestic materials and services—and to train workers for positions of responsibility within firms. Selectivity in choosing maquila operations in fields that are growing and attention to technology transfer and the improvement of skill levels are traditional concerns that have remained problematic. Mexican policymakers underutilize their degree of leverage vis-à-vis foreign investors if they simply exchange cheap labor for foreign investment.

Managing Interdependence

The capacity of the two countries to manage their interdependence has not kept pace with the increasing complexity of the relationship.[17] Decision-makers in both countries need to be sensitive to the ways in which policies on technology affect other areas of the bilateral agenda, as well as to the fact that policies seemingly unrelated to technology—or to the bilateral relationship—have significant spill-over potential. For example, as Joan Brodovsky points out, disputes involving intellectual property rights in the pharmaceutical field caused tension in the broader bilateral relationship in 1984-85.

Faced with the clamor of competing interest groups, no recent U.S. administration has been able to implement a sustained and coherent policy toward Mexico. U.S. foreign policymaking tends to be fragmented, and policies toward Mexico are no exception. As domestic and foreign policy issues become increasingly interwoven and as the stakes increase, more actors—both public and private—demand a say in policy formulation. As separate government agencies pursue their own particular interests with regard to Mexico, certain domestic constituent interests may be well served, but general U.S. interests are not. This fragmentation enables relatively minor actors within a given administration to suddenly play a disproportionate role in the elaboration of U.S. policy toward Mexico, thus making the overall relationship hostage to parochial concerns. In the absence of a general coordination of U.S. policy toward Mexico, there is no entity to evaluate, assign priorities to, and regulate the flow of demands placed on the Mexican system.

Mexico has not fared much better in developing a consistent policy toward the United States. A history of U.S.-Mexican conflicts —and vivid memories of them in Mexico—makes all policies toward the United States potentially controversial. Nationalistic feelings, heightened by the desire to preserve the country's integrity relative to its powerful neighbor, cut across all Mexican political constituencies. At the present time, in the midst of sweeping changes in economic philosophy, the nation's leaders recognize that they have provoked a domestic debate with profound implications for the bilateral relationship. Referring to emotional resistance to the structural changes his government seeks, Mexican President de la Madrid has acknowledged that differences of opinion in Mexico about trade and investment ties with the United States have thus far prevented the formation of a "broad social consensus."[18]

In 1982, in the absence of a coordinated policy toward Mexico, the United States found itself simultaneously helping to bail Mexico out of a debt crisis and engaging in an increasingly contentious series of trade disputes that exacerbated Mexico's foreign exchange crisis. The cumulative impact on Mexico of these ad hoc pressures is tremendous and potentially damaging to U.S. long-term interests. Tough U.S. policies toward Mexico and inconsistencies among the positions taken by the various U.S. agencies may polarize both the bilateral and national debates and undercut the position of those Mexicans who support economic liberalization and political reform.

Cross-National Coalition Building

The variety of domestic interests and the absence of a national policy consensus in either country opens up possibilities for cross-border coalitions and cooperation. Although there may be a great deal of infighting among the various domestic interest groups on each side of the border, future cooperation *across the border* will frequently originate outside government-to-government channels—reflecting growing recognition of a commonality of interests among some of these groups.

Joint ventures and U.S. investment in manufacturing facilities in Mexico are already making this a reality. U.S. companies, with or without joint-venture partners, on occasion have acted as *domestic* pressure groups in Mexico. For example, in discussions about whether or not to allow IBM to establish a 100-per-cent foreign-owned facility in Mexico, U.S.-based multinationals with Mexican joint-venture partners—companies which, like Apple Computer and Hewlett-Packard, stood to lose by the eventual decision to change the rules of the game—pressed the Mexican government, albeit unsuccessfully, for continuation of the status quo.

In the case of labor, the establishment of cross-national coalitions is more difficult. Despite statements by U.S. labor that it objects to the maquila industry because of the poor working conditions it offers to Mexican workers, it is the loss of U.S. jobs that really hurts. A color TV worker in Evansville, Indiana, clearly does not want to lose his or her job to a maquiladora worker in Ciudad Juárez, Mexico. Common interests such as skill upgrading, improved health conditions, and greater job stability unite workers on both sides of the border, but in such a highly competitive atmosphere, solidarity is elusive.

There are grounds for cross-national coalitions on the debt issue. For example, at a U.S. congressional hearing in early 1987, the vice president of the American Soybean Association stated that between 1981 and 1985, U.S. farm exports to Mexico dropped by 41 per cent, partly as a result of that country's economic crisis. He concluded that, "a policy such as debt forgiveness in exchange for debtor nations lifting import restrictions to their markets would benefit both U.S. farms and the population of these impoverished nations."[19] At that same hearing, the secretary of agriculture of Kansas stated: "We must find new and innovative ways to solve the Latin American debt crisis. The Kansas farmer and the Latin American *campesino* have very nearly equal stakes in that solution."[20]

Policy Implications

Development and international competitiveness require integrated approaches that include trade, finance (both relief on debt and fresh investment), and industrial policy. The stark dichotomies of the past—capital-intensive versus labor-intensive production, and import substitution versus export promotion—are fast being superseded by events. The nature of the trade-offs between public and private investment and between foreign and domestic investment is also changing rapidly. New models of development will characterize the next twenty years. The East Asian countries are important to both Mexico and the United States today not as models to be imitated—for their experience is culturally and historically specific—but as competitors.

Given macroeconomic constraints (such as a lack of capital) and a relatively more protected U.S. economy actively seeking commercial reciprocity, Mexico has a narrower range of options open to it today than did Brazil, when it opted for greater autonomy in its technological development, or Taiwan, when it chose a greater degree of integration with foreign firms. Mexico is left to pursue a path that will see the exchange of domestic market access for advanced technology (not more than six to twelve months old), increased exports, and fresh flows of foreign capital. To gain any chance of becoming internationally competitive, Mexico must both *create* and *assimilate* new technology.

In the United States, the challenge facing policymakers is to focus the discussion of declining competitiveness less on trade retaliation and more on the correction of domestic shortcomings. The need to attend to pressing domestic concerns, the interdependence of the two economies, and the growing internationalization of both R & D and manufacturing all make it important for policy development to take place simultaneously in the national, bilateral, and international arenas.

National Strategies

In light of the trend toward internationalization—discussed in depth by Alan Madian—both the U.S. and Mexican governments must work assertively to shape the nature of technology transfer and to promote indigenous R & D in order to retain some degree of control over their economic futures.[21] Policies designed to promote, protect, and transfer technology should be paired with others formulated to adjust to the effects of technological change. Some problems can be addressed specifically by technology policy, while others should be the focus of fiscal policy (to achieve certain distributional objectives, for example), trade, industrial, or labor policies.

A dynamic public sector role must be joined with greatly improved cooperation between business and government. Since the private sector controls great technological know-how and vast financial resources, its role—which varies significantly from sector to sector—is pivotal. For example, half of national R & D in the United States is financed by industry and three-quarters of R & D is carried out by industry. In Mexico, the government should encourage the private sector to engage in longer-range planning, to develop new alternative technologies through increased R & D, and to support technical training for local engineers. As Mauricio de Maria y Campos points out, the capacity of Mexican industry to bargain for, select, and assimilate foreign technology also must be strengthened.

Funding for education—both to train highly skilled engineers and to prepare the general work force to adapt to a changing work environment—is one of the most significant contributions that both private- and public-sector policymakers can make toward the strengthening of each country's technology base. Technology is knowledge, not just machines.[22] Mexico's economic crisis has made it increasingly difficult to provide high-quality training in Mexico in the "cutting edge" technologies, and it has reduced the system's capacity to finance study abroad. Even in the United States, where substantial resources are devoted to education, industry leaders complain of a situation in which vocational training still focuses on traditional skills and the labor force is generally technologically unprepared and sometimes functionally illiterate.

To increase its ability to export while simultaneously building up its domestic economy, Mexico must create its own comparative advantage. In this process, it must pay close attention to enhancing both its manufacturing and marketing capabilities.[23] In the past, protectionism played a vital role in strengthening certain sectors of the Mexican economy. Today, however, increasing the level of domestic competition in certain sectors will be equally important to the future vitality of the economy. To strengthen its technological position, Mexico must take action simultaneously in a number of areas. Public policymakers need to improve communication and linkages between research centers and production centers; to enhance backward and forward linkages among industries; to improve coordination of national R & D efforts with technology transfer (and in the case of the latter, to pay more attention to assimilation and "blending"); to extend greater support to private-sector initiatives; decentralize and deregulate industry to promote more balanced regional development and greater efficiency; to give far greater attention to quality control; and to compete and negotiate vigorously for access to foreign markets.

As difficult as it may be, Mexican public and private sector policymakers must look 15-20 years hence as they gauge future niches for Mexican production. Their assessment should be informed by the nature of industrial restructuring in the United States, and take into account the impact that U.S. technological choices will have upon Mexico's options. It may be advisable to place special emphasis on the development of export sectors in which the rate of diffusion of technology is relatively slower, thus providing Mexican firms with the opportunity to respond more effectively and to remain competitive over a longer period of time.[24]

The motor vehicle industry, discussed in this volume by James Womack, is an area in which Mexico already has had considerable success in increasing exports of finished cars and auto parts. Next to oil, automobile engines are today the single largest export earner for Mexico. The informatics industry is also strong, making Mexico the second largest producer and consumer of computers in Latin America. Since 1983, developments in this sector—originally spurred by a ban on most imports of finished computers and reliance on foreign technology and capital to develop domestic production—have been impressive.[25]

Another particularly promising avenue of development for Mexico is biotechnology—given Mexico's diverse genetic wealth and the strategic importance of biotechnology's application to agriculture and food production. Furthermore, as Cassio Luiselli points out in discussing this sector, biotechnology is a field particularly amenable to "technological blending," the joining of the cutting edge of technological advance with traditional agricultural practices. The United States is the driving force in this field, but—except for areas that require a massive initial investment or a large-scale operation—Mexico is relatively well endowed with the industrial and scientific infrastructure for biotechnology.

In contrast, the pharmaceutical industry, as Joan Brodovsky points out, is one in which Mexico has been losing relative competitiveness. In part, this is due to the lack of resources to invest in the new drug delivery systems or in high-risk, high-profit drugs. It is also the result of continued reliance on foreign active substances and technology, excessive product differentiation, and Mexican patent policies that U.S. investors still consider to provide insufficient protection and thus to discourage the transfer of technology.[26] In the case of the pharmaceutical industry, this approach—originally responsible for the promotion of certain social objectives and the development of a strong industrial sector that in the 1960s supplied virtually the entire Mexican market for pharmaceuticals—became an obstacle to the continued development of that sector. As Mauricio de Maria y Campos argues, however, a program has been implemented by the Mexican government to strengthen this sector with the result that many active substances, previously imported, are now being processed in Mexico and the industry's trade deficit has been reduced by half.

U.S. policymakers, too, must reexamine the entire range of U.S. trade, finance, and industrial strategies if they are to strengthen the country's international economic position and avoid having to choose between employment and an open trading system. The "unfair trade" issue has been overplayed; fairness is relative, and policies that differ from those of the United States are not necessarily unfair. Protectionism is a short-term palliative that, when elevated to a permanent development strategy, becomes part of the problem rather than a policy for growth. Circling U.S. trade wagons may be an easy response to public pressure, but it does not resolve the larger problem of declining U.S. competitiveness.

U.S. protectionism also effectively negates Mexico's attempts to prosper through export-led growth and aggravates an already critically difficult foreign exchange situation. James Womack suggests, as one alternative, that by prioritizing motor vehicle imports by country of origin (as is already done in the case of Japan), the United States could make Mexico a special case in terms of U.S. trade and investment policy. If deemed successful, this approach could be expanded to other sectors.[27]

Bilateral Options

Clarifying and pursuing national objectives is important, but the United States and Mexico must also reach beyond national decision-making on technology to look for bilateral approaches that enhance the complementarity of goods and markets. The two countries' asymmetry of economic power makes this a difficult task. U.S. goals may include the maintenance of high-wage employment, but Mexico has as yet to secure a minimum standard of living for all its citizens. Despite such differences, a bilateral approach can help ensure the complementarity of growth strategies needed by both nations. One possible initiative would be a bilateral agreement on trade and investment designed to set forth principles, to establish forms of consultation and dispute resolution, and to provide a framework for sectoral agreements.

Although there have been joint programs for technological cooperation in the past, their budgets have been far too small to be really effective. Much more collaborative research needs to be done by U.S. and Mexican private- and public-sector specialists. One possibility that Cassio Luiselli suggests is that Mexican capital and technicians participate in U.S. biotechnology companies. Joint R & D in the agricultural field is also a good prospect, given Mexico's relative strength in the area of biotechnology and the capacity of the United States to provide assistance to Mexico so that it can better anticipate and prepare for new technological developments in this field. Collaborative research in the health field would be particularly beneficial for Mexico—a country that had developed a strong pharmaceutical industry in terms of traditional production, but has fallen behind in terms of the new technology.

Galbraith, Womack, and Sanderson all suggest that production sharing is one of the few viable, short-term routes for Mexican development. James Galbraith points out that autonomous routes of development seem less available to Mexico, given the twin dilemmas of Mexican debt and U.S. protectionism. Absent a willingness or ability to alter the parameters of either dilemma, there seem to be few alternatives. But as Cassio Luiselli and Galbraith both point out, production sharing implies much greater economic integration with U.S. firms and the U.S. economy. Such an approach must be designed carefully if it is to be politically palatable; Mexico needs to be assured an equitable share of the economic benefits and significant influence over key investment and management decisions.

Clearly U.S.-Mexican relations involve much more than government-to-government contacts; the private sector's involvement in technological R & D increases the potential of business-government relations and business-business relations between the two countries to enhance or endanger the pursuit of technological advance. Thus bilateral efforts should go beyond government-to-government initiatives to include more attention to firm-to-firm negotiations over issues such as licensing.

International Arena

Technological advance in the United States and in Mexico takes place in a global context. The national and bilateral strategies of the two countries inevitably will be affected by a variety of outside actors, posing either a competitive challenge or a potential for cooperative ventures. In this connection, Japan and the countries of Latin America promise to be of special importance to the United States and Mexico.

Japan—currently Mexico's second largest trading partner—foresees large-scale involvement in trade and technology exchange in the Pacific Basin. Japan's burgeoning interest (perhaps to be followed by South Korea's and Taiwan's) in Mexico's in-bond industry—particularly that located in Tijuana, right across the border from parent firms in the United States—promises to be one of the most important economic developments of the late 1980s.[28] As James Womack points out in his chapter, any future U.S.-Mexican agreement on auto manufacture—a bargain he elaborates in some detail—would have to involve Japanese-based multinationals.

Japanese investment in Mexican maquila production stems from a desire to be close to major markets (notably the United States) to assure a faster supply of key components and—like its U.S. counterpart—to take advantage of low wage rates. Some Japanese firms are moving to Mexico from the United States. A Sanyo plant making compact refrigerators in San Diego moved to Tijuana, Mexico, in early 1987 for the same cost-cutting reasons that the U.S. company Wham-o has moved its entire Frisbee production from San Gabriel, California, to La Mesa, Mexico.

In addition to providing Mexico with much-needed capital, Japanese investment in the Mexican maquila industry allows Mexico to diversify its financial and technological dependence on the United

States. If U.S. concern about Japanese competition grows as Japanese investment in Mexico improves Japan's ability to compete in the U.S. market, Mexico may have an important negotiating tool for its commercial dealings with the United States. Currently, only 2 per cent of the materials used in U.S. in-bond plants in Mexico are purchased in Mexico. A significant portion of the other 98 per cent is initially imported by U.S. firms from Southeast Asia and then sent to Mexico for use in the maquiladoras. It is not inconceivable that an agreement could be reached that would see the United States agreeing to increase Mexican domestic content in maquila operations if Mexico agrees to impose tougher regulations on Japanese investment in these in-bond industries.

As Mexico moves up the technological ladder, it will compete with other advanced developing countries (ADCs) for access to foreign markets. If all the ADCs pursue export-promotion strategies aimed at the United States and other industrial markets, pressure on the U.S. trade balance will increase, fanning protectionist sentiments. As Cassio Luiselli points out, Latin American regional cooperation in terms of both R & D and (more ambitiously) marketing thus will be increasingly important. Possible cooperative ventures—pooling ideas and financing—might include joint Latin American R & D efforts, particularly in the early stages of research when competitive pressures are felt less acutely; Latin American direct investment in U.S. high-tech companies; the establishment of regional priorities for technological development; and the elaboration of policies designed to protect the region's genetic diversity.

Channeling Technology

There is a certain autonomous momentum to technology's advance, but this does not argue for a deterministic view that it is impossible to channel its future direction. Policymakers have a public responsibility to actively direct technology, not just passively watch it happen. While it is important to avoid overregulation and its potential to thwart creativity in technological innovation, policymakers—both public and private—cannot abdicate their responsibility to the general welfare. Answering the question "technology for what?" must take into account social needs alongside other government and business objectives.

For Mexico, of course, a key problem is to find the resources to take advantage of the opportunities for development that the new technology potentially offers. For the United States, the key is to develop its future competitive edge rather than to try to recapture and protect past glories. Both tasks are made more difficult by the extremely dynamic and unpredictable rates of technological and organizational change brought by the new technology. What *is* predictable is that the United States and Mexico will fall far behind in the race for international competitiveness if they do not each pursue policies that vigorously promote technology research and development. National efforts should be linked to cooperative bilateral initiatives based on respect for each other's national interests. Such an approach will increase the prospects for sustained prosperity and technological advance in both countries.

Notes

[1] For a skeptical view of the future viability of global sourcing of production, see Michael J. Piore and Charles F. Sabel, *The Second Industrial Divide* (New York: Basic Books, Inc., 1984), p. 355. For an alternative view, see Dieter Ernst, "Automation and Worldwide Restructuring of the Electronics Industry: Strategic Implications for Developing Countries," *World Development*, Vol. 13, No. 3 (March 1985), pp. 333-352.

[2] The *maquila* (in-bond) industry is a type of offshore production initiated in 1965 that allows U.S. companies to ship raw materials and components to Mexico to be assembled there and re-exported to the United States. Only the value added during this process is then assessed a duty.

[3] Gerardo Bueno, "Alternative Forms, Fashions and Politics for Technology Transfer: A Mexican Perspective," *Mexican Studies/Estudios Mexicanos*, University of California, Irvine, Summer 1986, Vol. 2, No. 2, p. 237.

[4] U.S. Department of Commerce, *Foreign Economic Trends and Their Implications for the United States* (Washington, D.C.: November 1986), p. 11.

[5] New process patents were established in chemicals, pharmaceuticals, biotechnology, and other areas; the patent term was increased from ten to fourteen years; and trade-secret protection and patent-lapse provisions were strengthened.

[6] For more on the origins and development of thinking in Mexico on technology policy, see Victor L. Urquidi, "Technology, Planning and Latin American Development," *International Development Review*, No. 7, 1971, pp. 8-12; and Miguel S. Wionczek, "On the Viability of a Policy for Science and Technology in Mexico," *Latin American Research Review*, Vol. 16, No. 7, 1981, pp. 57-78.

[7] For a case study of successful Mexican bargaining in the auto industry, see Douglas C. Bennett and Kenneth E. Sharpe, *Transnational Corporations Versus the State—The Political Economy of the Mexican Auto Industry* (Princeton, New Jersey: Princeton University Press, 1985), pp. 262-263.

The latitude of choice of policymakers is greatest at the outset both in terms of the creation and assimilation of technology. See Landon Winner, in symposium discussion entitled, "Some Issues of Technology," in "Modern Technology: Problem or Opportunity?", *Daedalus*, Vol. 109, No. 1, Winter 1980, pp. 8-9.

[8] For a sense of the industrial policy debate in the United States, see Gar Alperovitz and Jeff Faux, *Rebuilding America: A Blueprint for the New Economy* (New York: Pantheon Books, 1984), p. 319; Barry Bluestone and Bennett Harrison, *The Deindustrialization of America* (New York: Basic Books, 1982), p. 323; Robert Z. Lawrence, *Can America Compete?* (Washington, D.C.: Brookings Institution, 1982), p. 156; Ira C. Magaziner and Robert B. Reich, *Minding America's Business* (New York: Harcourt Brace Jovanovich, 1982), p. 387; Michael J. Piore and Charles. F. Sabel, op. cit.; Charles L. Schultze, *The Public Use of Private Interest* (Washington, D.C.: Brookings Institution, 1977), p. 93; John Zysman and Laura Tyson, *American Industry in International Competition* (Ithaca and London: Cornell University Press, 1983), p. 436.

[9] For analyses of the way in which technology affects national autonomy, see Harald B. Malmgren, "Technological Challenges to National Economic Policies of the West," *Washington Quarterly*, Vol. LX, No. 2, Spring 1987, p. 30; and Richard N. Cooper and Ann L. Hollick, "International Relations in a Technologically Advanced Future," in *Technological Frontiers and Foreign Relations* (Washington, D.C.: National Academy Press, 1985), pp. 227-265.

[10] U.S. Department of Commerce, Bureau of Economic Analysis, "Labor Force, Employment and Earnings Table," *Survey of Current Business*, April 1987, Vol. 67, No. 4, pp. S-9, S-10.

[11] Department of Commerce, Bureau of Economic Analysis, "Labor Force, Employment and Earnings Table," *Survey of Current Business*, August 1982, Vol. 62, No. 8, pp. S-9-S-13 and March 1987, Vol. 67, No. 3, S-9-S-13.

[12] Some 300,000 U.S. jobs have been lost since 1982 as a result of the Mexican recession. See John W. Sewell and Stuart K. Tucker, "Swamped by Debt: U.S. Trade with the Newly Industrializing Countries," to appear in *Tomorrow's Competitors: The U.S. and the Newly Emerging Industrial Countries*, ed. by Daniel F. Burton, Jr. (New York: Economic Policy Council of the United Nations Association, 1987).

[13] For discussion of the role of the domestic interest groups in the elaboration of U.S. trade policy, see I. M. Destler and John S. Odell, *The Politics of Antiprotection*, Institute for International Economics, forthcoming.

[14] William B. Johnston, in "Demographics as Destiny: The U.S. Workforce in the Year 2000," (unpublished paper, The Hudson Institute, June 15, 1986).

[15] Testimony by Alexander H. Good, Director General for the U.S. and Foreign Commercial Service, Department of Commerce, before the Subcommittee on Economic Stabilization, House Committee on Banking, Finance and Urban Affairs, November 25, 1986.

[16] Ellwyn R. Stoddard, *Maquila Assembly Plants in Northern Mexico* (University of Texas at El Paso: Texas Western Press, 1987).

[17] Guy F. Erb and Cathryn L. Thorup, "Mexico and the United States: National Strategies and Bilateral Interests," El Colegio de México, forthcoming, 1987.

[18] "Meeting of Miguel de la Madrid, President of Mexico, with the Mexico-U.S. Business Committee, Los Pinos, Mexico City, February 16, 1987," Mexico, D.F.: Presidencia de la República, Dirección General de Communicación Social, 1987, pp. 2-3.

[19] Testimony by James Lee Adams, Vice President, American Soybean Association, before the Subcommittee on International Debt of the Senate Finance Committee, March 9, 1987.

[20] Testimony by Sam Brownback, Kansas Secretary of Agriculture, before the Subcommittee on International Debt, Senate Finance Committee, March 9, 1987.

[21] For a comprehensive analysis of the role of government in the elaboration of technology policy, see Frances Stewart (ed.), *Macro-Policies for Appropriate Technology in Developing Countries* (Boulder and London: Westview Press, 1987), pp. 315.

[22] Enrique Martin del Campo, "Role of Multinationals in R&D in Developing Countries," (unpublished paper presented at the Annual Meeting of the American Physics Society, Phoenix, Arizona, March, 1981), p. 4.

[23] For more on the importance of international markets and on the need to build up manufacturing and market capabilities through national technology policy, see Henry Nau, "National Policies for High Technology Development and Trade: An International and Comparative Assessment," in Francis W. Rushing and Carole Ganz Brown (eds.), *National Policies for Developing High Technology Industries* (Boulder and London: Westview Press, 1986), pp. 9-29.

[24] Kurt Hoffman, "Microelectronics, International Competition, and Development Strategies: The Unavoidable Issues," *World Development*, op. cit., pp. 263-272.

[25] For more on the Mexican informatics industry, see Debra Lynn Miller, "Mexico," in *National Policies for Developing High Technology Industries*, op. cit., pp. 173-200.

[26] Because of continued dissatisfaction with Mexico's regulations involving intellectual property rights, the United States reduced Mexico's benefits under the Generalized System of Preferences (GSP) by 16 per cent in early 1987.

[27] For recommendations on improving U.S. competitiveness without resorting to excessive protectionism, see John W. Sewell and contributors, *U.S. Foreign Policy and the Third World: Agenda 1988*, Transaction Books for the Overseas Development Council, December 1987.

[28] According to some calculations, almost half of the 27,000 Mexicans who work in Tijuana's *maquiladoras* are now employed by Japanese companies. See Kathleen K. Wiegner, "How to Mix Sake and Tequila," *Forbes*, March 23, 1987, pp. 48-51.

Summaries of Recommendations

Summaries of Recommendations

1. Technology and the Changing Industrial Balance (Alan L. Madian)

Changes in technology, materials, communications, and transportation—and related changes in economic strategies—are reshaping the global economy and the economic policy options of both developed and developing countries. Economies that until recently were technologically backward and uncompetitive are now capable of producing many products that are up to the standards of advanced industrial societies, and that capability is increasing rapidly.

These changes are the result of a number of factors, including:

• The embodiment in machines of skills that formerly required years of technical training;

• The increasing flexibility of machines—allowing for greater product differentiation and receding scale economies;

• New materials;

• Attainment by an increasing number of countries of the critical mass in skills and infrastructure required to sustain world-quality industrial activity;

• Significantly improved and less expensive international transportation and communications;

• Increasing acceptance of development strategies based on export-led economic growth rather than import substitution;

• Increasing emphasis on quality control and inventory minimization.

At the same time that these changes have been taking place, the developed countries have experienced a decline in growth rates and rates of productivity. This is attributable to a number of factors, including:

• New materials, technologies, and products that have rendered significant amounts of physical and human capital in the developed countries obsolete;

• The OPEC oil price increase;

• Increased employment in services.

The new technologies have greatly affected the development of the Asian newly industrializing countries (NICs). The adjustments required of the European and U.S. economies reflect the global adaptation of the new technologies. The protectionist reactions of the Europeans and Americans are due partly to a failure to distinguish adjustment due to global technological change from that due to the increased competition from new producers aided by the new technologies. This is compounded by a failure to distinguish imports from Japan from those of the NICs.

If Mexico is to compete successfully in this new global environment, its manufacturing sector must be reoriented toward exports—that is, toward greater volumes, higher quality, and lower operating margins—and toward competing with imports at home and with producers from developed countries and NICs abroad. The Mexican government also must use the clout it possesses by virtue of proximity to the United States to assure that its exports are exempted to the greatest possible extent from U.S. trade restrictions.

2. Mexico's New Industrial Development Strategy (Mauricio de Maria y Campos)

Technological changes have a strong impact on all aspects of the U.S.-Mexican bilateral relationship. Vastly different stages of development and a common border exacerbate the impact, making it all the more important to develop cooperative policies that will serve both countries in their efforts to compete and prosper in the rapidly changing world economy.

Major structural changes are necessary in order for Mexico to remove existing obstacles and establish internal and external economic equilibria. In recent years, the government has instituted various reform measures designed to reduce the barriers between Mexico and the international economy and raise the country's industrial productivity and competitiveness. Promoting the growth of the manufacturing sector is the principal aim of the nation's current development strategy. The development of a strong technological base is a key element of this approach.

To date, special policy packages have been implemented in three key industrial sectors; motor vehicles, pharmaceuticals, and electronics. The expansion of the *maquila* sector has also received strong governmental support. The achievements attained so far in these areas constitute clear signals of the type of industrial policy that can and should be implemented in selected strategic industries. These efforts all combine regulatory and promotional measures. While trade restrictions and public sector involvement in the economy have been reduced in recent years, in the future, further deregulation will be needed in order to promote a more creative climate for growth and development.

Technology plays a fundamental role in determining Mexico's ability to compete in the international market, particularly as the threat of a more open economy gradually becomes a reality. Mexico will continue, through medium- and long-term sectoral policies, to support technological development and industrial restructuring as the most viable means of confronting the changing conditions of the world economy and achieving self-sustained growth.

3. U.S. Macroeconomic Strategy and the Advanced Developing Countries (James K. Galbraith)

The main features of the present U.S. macroeconomic strategy are high budget deficits, relatively high real interest rates, and a dollar that, despite everything, remains high relative to what would be required to restore trade balance. This mix is unsustainable in the long run, but for the present it serves the political purpose of supporting U.S. economic expansion and employment while repressing inflation. It is therefore likely to persist for some time yet.

If this mix does persist, U.S. macroeconomic strategy will sustain the market position of "inward-looking" consumer-goods manufacturing companies in the United States and overseas, while the position of "outward-looking" U.S. capital-goods producers and exporters continues to erode. The advanced developing countries (ADCs) may seek to exploit strong U.S. demand for imported manufactures and can expect such demand to recover quickly even from a U.S. recesssion, as long as the high dollar remains the principal instrument of U.S. anti-inflation policy.

But the ADCs will find their structural options constrained by the pattern of U.S. protection on the one hand and by the debt crisis on the other. Protection will work against rapid expansion of ADC exports in traditional manufactures and agriculture, as these sectors are the most effectively protected in the United States. The debt crisis severely limits the ability of ADC governments and national companies to import advanced capital equipment, which is required for the production of middle-technology exportable manufactures.

Further growth of direct foreign corporate investment is therefore likely to prove the path of least resistance toward higher exports for Mexico and countries in a similar position. Yet these investments may differ sharply in form and content from what the ADCs would choose on their own and in their own national interest. Hence the political tensions of the present U.S. relationship with the ADCs are likely to grow as long as the underlying U.S. macroeconomic strategy persists.

4. Prospects for the U.S.-Mexican Relationship in the Motor Vehicle Sector (James P. Womack)

Current technological and organizational trends in the world motor vehicle industry argue for a dramatic restructuring of U.S.-Mexican relations in this sector. In the 1990s, new technologies, simplified product designs, and new approaches to production organization will eliminate much of the unskilled and semi-skilled labor from motor vehicle manufacture. These unskilled activities have traditionally been envisioned as the major opening for Mexico in the international motor vehicle industry, as witnessed most recently by the boom in *maquiladora* plants producing seat covers and wiring harnesses.

Yet evidence is mounting that developing countries such as Mexico are now able to absorb very rapidly the new approaches to production organization pioneered by the Japanese. The latest example is the Ford Motor Company assembly plant at Hermosillo, which was built and is being operated with technical assistance from Mazda. Mexico should now be able to rapidly change its international image from that of a low-wage, low-quality manufacturing site using the simplest machinery to that of a low-wage site able to utilize state-of-the-art organizational techniques and complex machinery to attain world-class quality.

At the same time, the growing flood of imported vehicles and parts from many developing countries as well as from Japan and Europe seems likely to push the United States toward a much more protected market in motor vehicles in the 1990s. (The U.S. trade deficit in motor vehicles reached a staggering $55 billion in 1986.) In this situation, it is unclear how Mexican motor vehicle imports to the United States, now growing very rapidly, will be treated.

In light of these trends, what new relationship between the United States and Mexico is appropriate in this sector? The author proposes a U.S.-Mexican motor vehicle pact that is similar in some ways to the U.S.-Canada Auto Pact of 1965, but incorporates greater safeguards for the Mexican motor vehicle industry.

Such a pact would allow open trade in motor vehicles and parts between the United States and Mexico (and ideally Canada as well) for qualifying assemblers. It would eliminate all of the traditional Mexican local-content requirements. However, to qualify, motor vehicle assemblers (e.g., General Motors, Ford, Toyota, Honda, Nissan, Volkswagen) would need to maintain a large, positive trade flow from Mexico to the United States. In addition, qualifying assemblers would be required to guarantee that a substantial fraction of their Mexican manufacturing activity would consist of "high value added" activities such as engine manufacture, engineering, and research and development.

Why should the relevant parties—the Mexican and U.S. governments and the multinational assemblers—favor this new approach? The U.S. government must soon prioritize its trade relationships in the motor vehicle sector. (At present, Japan is in one category, with a quota, while the rest of the world, including Mexico, is in another.) In this situation, a motor vehicle pact that in fact liberalizes many aspects of U.S.-Mexico trade may be very attractive. In combination with restraints on other producing regions whose economic and political stability are less important to the United States, the proposed motor vehicle pact could even be implemented with positive results for U.S.-based motor vehicle manufacturing.

For the Mexican government, the motor vehicle pact could guarantee expanded access to the U.S. market while helping overcome two traditional weaknesses of the Mexican industry: a lack of scale economies (caused by the rigid local-content rules) and a lack of participation by the leading Japanese producers (due to the high investment cost of market access and uncertain long-term access from Mexico to the United States).

For the U.S. and European multinationals, the motor vehicle pact would permit the rationalization of their U.S.-Mexican operations that they have long sought. The Japanese multinationals, by contrast, would suddenly have much easier access to a new market and a new site for low-wage manufacturing with guaranteed access to the United States.

A new relationship of the type proposed would of course be complex and difficult to negotiate. However, current trends strongly suggest that such a new relationship would be worth the effort for all of the parties concerned.

5. Automated Manufacturing and Offshore Assembly in Mexico (Susan Walsh Sanderson)

Offshore assembly plays a very important role in the Mexican economy, employing over 300,000 workers and serving as the country's second most important source of foreign exchange. Increasing automation in manufacturing—specifically in the electrical and electronics industries that comprise two-thirds of Mexico's offshore assembly activity—and subsequent changes in methods and organization have the potential to alter existing co-production relationships and pose serious dilemmas for Mexican policymakers.

One principal impact of computer-aided design and manufacturing (CAD/CAM) and robotics has been to reduce the importance of low-cost labor in the production process. For U.S. firms attempting to keep up with the Japanese, automation has become imperative. Given the inextricable links between U.S. and Mexican manufacturing, this promises to result in a direct loss of jobs, primarily among unskilled and semi-skilled laborers. Mexico must make it a policy priority to train and retain workers, particularly in disciplines related to design and engineering, if Mexico hopes to develop an independent, competitive manufacturing sector. Although developing industries of the future will require substantial capital and expertise and will reduce the need for certain unskilled or semi-skilled workers, automation is a "must" if Mexico is to avoid falling even further behind in an increasingly competitive global marketplace.

Another option that Mexico should explore is that of forming production alliances that include Japanese manufacturers, posssibly sourcing parts for Japanese production facilities in the United States. If these or any other new production alliances are to make a real difference to Mexican long-term economic development, however, it will be essential to link them to domestic suppliers and producers.

To make such links feasible, incentives must be offered to domestic suppliers and producers to improve both the quality and the cost of their goods. Protectionism, which has long characterized Mexican industrial policy, tends to contribute to inefficiency and hence must be replaced by policies that lead toward greater trade liberalization. Opening up the Mexican market to inputs such as semiconductors, controllers, microprocessors, and computers—goods that form that basis of production in many sectors of industry—is imperative if the Mexican manufacturing sector is to keep pace with the rapid rate of innovative change taking place.

6. Technology and Employment Along the U.S.-Mexican Border (M. Patricia Fernández Kelly)

Mexican officials consider the *maquila* sector to be a key feature in the country's development strategy. Mexico currently ranks first among newly developed countries doing assembly work for U.S.-based multinationals, and domestically the maquila industry is the fastest growing sector of the economy. Since it was launched in 1965, the industry has appealed to public officials in Mexico as a promising mechanism for creating jobs, upgrading worker skills, and facilitating technology transfer. To realize this potential, however, the Mexican government must design concrete policies to assure that the development of the maquila sector results in greater benefits for Mexican workers and their communities.

Advanced technological processes have allowed for the decentralization of production and reorganization of labor by converting complex tasks into a series of unskilled operations that can be geographically dispersed. This manner of organizing production has made it possible to generate considerable employment in low wage regions of the world. In Mexico, the maquila industry has primarily opened up jobs for young, unskilled women previously considered "unemployable." Most of these women are the primary wage earners in their families, yet their jobs often are viewed as merely a source of supplemental income. A critical first step for Mexican policymakers is to overcome the barriers in perception that prevent them from recognizing the importance of these women's jobs to the subsistence of their families and to national development.

The author outlines other policy recommendations to facilitate the integration of the maquila sector into a broader Mexican development strategy. Prominent among these is the strengthening of links between the maquila sector and the rest of the domestic economy. Measures that would encourage this process include a) offering incentives to foreign companies and tax exemptions to encourage them to "buy Mexican," and b) encouraging the development by Mexican firms—aided with public and private loans—of services and manufactures related to transportation, packaging, and the processing of waste and residues.

To stimulate technology transfer and worker training, tax incentives should be awarded to firms willing to participate in experimental projects aimed at equipping Mexican-owned sister firms with technology to facilitate their expansion. Incentives should also be offered to firms to promote personnel training—a policy that would require a reconsideration of the role of women in the work force.

The maquila sector's role in national development would also be enhanced by weeding out those industries that have either a negative effect or very limited positive impact on the Mexican economy. The prevalent attitude has been that even the slightest pressure on foreign companies would result in the loss of investment and jobs. This attitude should be abandoned in favor of a more discriminating approach.

Businesses should be encouraged to utilize and further develop the skills of *maquiladora* workers by promoting qualified assemblers to positions of greater responsibility. The traditional approach has been to hire engineers to fill supervisory and administrative positions, yet clearly many employees acquire on the job the necessary skills to assume such responsibilities.

To date, the maquila sector has functioned almost as an island within the Mexican economy. The role and gains for Mexico have been limited primarily to the provision of unskilled laborers who bring home very low wages. There is potential, however, to integrate this sector more fully into the Mexican economy—for the benefit of the sector's predominantly female work force and their dependents as well as for the strengthening of the Mexican economy.

7. Biotechnology and Food: The Scope for Cooperation (Cassio Luiselli Fernández)

Biotechnology has emerged as a field of profound innovation, holding the promise for Mexico of providing the means to address some of its most pressing social and economic needs. The development of coherent policies to promote and regulate progress in this field, both at the national and international level, merits policy attention in both the United States and Mexico as this field holds potential to serve as a showcase for compromise and cooperation. Such an approach would benefit both countries and could offer an example of the creative management of interdependence.

Agriculture, food production and processing, health, energy, and pollution-control efforts all stand to benefit from changes taking place in this field—changes that are occurring at an increasingly rapid rate. Mexico has many of the necessary resources to allow it rapidly to develop and take advantage of the new biotechnology. There are, however, also numerous obstacles to overcome. Research costs are very high, and fiscal and investment incentives are severely lacking; linkages between the research level and industry are very weak; and the development of relevant infrastructure has been uneven and disjointed.

The author argues that the Mexican government must recognize the importance of biotechnology for the country's development progress, particularly in agriculture, and formulate programs and policies to overcome the obstacles identified and promote the development of this field. A national strategy must integrate the pursuit of a number of policy aims, including the following: the training of skilled personnel; the development of appropriate financial instruments; the linkage of academic, government, and private sectors; and the reshaping of the regulatory framework to attract foreign capital and technology while continuing to protect Mexican national interests. It is also essential to ascertain the extent to which the biotechnology strategy can function within the existing *minifundio*-based agricultural system.

At the international level, there is a need to develop policies to improve the security and regulation of the field of biotechnology. Evaluation and oversight mechanisms are needed to monitor the impact of new developments, and international standards and regulations must be established to govern the handling and transport of biological materials.

In Latin America, efforts should also be made to promote cooperative regional development in this field. Given their level of development, natural resources, and industrial maturity, cooperation among Latin American countries would allow them to reach the "cutting edge" of biotechnology in some strategic areas. A networking program should be initiated and might usefully start by defining the more promising and critical areas for development in the region.

A cooperative bilateral U.S.-Mexican biotechnology strategy should also form part of Mexico's overall approach to this field. The United States has an overwhelming worldwide advantage in biotechnology while Mexico, for its part, has the industrial and scientific infrastructure to adopt and rapidly adapt new biotechnologies. Given the open nature of the U.S. economy and the proximity of the United States and Mexico, serious consideration should be given to the possibility of Mexican capital and technicians participating in U.S. biotechnology companies. This would allow for the transfer of both technology and expertise in management. The challenge for Mexico is that it can take advantage of the benefits offered by the level of development and proximity of the United States only to the extent that it has itself developed in this pivotal area.

8. The Mexican Pharmaceutical and Pharmochemical Industries (Joan Brodovsky)

Pharmaceutical and pharmochemical industries worldwide are experiencing a period of technological change and growth. In Mexico, for over forty years, the government's policy of trade protection has successfully assisted the expansion and development of the country's domestic pharmaceutical and pharmochemical industries while holding down consumer prices. Today, however, these same policies are contributing to the industries' currently slowed technological development. An inadequate scientific infrastructure further hampers the acquisition and assimilation of new technology in these areas.

Official control of the prices of all finished pharmaceuticals is the dominant characteristic of the Mexican market for medicines. It is also the most important point of contention between the industry and the government.

Mexico's pharmochemical and pharmaceutical industries are fully developed technologically in traditional manufacturing methods, but they are neither acquiring and assimilating the new technologies from abroad nor developing them domestically. Both the patent laws which prohibit patents on health products, and the technology transfer laws, which limit royalties and regulate licensing contracts, have served as major disincentives for potential foreign licensors, and, to some degree, for Mexican research in new pharmochemicals and pharmaceuticals.

Mexico's Pharmaceutical Decree of 1984 provoked a sharp reaction from the U.S. pharmaceutical companies with operations in Mexico. Among other restrictions that it imposed, the Decree limited the ability of these firms to capitalize on their trademarks by requiring them to display prominently the generic name of the product. The differences of opinion and in point of view on this issue between the U.S. government, which supported the U.S. pharmaceutical firms with operations in Mexico, and the Mexican government, which deeply resented the interference by a foreign government, illustrate the differences in political tactics and philosophy of the two countries.

Sustaining a constructive working relationship is both economically and politically important to Mexico as well as the United States. Diplomatic disputes—in this sector as in other areas—can be minimized if policymakers on each side see their own country's broad as well as specific interests clearly, recognize and understand the viewpoint and political philosophy of the other country, and measure in those terms the consequences of their actions.

The United States and Mexico: Face to Face with New Technology

Chapter 1

Technology and the Changing Industrial Balance

Alan L. Madian

This essay examines the interaction of technology with the other forces that have shaped and will continue to shape trade and economic relations between the United States and Mexico—as well as between other industrial and advanced developing countries. The reason for focusing on trade is simply that the most successful of the advanced developing countries—the Asian newly industrializing countries (or NICs)—owe their success to a relatively open system of world trade, to their ability to combine labor-intensive production with modern high-technology, and to their ability to produce extremely high-quality products demanded by the developed countries at costs that are frequently substantially lower than the costs of industries in those countries. A large part of the success of the Asian NICs is attributable to organizing production so that the benefits of new technologies can be realized quickly.

The transfer of technology to the NICs has been facilitated by the proliferation of machinery-making companies that sell to all comers, and by the use of microelectronics, which allows production techniques—that once required years of worker training—to be carried out by machines operated by semi-skilled workers. Programmable machines have provided new opportunities for import substitution and export growth, and they have enabled manufacturing industries in the NICs to compete successfully with developed countries for shares of the world market for manufactured goods.

Exports from the NICs and other advanced developing countries increasingly have shifted from raw materials and semi-finished goods to sophisticated manufactures. In the long run, as lower-cost substitutes for raw materials continue to proliferate and as agricultural subsidies and overproduction continue, terms of trade can be expected

41

to continue to favor manufactures even though the price levels of manufactured goods are likely to decrease as manufacturing expands in an increasing number of relatively low-wage countries. The *export-based, market-driven economic development model*—originating in Japan, with applications in Taiwan, Korea, and elsewhere—and the *import-substitution development model*—dominant during the decades following World War II and still lingering in Mexico and prevalent in other countries in Latin America—are in a contest for the allegiance of emerging developing-country elites. The outcome is not preordained.

The Limits of Prophecy

During the 1960s, some of those concerned with the future of the U.S. economy and the economies of developing countries attempted to forecast the international division of labor in the year 2000. Perhaps the most prominent figures associated with these efforts were Daniel Bell and Herman Kahn.[1] But forecasting the impact of technological change is an extremely risky activity. The forecasts of the 1960s predicted that the Western industrialized countries and Japan would dominate research and development, as well as high-technology manufacture, and that their rates of growth consequently would be robust. After all, these countries had a near monopoly on skilled labor and on the technical infrastructure necessary to use the computers and robots that were soon expected to transform manufacturing. The forecasters thought that developing countries—due to their proximity to emerging markets and their lower costs, as well as to their diverse national tastes—would become secondary sites of multinational manufacturing (in keeping with a version of the product cycle theory that was developed and popularized by Raymond Vernon.[2])

Although some of the forecasters said that Japan would join the U.S. and European leadership in technologically sophisticated manufacturing and in traditional capital-intensive heavy industry, they failed to foresee the emergence of the NICs. The forecasters assumed that effective plans could be devised to move the world toward the forecasted division of labor and that doing so would optimize development. In the 1960s, a great deal of thought and research in the United States was devoted to anticipating the impact of automation on the future of manufacturing and on the future organization of the domestic economy and society. Commentators believed that automation would cause a significant decrease in employment of skilled workers in manufacturing as robots took over their jobs, but that profits would be sufficient to enable unions, following the pattern set by the United Auto Workers, to bargain for increased leisure through sabbaticals, early retirement, and longer vacations. There was a consensus that the new high-technology markets would be dominated by the most advanced countries, using highly automated processes; more labor-intensive "appropriate technologies" would provide employment and import-substituting industrialization in the developing world. The problem for the advanced industrial countries would not be production, but the division of the profits and employment creation for those whose skills were no longer needed in the high-technology industries that were expected to prevail.

Of all of these forecasts, the only one that proved to be correct was that the least-skilled workers in the developed countries would face increased employment difficulties. The conventional wisdom neglected the changes already brought about in developing countries by increased communications and automation, and it failed to anticipate the changes that this potent combination would make possible. It likewise, understandably, failed to anticipate the impact of changing energy costs on the uses of many traditional materials and on the industries that produced and utilized those materials. For example, markets have disappeared as new materials have been substituted for traditional materials, and only the least-cost producers of such basic traditional materials as copper and steel have continued to be profitable. The forecasts of the 1960s also neglected the impact on industries in developing countries of the unprecedented numbers of their technical professionals educated in industrialized societies and the skills developed by indigenous employees of multinational companies.

Automation and developments in communications have made possible transfers of technology on a scale and with a speed previously unimaginable. Vastly increased international trade and financial flows of course mean that national economies—regardless of their size—are far more influenced by what goes on elsewhere.

There are those who refer to the current development of robotics and microprocessors—sometimes in combination with the "green revolution"—as the cause of a third industrial revolution (the earlier two having been the combination of steam and machinery in the late eighteenth and early nineteenth centuries, and the development of mass production in combination with electric power and chemical fertilizer in the early twentieth century). It is, however, too soon to know whether these new developments will bring about changes as profound as those associated with the first two industrial revolutions—or whether new developments in areas as diverse as superconductivity and bioengineering will result in similarly profound changes in the near future. But there is no question that robotics and microprocessors are radically restructuring the large-scale industrialization that resulted from the second industrial revolution.

The impact of the new electronics has been magnified by its coincidence with the restructuring of industrial production due to two other significant changes. First, changes took place in the materials used in manufacturing; for example, plastics, carbon composites, and fiber optics reduced demand for metals. Second, greatly improved communications made it far easier to locate and successfully operate manufacturing plants in less industrialized countries.

In industries as diverse as automobiles and pharmaceuticals, the emergence of flexible, electronically programmed machine tools and laboratory instruments, enhanced by computer-aided design, produced "receding scale economies"—or the capacity to sustain world-scale plants with substantially lower market shares and total sales than was the case during the past several decades.

Since the 1960s, new technologies and new ways of organizing production have been emerging in greater numbers and with increasing speed and geographical dispersion. Earlier models of the process and the time required to go from an underdeveloped to a developed economy have been shattered. In East Asia, entire societies have been transformed at unprecedented speed. In Korea, for example, the proportion of the population employed in agriculture declined from 56 to 26 per cent between 1965 and 1984. In the United States, a similar transformation took nearly sixty years.

All of these factors—and the political responses to them—will shape the future of economic development and economic relations between the developed and the advanced developing countries. The forecasting misjudgments of the recent past provide a useful cautionary note about the very feasibility of predicting longer-run outcomes with any certainty.

Created Comparative Advantage: Theoretical Origins

The forecasters failed to grasp a fundamental truth about comparative advantage that is integral to the Asian economic development model. In the modern era, comparative advantage is at least as much *created* as it is a result of natural and human endowments—a fact long recognized by Western economists when dealing with microeconomics, or the economics of firms. Until recently, however, economists (with the notable exception of Joseph Schumpeter) have rarely recognized this truth when dealing with macroeconomics and international trade.

The Asian trends derive from efforts to create comparative advantage without significant natural resources. The strategies of the Asian NICs—whether directed in part by government, as in Korea or Singapore, or relying more on entrepreneurial decisions, as in Taiwan or Hong Kong—have much in common with the strategy of Japan. Thus the Japanese view of industrial planning can provide important insights into aspects of all of these countries' national strategies. Japan's approach has been described with considerable candor by Miyohei Shinohara, a former head of the economics section of the Japanese Planning Agency:

> Ironically, . . . Japan's industrial policies achieved unprecedented success by going against modern economic theory. Whether it was steel, petrochemicals, or other industries . . . the government tried to introduce protective measures in industries which appeared to have potential for achieving an advantageous position over the next decade. . . . The problem with classical thinking undeniably lies in the fact that it . . . does not take into account the possibility of a dynamic change in the comparative advantage or disadvantage of industries over a coming 10 or 20 year period.[3]

The new policy concept as described by Shinohara was followed by economic planning officials and, perhaps less explicitly, by entrepreneurs:

> The two basic criteria to which the industrial structure policies adopted by MITI [Ministry of International Trade and Industry] conformed . . . were an 'income elasticity criterion' and a 'comparative technical progress criterion'. . . . The 'income elasticity criterion' provides a suggestion that an industry whose elasticity of export demand with respect to world real income as a whole is comparatively high should be developed as an export industry. . . . The 'comparative technical progress criterion' pays more attention to the possibility of placing a particular industry in a more advantageous position in the future through a comparatively greater degree of technical progress. . . .

Shinohara's observations on labor or capital intensity indicate that the old "labor-intensive versus capital-intensive" dichotomy has only limited usefulness as applied to Japan and the Asian NICs:

> Both in Japan and in Korea, the fostering of basic industries that are highly capital-intensive (e.g., steel and petrochemicals) was planned at a time when labor supply was in excess. . . . There are indications that many production methods, no matter how capital-intensive, could certainly become paying industries in the LDCs [less developed countries] and NICs—provided . . . a high standard of technology is embodied within the capital stock, thus eliminating the necessity for the labor force to be equipped with high technology and skills. . . . However, . . . the phrase 'in parallel with development of other labor-intensive industries' should be hastily added as a necessary condition. . . . The point here is the parallel development of . . . basic industries and processing indus-

tries. . . . Of the so-called heavy industries in Japan, the industries achieving the most outstanding growth have been the labor-intensive industries involving a high degree of processing, such as automobiles and electronics.

In comparative technical progress analysis, the question that must be addressed is how to become a low-cost—or possibly the lowest-cost—producer. In the absence of natural resources, a favorable answer would depend on scale economies that sometimes involve protecting the home market for a prolonged period (a course that is no longer acceptable internationally), or on labor-rate economies and innovations in production technologies and logistics.

The success of Japan is based on an export strategy that takes advantage of being second or later in the marketplace, rather than of being the product innovator—although that has recently been changing. (Japanese companies are making significant investments in research and development of new consumer products, as well as in super-computers and robotics, among others.) For years, innovation took place in the organization of production and in the technical means selected to produce final products—whether these were producer goods such as steel sheets, or consumer goods such as automobiles. Despite the significant labor-cost advantages that it enjoyed in the 1950s and 1960s, Japan was very quick to adopt the most advanced technologies used in high labor-cost societies, provided that such technologies reduced costs and increased competitiveness.

The succesful East Asian NICs have been following Japan's strategy of rapid industrialization. Like Japan, they all started to build from a base of low-cost labor but are increasingly reliant on state-of-the-art technologies as well. Japan's success, however, has changed the conditions for later entrants by provoking significant protectionist reactions in the developed economies. Consequently, latecomers have faced increasing trade difficulties even if they are otherwise successful in imitating the Japanese model.

Relations Between Advanced Developing and Developed Countries

Those who urge protection of industries in developed countries frequently assume that the decline in industries in the United States and Europe is the direct result of the emergence of identical industries in Japan and in the advanced developing countries. Reality, however, is not so simple. The experience of the steel industry shows that the use of alternative materials and the elimination of some uses of steel may be as important as—or even more important than—the emergence of new steel producers. But it is the *belief* that the decline of developed-country industries is due to the emergence of those of other countries that shapes policy in the developed countries. American attitudes toward international trade have been changing as a result of the emergence of Japan and the Asian NICs at a time when industries in which Europe and the United States dominated were declining. This protectionist attitude will make the repetition of the Japanese approach to development (which involved protecting the home market while building industries capable of significant exports) impossible for countries such as Mexico that are latecomers to international industrial competition.

The Success of the Asian NICs

Since 1960, the Asian NICs have caught up with or surpassed the most developed countries of Latin America in per capita GNP, education, life expectancy, economic growth rates, and the amounts earned by production and other workers. They have done so despite their relative paucity of natural resources and despite large expenditures by some of them on national defense. The Asian NICs have gone through a remarkable series of transformations in the goods that they produce. Product complexity and quality have been upgraded continually. These countries also have much higher ratios of exports to gross national product and much higher percentages of manufactures in their exports than do the Latin American countries. For example, in 1981 manufactures accounted for only 39 per cent of the exports of Brazil and Mexico, but for 82 per cent and 90 per cent, respectively, of the exports of Taiwan and Korea. Increases in the growth of manufacturing have been somewhat higher in the Asian industrializing countries than in Latin America, as can be seen in Table 1—although the difference in rates achieved by producing largely for export rather than for home markets is not as great as might have been expected.

Gross National Product. A comparison of the rate of increase in GNP in the 1960s, 1970s, and 1980s shows that while the rate of increase has fallen most in the developed countries and the advanced developing countries of Latin America, it has fallen least in the Asian NICs (Table 2).

Trade with the United States. Table 3 breaks down U.S. import and export shares by national origin. Table 4 shows the composition of U.S. merchandise trade. In 1986, Japan's total exports amounted to $209.2 billion, of which the U.S. share was $85.5 billion. In the same year, the total exports of the Asian NICs were $127.3 billion, of which the U.S. share amounted to $49.1 billion. In percentage terms, Japan and the Asian NICs together accounted for about 35 per cent of U.S. imports—and for a substantially higher share of U.S. manufactured imports.

Table 1. Average Annual Growth Rate in Manufacturing (percentages)

	1960–70	1970–81
United States	5.3	2.9
Japan	13.6	6.5
Germany	5.4	2.1
France	7.8	3.2
United Kingdom	3.3	−0.5
Taiwan	17.3	13.3
Hong Kong	13.6	10.2
Singapore	13.0	9.7
Korea	17.6	15.6
Brazil	9.7	8.7
Mexico	10.1	7.1

Source: World Bank, *World Tables* (third edition), 1984.

Remarkably, Japan's share of U.S. imports rose from 17.7 per cent in 1984 to 22.1 per cent in 1986 and that of the Asian NICs rose from 11.5 per cent to 12.7 per cent over the same period. In contrast, the share of U.S. imports accounted for by the Western Hemisphere developing countries declined from 14.7 per cent in 1984 to 11.4 per cent in 1986; Mexico's share fell from 5.4 per cent to 4.5 per cent.

In terms of the balance of trade, the special place of Japan and the Asian NICs can be seen in the following data. In 1986, the smaller Asian exporters had a favorable trade balance of $30.8 billion with the United States; Japan's favorable balance was $58.6 billion. By contrast, if oil is excluded, trade with Mexico is favorable to the United States— despite Mexico's debt crisis, which has significantly reduced Mexican imports; and Brazil, which has a larger population than the combined population of the Asian NICs, had a favorable balance of trade of less than $3.5 billion with the United States in 1986.

Until recently, the smaller Asian exporters had a very modest effect on the U.S. balance of trade; as late as 1982, for example, Korea had a lower value of exports to the United States than imports from the United States. Japan, by contrast, has maintained substantial surpluses for over a decade. In comparison to Japan, the other Asian

Table 2. Gross National Product: Average Annual Growth Rate, 1960–1985 (percentages, constant currency units)

	1960–70	1970–81	1981–85[a]
United States	4.3	3.0	2.6
Germany	4.4	2.6	1.6
France	5.4	3.4	1.3
U.K.	2.9	1.7	2.2[b]
Japan	10.4	4.6	3.7[b]
Hong Kong	10.0	10.0	5.0
Singapore	8.7	8.3	5.2
Korea	8.7	8.7	7.6
Brazil	5.4	7.5	0.7[b]
Mexico	7.5	6.4	− 0.7[b]

[a] GDP.
[b] 1981–84.
    Sources: 1960–81: *World Tables*, op. cit.; 1981–84: United Nations, *Monthly Bulletin of Statistics* (January 1987).

exporters (despite their much lower level of per capita GNP) have been relatively open to U.S. imports. Yet recent U.S. legislative proposals show that this has not saved them from intense protectionist reactions.

The Industrial Employment Crisis in the United States and Europe: Perceptions and Reality

The industrial employment crisis in the United States and Europe has many causes and reflects only in small part the changing industrial balance between industrial societies and the NICs. Unlike Europe, the United States has had serious and growing balance-of-trade deficits. Table 4 provides the 1986 composition of trade; imports of manufactures exceeded exports by over $130 billion. Industrial output as a proportion of GNP has declined far less than industrial employment, and for many industries output has increased. Nonetheless previously privileged industrial workers in autos and steel and less privileged workers in textiles and shoes, for example, have faced plant closings and unemployment.

Table 3. Direction of U.S. Merchandise Trade with the World, 1986 (billions of U.S. dollars)

	U.S. Exports		U.S. Imports		U.S. Balance
Canada	$45.3	20.9%	$68.7	17.7%	−$23.3
Japan	26.9	12.4	85.5	22.1	−58.6
European Community (12 countries)	53.2	24.5	79.5	20.5	−26.4
East Asian NICs	18.3	8.4	49.1	12.7	−30.8
Other Asian countries	7.8	3.6	14.3	3.7	−6.5
Middle East	8.4	3.9	8.6	2.2	−0.2
Western Hemisphere developing countries	31.1	14.3	44.1	11.4	−13.0
(Mexico)	(12.4)	(5.7)	(17.6)	(−4.5)	(−5.2)
African LDCs	4.8	2.2	8.6	2.2	−3.8
Centrally planned economies	5.1	2.4	7.4	1.9	−2.3
Other	16.1	7.4	21.7	5.6	−5.6
TOTAL	$217.3		$387.1		−$169.8

Source: U.S. Department of Commerce, 1986 *Foreign Trade Highlights* (unnumbered proof pages). Totals may not add due to rounding.

Table 4. Composition of U.S. Merchandise Trade with the World, 1986 (U.S. $ billions and percentages)

	Imports	Exports
Total	$387.1	$217.3
Machinery and transportation equipment	42.9%	45.7%
Chemicals	4.1	10.6
Basic manufactures	13.4	6.8
Miscellaneous manufactures	15.5	8.3
Beverages and tobacco	10.3	1.4
Food and animals	1.1	8.2
Mineral fuels	5.8	3.8
Crude materials	2.9	8.1
Fats and oils	0.2	0.5
Other	3.8	6.6

Source: U.S. Department of Commerce, *1986 Foreign Trade Highlights* (unnumbered proof pages). Totals may not add due to rounding.

It is widely assumed that the cause of the crisis is foreign competition—particularly competition from Japan and the NICs. Economists, however, have pointed to the diminishing rate of productivity improvements as a fundamental cause and explanation of declining competitiveness and export sales. But it should also be noted that, other things being equal, increased productivity means reduced employment.

Declining productivity gains are primarily a reflection of changes in economic and demographic structure as agriculture and industry employ ever smaller proportions of the labor force, while services employ ever larger proportions. Within industry, there are also changes in industrial composition as new products are developed and as new technologies and materials replace those that were formerly dominant. Thus the role of foreign competition, while not insignificant, is a *secondary* cause of the employment crisis in the United States and Europe.

The crisis is even more serious in Europe than in the United States. Despite an improvement in the European Community's (EC) trade balance from a negative $66 billion in 1980 to a positive $4.8 billion in 1986, economic dislocation has been a more serious problem in Europe than in the United States. Because levels of unemployment and the fate of major industries are seen to be more a matter of public policy in Europe than in the United States, demands for remedial measures are far more frequent. In some European countries, unemployment is at levels above those reached during the Great Depression—without taking into account the "guest workers" who have returned home to Turkey, Yugoslavia, North Africa, and elsewhere. Between 1970 and 1984, labor participation rates in the European member states of the Organisation for Economic Co-operation and Development (OECD) declined from 67.4 per cent to 65.2 per cent of the working-age population. In the United States, in contrast, the rate increased from 66.8 per cent to 73.3 per cent; the United States has succeeded in creating over twenty million more jobs in the period between 1973 and 1984, while the EC lost between one and two million. Moreover, the much greater role that trade in manufactures plays in the EC makes it far more vulnerable to adverse changes in international trade. The current dollar exchange rate will enhance the U.S. trade position, while Europe's trade position can be expected to deteriorate, further worsening its employment situation.

Developed-Country Industrial Decline: A Closer Look at the Causes

Three industries—steel, automobiles, and semiconductors—have been held up as examples of ruinous competition from Japan and the Asian

NICs. In both the United States and Europe, however, the impact of Japan on all three of those industries is far more significant than that of the Asian NICs, and other causes have also contributed to their decline.

Steel

In the steel industry, the use of alternative materials and the elimination of some uses of steel have been more important than the emergence of new producers.

Materials substitution began before the energy crisis but was hastened by changes in the relative costs of inputs and by the redesign of products to reduce weight. This led to the restructuring of major industries, including an increasing substitution of injection-molding equipment for machine tools as plastic and carbon fiber materials replaced metal. These changes made a lot of high-cost capacity for metal production and processing redundant.

As Table 5 shows, industrial-country consumption and production of steel fell significantly in the decade 1974–1984, during which other countries increasingly provided for their own needs and in some cases exported quantities that were of considerable significance for their economies.

Certainly there have been cyclical fluctuations in steel output, as well as significant reductions in steel use per automobile and per $1 million of GNP, as other materials have been substituted. Yet, as a result of economic growth, the total level of production in 1984 was 1 per cent more than in 1974. Between 1974 and 1984, the United States, Japan, and the EC countries reduced their total output by 95,825,000 metric tons (representing nearly a quarter of their 1974 production); over the same period, however, they cut their consumption by 57,908,000 metric tons. Thus about two-thirds of the output decline reflected a dramatic decline in consumption. The Western developed-country market shares of world production fell from 58 per cent in 1974 to 44 per cent in 1984. During that time, Brazil, Mexico, and the Asian NICs increased their production by about 29 million metric tons—or less than a third of the amount by which the three major producers reduced their shares.

Thus it appears that, at least in terms of quantities of crude steel manufactured, the distress in the steel industries of the developed countries was only partly, and not mainly, attributable to the production and export increases of the advanced developing countries.

Motor Vehicles

World motor vehicle production rose from 16.5 million in 1960 to 42.3 million in 1984 (Table 6).

Table 5. Steel: Changes in Production and Consumption, 1974–84 (thousands metric tons crude steel)

	1974		1984		1974-84	
	Production	Consumption	Production	Consumption	Changes in Production	Changes in Consumption
United States	132,195	144,120	83,900	114,300	−48,295	−29,820
EC	156,224	123,140	120,241	94,100	−35,983	−29,040
Japan	117,131	75,753	105,584	73,800	−11,547	−1,953
Brazil	7,515	12,799	18,391	11,000[b]	10,876	1,799
Mexico	5,138	5,880	7,482	6,600[b]	2,344	720
Korea	1,947	3,256	13,033	7,000[b]	11,086	3,744
Taiwan	597	2,544	5,010	2,800[b]	4,413	256
Singapore	194	1,762	359[a]	2,500[b]	165	738

[a] 1982.
[b] Estimate.

Sources: International Iron and Steel Institute, *Steel Statistical Yearbook* (Brussels: various years); American Iron and Steel Institute, *Steel and America, An Annual Report* (Washington, D.C.: various years); Statistical Office of the European Communities, *Eurostat: Iron and Steel Yearbook, 1984* (Luxembourg); IISI, *Steel Statistics of Developing Countries, 1985*; IISI, *World Steel in Figures, 1985*; AISI, *Annual Statistical Report* (various years).

Table 6. Motor Vehicles: Changes in Shares of World Market (thousands and percentages)

	Units Produced	U.S.	EEC	Japan	Combined
1960	16,488	48%	36%	3%	87%
1965	24,267	46	34	8	88
1970	29,403	28	37	18	83
1975	32,998	27	31	21	79
1980	38,514	21	29	29	79
1984	42,330	26	26	27	79

Sources: Motor Vehicle Manufacturers Association, *World Motor Vehicle Data* (Detroit: various years); MVMA, *Automobile Facts and Figures* (various years); Automotive News, *1985 Market Data Yearbook* (Detroit).

From 1960 to 1984, passenger car production increased from less than 13 million to nearly 31 million. Since 1960, the U.S. share of the world market has diminished significantly as the shares of Japan and the European Community have increased. Yet the *combined* share of the three major producers remained remarkably stable between 1975 and 1984.

Production increases in the NICs are dwarfed by those in Spain and Canada. Between 1970 and 1984, Canada increased its production by 718,000 units and Spain by 773,000. With the success of Brazil and Korea, the NICs are just beginning to have an impact on motor vehicle production in the developed countries.

Solid-State Electronics

Solid-state electronics, including semiconductors, is viewed as the essence of high technology. In this industry perhaps more than any other, U.S. companies have established manufacturing facilities abroad. If the production of U.S. subsidiaries abroad is included with the U.S. production, the U.S. share of the world industry is extremely high. Unfortunately, however, exact figures on the world industry are not readily available.

Between 1975 and 1985, U.S. exports of solid-state electronic products increased over 400 per cent in current dollars. This surely would be cause for celebration, had imports not increased over 700 per cent and apparent consumption[4] by nearly 600 per cent (Table 7).

Imports as a share of U.S. apparent consumption rose from 29 per cent in 1975 to 36 per cent in 1985. Exports as a share of U.S. apparent consumption fell from 38 per cent to 27 per cent. The last year in which the United States had a trade surplus in these products was 1977. These figures are of course misleading, given the large proportion of imports (perhaps as much as 75 per cent) that comes from U.S. foreign operations or subsidiaries.[5] In semiconductors, for example, the U.S. balance of trade with the Asian NICs and Japan is significantly adverse. At least through 1984, however, most of the non-Japanese imports and a significant amount of the Japanese imports were from subsidiaries of U.S. multinational corporations.

Policy Choices

Increasingly, economic policy decisions are constrained by *global* trading possibilities. Yet political decisions about economic policy still tend to be based on local, or at most, national considerations. This discrepancy results in serious conflicts and inefficiencies.

In the case of Mexico, economic policy debates since the crisis of 1982 have increasingly focused on the choice between an outward-

Table 7. U.S. Production and Trade in Solid-State Electronics
(U.S. $ millions and percentages)

	1975	1985	Change, 1975–85
U.S. factory shipments	$3,002	$14,430	480.6%
Imports	803	5,713	711.7
Exports	1,049	4,242	404.5
Apparent consumption	2,756	15,901	576.9

Source: Electronic Industries Association from U.S. Department of Commerce data, *Electronic Market Data Book* (Washington, D.C.: 1986).

looking economic strategy, which assigns a key role to the development of internationally competitive industries, and the country's traditional import-substitution model. Economic, commercial, political, and social interests are at stake, and the struggle is far from over. The degree of openness of the U.S. economy to Mexican exports will affect the attitudes of those who pursue the export strategy.

The Advanced Developing Countries

Since the terms of trade for manufactures continue to improve, developing-country entrepreneurs and policymakers are seeking to increase their ability to compete for a significant share of internationally traded manufactures. Many are examining the experience of the Asian NICs in search of lessons that they, too, can apply. Given the diverse traditions and institutional arrangements of the developing countries, the goal of increasing both manufactured exports and economic growth is likely to be pursued in ways that differ from those of the original Asian models.

In Mexico, for example, access to the home market has been used to lure developed-country manufacturers who provide reciprocal access to foreign markets, or who invest in return for access to a protected market. Agreements with the major U.S. automobile manufacturers have resulted in the construction in Mexico of world-class engine plants that export much of their output to the United States. These facilities have every prospect of remaining competitive as Mexican protection erodes.

In contrast, investments in aluminum manufacturing were made in the absence of scale economies and despite high electricity costs to take advantage of a protected market with prices well above competitive levels. The short-term benefits resulting from the aluminum investment are more than offset by long-term costs. This is always the case when goods are internationally traded at costs below those of the protected producers. The purchasers of such producer goods cannot compete with producers elsewhere who can acquire lower-priced inputs.

In addition to pricing other industries out of the market, protected export industries will be increasingly vulnerable to the actions of importing countries—and therefore inherently unstable. More emphasis should therefore be placed on getting plants with competitive economies—so that competitiveness remains as protection erodes.

Export Orientation versus Import Substitution. The experience of the Asian NICs requires reconsideration of the import-substitution model. What have been its shortcomings? In the absence of substantial manufacturing for export, a protected home market frequently has meant manufacturing costs in excess of world competitive levels; this has often been the case for Mexico. For domestic consumers, it has meant costs well above world market levels. New technologies are reducing the economies of scale in some industries, such as automobiles, but full scale economies still require substantial markets. Since technological obsolescence now occurs much more rapidly than it did even a decade ago, import substitution may lead to technological obsolescence.

The shortcomings of import substitution do not imply that there should never be subsidies or temporary protection, but rather that both should be *transitional* and *market-oriented*. Subsidizing an infant industry that produces an input used by other industries so that the input costs of the other industries are at world market levels may make sense—*if* it is reasonable to expect that the input-producing industry will be capable of competitive pricing in a few years. Japan followed just such a pattern in the cases of steel and semiconductors, among other products.

If a country chooses to follow the model of the Asian NICs, it must take care to link import substitution to export promotion. If a particular product is not a candidate for export promotion, then its candidacy for import substitution should be questioned. Products with the best export prospects should be chosen first. The pursuit of unsubsidized exports provides a useful cost discipline and a standard for project evaluation. Mexico is learning the hard way how difficult it is to reverse the course of import substitution undertaken without regard to export opportunities. Nevertheless, some companies in Mexico have succeeded, in 1985 and 1986, in substantially increasing manufactured exports.

Choice of Technology. Conventionally, investment is categorized as either high- or low-technology and as either capital- or labor-intensive. It is often assumed, incorrectly, that a labor-intensive industry is necessarily low-technology and has modest capital requirements—while a high-technology industry has high capital requirements and provides employment for a few highly trained individuals rather than for large numbers of less skilled workers. Stereotypes of high-technology are typified by the modern steel plant, or by the pharmaceutical factory staffed by a handful of chemical engineers and skilled operatives. Stereotypes of low-technology include garment factories before computerized cutting machines. This is a generally false dichotomy. Electronics and automobiles require inputs produced by high-technology *and* a large number of relatively unskilled workers. Within many industries, there are processing or fabricating tasks that have relatively low capital requirements and relatively high labor requirements.

In the present phase of developing-country industrialization, however, advanced technology frequently substitutes for skills and for labor. It is this embodiment of skills in machines, along with the substitution of materials that do not require skills, that has eroded the position of the skilled workers of the developed countries. Their position would have eroded regardless of whether or not that new technology was sent from the developed to the less developed countries. To understand the process, one has to go no further than a neighborhood auto repair shop, where electronic diagnosis has replaced the diagnostic skills of the mechanic and body putty has replaced the metalworking skills of the body shop craftsman.

Consequently the choice facing entrepreneurs and policymakers in the advanced developing countries is not between high- or low-technology, or between labor- or capital-intensive investment. Instead, they seek to maximize the potential for sales, profits, employment, and other benefits. From the perspective of the entrepreneur, the optimal investment is that which, combined with the other available inputs, will maximize profits. Insofar as policymakers are able to influence the costs of those other inputs, they are in a position to influence the choices of technology made by entrepreneurs.

Policymakers must evaluate the impact of an investment not only on the facility in which it will be operated, but on all the opportunities that will result from linkages to that facility. Eliminating excess costs in one area may enable the competitive manufacture of products that use the output of that industry as an input. Inputs that carry prices above world market levels are likely to reduce or eliminate the export potential of other industries that might otherwise be competitive, and these in turn will then require subsidies or protection from competitive exporters if they are to survive.

Industries also differ in the extent to which the most advanced technology is developed by the industry itself or by outsiders who sell it to all comers. Where technology is only available from a producer of the final products in the marketplace, new entrants can only obtain it through joint ventures or technology licensing. In such cases, if the export-promotion model is to be pursued, it is important that licensing and joint-venture agreements place no more than minimal limitations on exports.

Choice of Investor. Many developing countries restrict foreign investment; few restrict private investment, but many make public investments in industry and favor state industry over private industry.

The strategies adopted by the Asian NICs operate largely without public ownership of industry—but not without some public investment in research and development; considerable official guidance through licenses, permits, and other procedures in the selection of investment targets; and official limitations on the amounts to be invested in any single activity.

Mexico, in contrast, has attemped to guide development through government directives, including price controls, and through the creation of state enterprises in a variety of industrial and service sectors. In comparison to the framework for private endeavor established by Korea, for example, the Mexican government has not provided a consistent and clear direction for either public or private enterprise. Nor has Mexico encouraged exports.

Thus, where guidelines are modeled after the policies of the Asian NICs, government policy will avoid excess capacity and focus on exportable products. Private investment in industrial activities will be encouraged and the state role in industry will be reduced.

Investment and Capital Flows. As the NICs become more successful in the markets of the developed countries, they will no doubt make increasingly large investments in the markets of their customers. At the same time, the dynamic economies of the Asian NICs are already attracting portfolio managers from major institutions in the developed countries. As private companies in these Asian countries become stronger and better known internationally, they will have increasing access to international capital markets, and this will enhance their ability to compete.

In the Latin American advanced developing countries, private firms are in a much less advantageous position vis-à-vis private investment—due to the enormous burden of debt that these countries' private sectors and governments currently face and the far more cyclical nature of their economies. The perception is widespread—whether correct or not—that political as well as economic risks are greater in these countries than in the Asian NICs. This does not mean that opportunities to attract foreign investment have vanished for the Latin American advanced developing countries, but it does mean that in these countries foreign investors generally will seek to invest in ongoing operations rather than in new ventures, and that they will look for rates of return that compensate for the perceived risks.

The Developed Countries

The United States and other developed countries will face increasing supplies of high-quality manufactured goods from new competitors, and political leaders in the developed countries will continue to face demands from industrialists and trade unions for protection or, failing that, for policies that would reduce the pain caused by these emerging competitors.

The deterioration in the U.S. share of world trade preceded—and the commencement of a negative U.S. merchandise trade balance coincided with—the deterioration in real income that affected American workers throughout the 1970s and well into the 1980s. Both deteriorations were exacerbated by the two oil price shocks and the recessions they engendered. But it is important to recognize that both began before the Asian NICs became significant exporters; they were not brought on by the success of these countries.

There is no question that average annual growth rates of manufacturing have declined substantially since the 1960s in the United States and Europe while rising at unprecedented rates first in Japan and later in the Asian NICs and in the Latin American advanced developing countries. It should be noted, however, that while the NIC's growth rates of the 1970s were still high, they were lower than those they achieved in the 1960s—perhaps because of the oil price shocks and/or because of the success they had achieved in the previous decade.

Trade Policy. In the past two years, a large number of public officials who had formerly resisted AFL/CIO demands for protection of U.S. industries have changed their views. While free trade remains the dominant ideology among U.S. policymakers, the prospect of retaliating against those who limit U.S. access to their markets has gained substantial support—to the point where such demands are politically fashionable. As the current posture of the U.S. administration demonstrates, those who would resist protectionism at home must be seen to be forcing reciprocal market opening abroad.

The focal point of the U.S. protective reaction lies in the perception that the adverse trade balance is the cause of declining employment opportunities for skilled manufacturing workers—as well as in the belief that competition that hurts us must somehow be unfair. Despite extensive arguments to the contrary, it is still widely believed that a large share of the employment and welfare losses due to declining exports and increasing imports might have been avoided had U.S. multinational corporations not been so quick to ship their technologies abroad.

Whether the current combination of efforts to open foreign markets and reduce the value of the dollar will allow the United States to maintain the present degree of market access is open to question. At the very least, the NICs and other advanced developing countries must expect to be subject to increasing pressure to open their markets. In all probability, protectionism will become more acceptable as a retaliation against the real and supposed sins of others. Mexico will be affected by the backlash unless a special relationship is negotiated.

It appears extremely unlikely that the present U.S. trade regime can be liberalized unless major concessions are offered by developed-country, NIC, and other advanced-developing-country competitors. A significant reduction in non-tariff barriers and liberalization of trade in services is essential to bring about any liberalization of the present regime. Both may be required politically simply to maintain the status quo.

Industrial Policy. At present, it seems extremely unlikely that the developed countries will significantly increase the degree to which government gets involved in the investment decisions of the private sector. Indeed, the trend is away from such involvement in Japan, Europe, and North America.

Unlike the developing countries, the developed countries as a group cannot rely on a strategy that is based on taking advantage of being second into a market already developed by others by taking advantage of lower labor or overall manufacturing costs. They must be product innovators. The inability to rely on being second significantly reduces any advantages that could be gained by adopting the Japanese model of government direction of industry, which now is waning in Japan. France, which comes as close as any country in the developed West to providing economic policy guidance, has not been notably successful.

It is of course possible that there will be protectionist moves in the guise of industrial policy. Programs to protect "sunset" industries and the communities in which they are located have been advocated by a number of politicians and economists in the United States. The current wave of protectionist sentiment may allow some of their programs to be enacted, but that appears less likely now than in the recent past.

Technology Transfer. It appears most unlikely that technology transfers abroad—with the exception of technology with military applications—will be in any way curtailed. In fact, the pressure now seems to favor liberalization in this area. While it is true that U.S. or other developed-country producers could maintain a competitive edge for a longer period if exports of technology were reduced, the impact of retaliation would almost certainly far exceed any benefits provided by such a program.

Employment Strategies. The international division of labor has changed profoundly, often in ways that were not anticipated. It appears likely that if further trade liberalization is attempted, one of the requirements will be increased payments to workers displaced by trade. Even if the attempt at liberalization fails, those who favor such compensation programs are likely to attempt to have them implemented. Whether they will succeed, and in what form, cannot now be predicted. There appears to be a growing demand for benefits to those who are directly injured as a result of trade. The benefits would be used to provide help to those seeking alternative employment, retraining aid, and increased employment benefits.

Implications for the United States and Mexico

The effects of the changing global division of labor on the U.S.-Mexican relationship will be determined by market forces, bilateral and multilateral negotiations, trade litigation, capital flight, as well as by legal and illegal immigration, which will be profoundly affected by the implementation of the Simpson-Rodino bill. The discrepancy in per capita income between the two countries—and the fact that now the

United States is relatively prosperous while Mexico is in a deep depression due to low oil prices—makes the United States a magnet for skilled and unskilled Mexicans and for Mexican capital.

The Mexican economy is among the world's most porous: Adverse domestic economic circumstances quickly result in labor and capital flight, both of which have a direct impact on the U.S. economy. Consequently, Mexico has unique bargaining power vis-à-vis the United States, and at the same time some special weaknesses.

There is little doubt that the Mexicans can bargain for a special relationship with the United States, and that it is in their interest to do so. What might Mexico offer the United States that would relieve it of some of the current pressures it is facing from its $97–billion debt? One possibility is for the Mexican government to offer to sell oil *in situ* to the U.S. strategic petroleum reserve, or to oil companies. Such reserves might be drawn out at prearranged rates or at rates dependent on world supplies and prices. The price might be predetermined, or a fixed discount might be granted from the future market price. The purchaser of the oil might be allowed to buy Mexican government debt at a discount from U.S. banks and exchange it for the oil at an agreed ratio. If a sufficient quantity of oil were purchased on such terms, U.S. energy security would be enhanced and the Mexican debt would be significantly reduced.

The Mexicans have also encouraged debt/equity swaps. This option can be used much more vigorously to open the Mexican economy to private equity investment. Rules and regulations should be simplified so that extensive negotiations of each project with the government would not be necessary; and the program should be made more accessible to Mexican investors.

From the perspective of its domestic economy, Mexico could gain significant benefits by becoming far more oriented to the U.S. and international market. To some extent, the *maquila* industry has begun a transformation of the regions in the north of Mexico, but it remains to be seen whether that success can serve as the basis for an expansion into exports by Mexican firms that now primarily serve the domestic market. Increased exports will result in demands by the importing countries that the Mexican domestic market be more open to imports. While ultimately such an opening would be economically beneficial to Mexico, the short-term adjustment would be disruptive to protected Mexican industries and would require careful management to minimize bankruptcies and unemployment in the previously protected sectors.

A special relationship between the United States and Mexico cannot, however, fully compensate for Mexico's failures as an export manufacturer. While special arrangements, along with increasing competitiveness, will be necessary if Mexico is to gain a significant share of the U.S. market, additional measures will be required. It would be ideal from the perspective of both countries if illegal immigration could be greatly reduced and replaced by increased manufacturing for the U.S. market. However, since Mexico is not competitive with many of the Asian NICs in most manufactured products, this approach would require special arrangements—for example, a free trade area, or exemption from the Multi-Fibre Arrangement. And such special arrangements would require mutual recognition of U.S.-Mexican interdependence—which, while possible, does not at present seem likely.

Special arrangements such as that which led to Mexican production of U.S. auto engine blocks will still be necessary if significantly increased volumes of exports are to be achieved in the near future. In addition, Mexican manufacturers will have to become increasingly competitive with the Asian NICs if substantial export earnings from manufactures are to be a continuing source of foreign exchange earnings. This may well be feasible in the foreseeable future if market discipline is allowed a far freer rein than it has been to date. Recently there have been some signs—for example, the closing of the Fundidora Monterrey steel works—that the practice of subsidizing products that sell above world market prices will not continue indefinitely, but many ineffective parastatals continue to collect subsidies and sell their output at prices well above world levels.

The next step for Mexico should be to increase competition substantially by reducing import barriers, so that Mexican entrepreneurs can purchase inputs at world market prices. In the short run, such a policy would reduce profits and cause significant disruption for Mexican manufacturing firms that now provide such inputs. But over the intermediate term, such steps would vastly strengthen the Mexican economy.

For the United States, the implications of the present circumstances are that Mexico will be unable to fully service its foreign debt—and still less able to pay it off. Unless oil prices rise significantly, or unless a deal is made to sell a large quantity of oil in place as a petroleum reserve to the United States or other buyers, a continuing series of restructuring agreements, or a default, appear to be the only alternatives.

U.S. immigration from Mexico will depend on the effectiveness of the Simpson-Rodino Act employment provisions. Unless they are effective, immigration from Mexico is likely to increase substantially as the working age population grows far more rapidly than the capacity of Mexico to create jobs. On the other hand, if the Act is effective, Mexican unemployment is likely to increase significantly.

If oil prices remain at present levels, it seems likely that the export-driven models of the Asian NICs will have some influence in Mexico. If oil prices were to rebound, however, the likely outcome would be business as usual—with oil profits used to avoid the hard choices now being contemplated.

In closing, a forecast cannot be avoided: If present trends continue, it will become easier to operate high-technology, labor-intensive plants in less developed countries. A "demonstration effect" is to be expected from the most successful of the NICs to other developing countries. While it is far too early to predict the outcome of these attempts at emulation, the fact that poor societies can be transformed into dynamic, middle-income countries in less than a quarter of a century can be expected to inspire would-be imitators. At the same time, a similar "demonstration effect" may result in influences of Japan on the United States and Europe.

New global economic dynamics—the result of changes in technology, communications, and transportation, as well as in perceptions and policies—have forced both the developed countries and the rapidly industrializing developing countries to confront new opportunities and challenges.

One thing that has become clear is that technological innovations travel with increasing ease, but that the social organization of production is not easily transformed. Models borrowed from the most successful countries will be modified in their new environments with results that also are impossible to foresee. Whether Mexico will decide to pursue export-driven economic growth is uncertain, but if it does choose to do so, it will improve its prospects for economic success. In this age of increased competition, however, success will require continuous efforts and adaptation, and that has proved difficult for countries more favorably situated than Mexico.

Notes

Note: The author wishes to thank Hannah Boyle for her substantive assistance on the statistical material contained in the essay.

[1] "Commission for the Year 2000," American Academy of Arts and Sciences, Daniel Bell, Chairman, *Daedalus* (special issue), Summer 1967; and Herman Kahn and Anthony J. Weiner, *The Year 2000: A Framework for Speculation on the Next Thirty-Three Years* (The Hudson Institute, 1967).

[2] Raymond Vernon, *Sovereignty At Bay: The Multinational Spread of U.S. Enterprises* (New York: Basic Books, 1971), pp. 65–74. The product cycle theory holds that products will emerge, flourish, and diminish in market share, or become obsolete, in far shorter periods than formerly. It also holds that research, development, and initial manufacturing activities will take place in the developed countries, and that, as competition emerges or is anticipated, production will move offshore both to be closer to other markets and to take advantage of lower labor costs.

[3] Miyohei Shinohara, *Industrial Growth, Trade and Dynamic Patterns in the Japanese Economy* (Tokyo: University of Tokyo Press, 1982), pp. 24–26, 33.

[4] Apparent consumption is domestic shipments and imports minus exports.

[5] Estimate (1983) of the Electronics Industry Association.

Chapter 2

Mexico's New Industrial Development Strategy

Mauricio de Maria y Campos

Technological change, particularly when filtered through U.S. channels, has a significant impact on the political, cultural, social, and economic relationships between two neighboring countries such as Mexico and the United States. The impact is even more important when the two countries, unlike any other contiguous nations in the world today, are *unequal* neighbors, with contrasting levels of development.

The fact that the United States and Mexico are neighbors—whether they are "close" or "distant" neighbors—is terribly important. We share a common border, common weather, common services—and above all, a common history. As in any relationship between neighbors, our proximity is the source of problems, opportunities, and, above all, challenges—particularly given the contrasting levels of economic development, social welfare, and technological achievement that exist side by side.

It is important to discuss these issues since many opportunities exist for mutually beneficial U.S.-Mexican cooperation that could both assist the United States in maintaining world market competitiveness through trade, investment, and technology flows into Mexico and, at the same time, allow Mexico to take advantage of the relationship's potential to promote industrial development, modernization, and foreign exchange generation. The opportunities are numerous, and proper technological and economic forecasting—and common sense—should allow us to take advantage of some of them. The challenges, however, are also great. Never in the last four decades has Mexico been so economically strained and in such need of understanding of both our potential for change and the limits and obstacles before us. The biggest challenge, however, continues to be that of developing effective channels of communication, mutual understanding, creative problem-solving, and a common political will.

The Policy Background

By 1982, Mexico's industrialization process had resulted in the development of a sizable, dynamic, and diversified manufacturing sector that was, however, marked by insufficient levels of efficiency and international competitiveness, highly dependent on imported capital goods and technology, and very low in export capacity. Among the main reasons for this situation were past economic policies.

The industrialization strategy pursued in Mexico during the past four decades was founded on a policy of import substitution. This meant that industrial development took place in response to a growing domestic market, isolated from external competition through policies and instruments that led to levels of protection that were excessive, permanent, non-conditional, and indiscriminate in terms of dynamic comparative advantage and international competition.

During the 1970s, macroeconomic policy resulted in serious imbalances that had repercussions on the Mexican economy—specifically on the industrial sector. Between 1977 and 1981, the growth rate of domestic aggregate demand was higher than the growth rate of GDP. This was primarily caused by a high public deficit, which in 1982 amounted to 17.6 per cent of GDP and was accompanied by an increasing overvaluation of the peso—both of which aggravated Mexico's balance-of-payments situation.

This strategy and policy for growth, together with the structural problems characteristic of a developing country, accounted for the fact that activity in Mexico, despite efforts to the contrary, was highly dependent on imports and low in export capacity. Consequently, the greatest and most constant constraint on economic growth during the last four decades was the external disequilibrium that resulted from a growing deficit in the manufacturing trade balance, which during the 1977-81 period amounted to $46 billion.

Yet the domestic economy grew during this period, thanks to the fact that there were various sources for financing the external deficit. During the 1950s and 1960s, the main sources of financing were agricultural exports and tourism; during the second half of the 1970s financing came from foreign lenders and from oil exports. All of these permitted postponement of the implementation of policies geared toward macroeconomic adjustment and structural change—policies that were needed to correct the external disequilibrium.

It was the 1981 fall in the price of oil—which had become the source of 80 per cent of Mexico's foreign exchange and half of its fiscal income—that forced us to face the bleak reality of an enormous budget deficit, a deteriorating trade balance, and a growing external debt with very high interest rates. The crisis signaled not only the urgent need for short-term adjustment measures, but also the need for fundamental structural change. As a result of the macroeconomic imbalances recorded in 1982, the productive capacity was affected—simultaneously, and for the first time in more than forty years, by a significant reduction in demand, a rapid increase in prices, high financing costs, a shortage of liquidity, and a high degree of indebtedness to both Mexican and foreign banks.

The critical situation of Mexican industry made it necessary in early 1983 to design and implement a Program for the Defense of Productive Capacity and Employment. The aims of this program were to moderate the most harmful effects of the crisis, protect the nation's capital stock, ensure the survival of industry and the maintenance of employment levels, and establish a basis for making the most essential changes required in the country's productive structure.

This strategy for structural change combines supply and demand policy instruments so as to induce and increase the integration and efficiency of the productive plant in order to secure steadier growth and to cope with a constantly changing world economy. To give impetus to this new strategy, industrial policy needed to: (a) ensure that it was consistent with macroeconomic policy, (b) surmount structural obstacles to growth, and (c) be coherent in the design and use of its operative policies, instruments, and mechanisms.

The 1983 program explicitly identified existing structural problems and obstacles as well as provided specific measures to tackle them. The traditional instruments of economic policy—relative pricing and demand management—were essential for providing signals of profitability in investment and production in order to induce a certain allocation of resources among sectors. However, in countries like Mexico these two instruments, though necessary, are not sufficient to induce changes in the level and structure of supply because of the structural problems opposing them. Clearly, new and highly selective policies were needed on the supply side of the economy. It was recognized that the only way for the country to develop steadily was to eliminate obstacles and problems that had been accumulating for years by introducing major changes throughout the economic structure.

The structural problems arising from Mexico's traditional growth pattern can be summarized as follows:

1. Mexico's manufacturing industry has been unable to export enough to generate its own foreign exchange requirements, or to pro-

vide a satisfactory supply of basic domestic goods and services, intermediate products, and, particularly, capital goods.

2. The Mexican economy is highly dependent on imported technologies—due to excessive protection from external competition, the absence of a climate that promoted risk-taking and creativity, and low spending on research and development by both the Mexican government and the private sector. This problem has been exacerbated by weak linkages between the few existing technological research centers and the manufacturing sector.

3. In many cases, goods have been produced under less than optimal conditions of scale, productivity, price, and quality. In some industrial sectors—for example, petrochemicals, cement, glass, many foodstuffs, garments—Mexico is internationally competitive in terms of technology, plant scale, management practices, and product quality. This is the result of very important recent investments by innovative Mexican and foreign companies. However, most manufacturing sectors—particularly those related to mature industries such as steel, textiles, electrical appliances, and automobiles—require important improvements in their performance to reach current international standards.

4. The high concentration of industry in Mexico City and in a few large consumption centers far from the coasts and the borders constitutes an obstacle to exports and is the source of many social problems and growing inefficiencies for the country's economy as a whole.

5. Insufficient coordination among producers has led to: (a) overextended government participation in the manufacturing sector as well as unnecessary confrontation between the government and the private sector; (b) insufficient attention by both public and private investors to strategic industrial sectors critical to domestic development; (c) failure to fully develop and utilize the potential of each producer; and (d) inefficient integration of small and medium-size industries into the productive structure.

Mexico's New Development Strategy

At the end of 1982, President de la Madrid's administration announced its main economic objectives and corresponding strategy, both of which were more fully elaborated in 1983 in the National Development Plan and several sectoral programs. The principal purpose of the strategy was the attainment of external and internal equilibria.

The external objective—considered short-term—involved the implementation of an economic policy designed to correct Mexico's historical balance-of-payments problems, which included the permanent trade deficit, increasing foreign indebtedness, and an overvalued currency. The objectives relating to the problem of internal disequilibrium were to reduce the inflation rate and to protect the level of employment and production in the industrial sector. At the same time, the need to promote structural changes was recognized as a long-term objective.

The government decided to pursue these objectives by utilizing both traditional and non-traditional policy instruments. For example, to improve the balance-of-payments situation, efforts were made to promote foreign investment, in-bond plants, and non-oil exports; to reschedule the foreign debt; and to keep the peso slightly undervalued.

To curb inflation, domestic aggregate demand was lowered through contractionary public spending and monetary policies, and wage controls were tightened. To maintain the level of output and employment, some temporary incentives were granted, including tax reductions and preferential access and interest rates on credits from internal sources.

At the same time, the de la Madrid administration emphasized the importance of developing a strong manufacturing sector through its strategy of structural change. Recognition that the existing structure of the manufacturing sector hindered Mexican economic development prompted the adoption of this long-term strategy.

The de la Madrid administration made its decision to promote necessary changes in the manufacturing sector in order to achieve the following objectives:

1. Establishment of a new pattern of industrialization and specialization in foreign trade that could overcome external constraints and abate the foreign vulnerabilities of the Mexican economy in order to secure self-sustained growth.

2. Launching of a new approach to allow new technologies to be incorporated into the industrial plant in order to better meet the accumulated basic needs of the Mexican population.

3. The rationalization of industrial organization to make optimal use of the resources and the capacity of installed plant, in order to take advantage of economies of scale and to increase the degree of integration among industries.

4. The decentralization of policy instruments in order to promote more harmonious and balanced regional development, to induce firms to make more efficient and rational use of national resources, and to establish more competitive locations vis-à-vis both the Mexican market and foreign export markets.

5. Increased participation in industry by the public, social, and private sectors according to their characteristics and aptitudes, under a scheme of complementarity, mutual trust, and joint action aimed at the realization of common objectives.

6. The continuous generation of better-paid jobs and increasing

efforts to meet the basic needs of the Mexican population, which will mean a fairer distribution of income.

To achieve structural change in Mexican industry's output as well as in its foreign trade, the de la Madrid administration's strategy included an internally consistent set of policies geared toward the promotion, protection, and regulation of the manufacturing sector. Many of these policies have existed for years, but they are being updated, simplified, and adapted to clarify "the rules of the game." With the promotion of manufacturing made its principal aim, regulation should decrease in importance and eventually be applied only in those policy areas and industrial sectors where it is necessary for the achievement of basic goals.

Trade Policy

Traditionally, the Mexican economy has been highly protected, with economic growth oriented primarily toward the domestic market. In recent years, important steps have been taken to reduce barriers between Mexico and the international economy in order to raise the country's industrial productivity and competitiveness. It is important in this connection to highlight Mexico's recent decision to enter the General Agreement on Tariffs and Trade (GATT) and the adoption of trade policies designed to eliminate quantitative import restrictions and reduce tariffs. The most important efforts in this area include the following:

1. The current protection system is now based primarily on tariffs, whereas the previous one relied mainly on import licenses. More than 90 per cent of import tariff items, accounting for about 75 per cent of the value of imports, is now license free. This contrasts sharply with the situation in 1982, when only 20 per cent of the value of imports was free of quantitative restrictions.

2. Import tariffs already have been cut from levels where some were as high as 100 per cent to a range of 0-45 per cent. In April 1986, Mexico initiated a further gradual reduction of its tariff levels, with the aim of establishing an upper limit of 30 per cent by the end of 1988.

3. Other quantitative restrictions, such as prohibitions on the importation of certain goods, also have been relaxed.

The fact that these steps to lower trade barriers have been taken despite the country's foreign sector crisis contrasts sharply with trends observed in most industrial countries, where greater trade restrictions have become common practice in the last several years.

In addition, between 1982 and 1986, the government has encouraged non-oil exports, which in 1986 grew by 30 per cent and in the first quarter of 1987, by 50 per cent over the first quarter of 1986. With regard to foreign investment, Mexico has made great strides by opening up most industries to 100-per-cent equity participation (contingent on foreign participants providing new technologies and contributing to the expansion of exports), streamlining administrative procedures, actively promoting new investments, and, most recently, establishing mechanisms for the conversion of debt into equity. The number of in-bond plants exceeded 1,000 by early 1987, with employment growth in this sector at a 20-per-cent annual rate. However, in early 1987, foreign investment outside the *maquila* sector had only begun to recover, primarily because the Mexican domestic market is still depressed.

The de la Madrid administration's attempts to achieve greater industrial competitiveness began in 1982, with deliberate steps to promote the development and reconversion of strategic industrial sectors. The automobile, electronics, pharmaceutical, and in-bond industries, as well as small and medium-scale industry, have been the primary targets of these actions. To improve Mexico's export capacity so as to obtain the foreign exchange needed to meet foreign debt payments and to meet the demand for imports, industrial sectors and enterprises with export potential have been receiving official support in ways including the following:

1. Continual adjustment of the exchange rate to avoid an overvaluation of the peso, which would impair the price competitiveness of Mexican-manufactured products in international markets.

2. Duty-free entry for items that are to be incorporated in the production of exports.

3. The Mexican government will aim to grant credit conditions similar to those granted to exporters and their suppliers in the majority of countries under international agreements.

4. In general, the government is working to eliminate all structural and administrative obstacles that have limited the competitive production, transportation, and commercialization of exports.

Structural Change: Policy Implementation and Some Results

The importance of initiating long-term programs of structural change and industrial reconversion, recognized in Mexico since 1982, has gained in urgency as trade liberalization, the rationalization of the public sector, and the sale of non-strategic public enterprises have advanced. The new industrial strategy is directed toward decentralizing and strengthening the Mexican manufacturing sector and promoting the development of domestic technological capabilities. Its ultimate aim is the development of a more efficient, competitive, export-oriented economy.

To support this strategy, Mexico is actively using traditional promotional instruments such as credit and tax incentives as well as the purchasing power of government and big private sector corporations. In addition, efforts will be increased to strengthen the physical and social infrastructure in regions designated for new development, particularly by promoting technological development, creativity, productivity, competitiveness, management, and quality standards. These policy packages cannot, however, be applied across the board to all areas of manufacturing. The impact of the technological and industrial revolution taking place around the world does not affect all sectors in the same way. Needs and opportunities for structural change vary among industrial sectors and even among companies. We have identified three such variants in Mexico:

1. Industrial sectors in which Mexico is reasonably efficient and competitive—for example, petrochemicals, cement, glass, most food and beverage industries, and energy-related equipment. During the 1970s, a significant process of investment and incorporation of modern technology took place in these sectors, resulting in production scales as well as costs and quality levels competitive with the highest international standards.

2. Mature industrial sectors whose levels of technology, productivity, and competitiveness have not adjusted to world standards; these include industries such as steel, textiles, and electrical and electronic consumer goods.

3. Emerging industrial sectors such as telecommunications, computers, or new materials and biotechnology—sectors in which the technological gap between the industries of Mexico and the developed countries is quite large. In these areas, Mexico is trying on a selective basis to promote specific projects that either already are competitive, or can become competitive, in a reasonably short period of time.

According to this arbitrary classification—to which there are many specific exceptions—each of the situations just described requires a different line of action. Given existing resources, the present Mexican administration has been adopting and implementing various approaches to the extent possible. The following are examples of specific efforts under way.

The Mexican Automobile Industry

The automobile industry, a very important generator of employment, emerged in Mexico over the years with an excessive number of plants and models that could operate profitably only within a small but captive market. During the last two decades, the industry advanced in terms of attracting investment and increasing domestic integration. However, it always showed high production costs and a sizable trade deficit—despite successive government decrees aimed at increasing the level of domestic inputs and promoting a stronger export orientation. It became apparent that it would be difficult to achieve these objectives with small-scale plants producing for a protected and highly segmented market. In recognition of this, the Mexican government in early 1983 developed a new program designed to induce a major transformation of the Mexican automobile industry.

This Program for the Rationalization and Development of the Mexican Automobile Industry established a timetable for automotive firms to reduce production lines and models that were not highly export-oriented and required producers to fully compensate imports with exports. It also required that all new assembly and component manufacturing plants function on a competitive scale and attain world price and quality standards. As a result of this new policy, new investments and important processes of cost reduction and export promotion have been initiated in the automotive sector.

It is important to mention that because of Mexico's ongoing recession, which has reduced domestic automotive sales by 60 per cent since 1981, it has not been possible to carry out all of the projects stipulated by the program. However, the measures that have been adopted so far have contributed to the creation of a competitive, export-oriented capacity for most automobile manufacturers. This in turn has forced auxiliary industries to develop similar capacities. For example, the new Ford-Mazda assembly plant in Hermosillo, which marked the introduction of "state-of-the-art" technology and assembly processes into the Mexican automotive sector, fostered the establishment of nine new components plants in the vicinity and the development of new world-class suppliers in other parts of Mexico.

As a result of this initiative, the automobile industry, which in 1981 accounted for 60 per cent of the Mexican balance-of-trade deficit, in 1983 began registering surpluses expected to reach $1 billion by 1987. This has made the automotive industry, including components production, the most important exporter of manufactured goods in Mexico.

What the Mexican government would like to do now is deepen this process by giving components manufacturers the support required for them to undertake their own modernization, with technological assistance from the automobile manufacturers. If Mexico can achieve these objectives by 1988-89, it will in later years be in a position to gradually expose its automobile industry to more open competition and active participation in the rapidly changing world economy.

The Mexican Chemical-Pharmaceutical Industry

The 1982 economic crisis placed the Mexican pharmaceutical industry in an extremely difficult situation that required the adoption of an emergency rescue program in December of that year. This program included a set of measures designed to meet the industry's urgent demand for foreign currency, import permits, liquidity, and foreign financing. It enabled Mexico to overcome short-term supply problems and revealed the need to restructure this industry. What also became clear was that the basic problems of the pharmaceutical industry were not related to the competitiveness or quality of its products; Mexican products met international standards, and actually were much cheaper than in most other countries. The industry's fundamental problems were its high dependence on foreign active substances and technology, excessive product differentiation, the growing trade deficit, and a very low level of participation of Mexican investors—particularly risk-taking entrepreneurs—in the industry.

The Mexican government, working closely with the pharmaceutical industry, therefore developed a comprehensive policy, supported by a presidential decree, that sought to regulate and promote the development of the industry. The policy, implemented in 1984 after long negotiations with international corporations, resulted in the following regulatory requirements:

(a) The obligation to print the generic names of pharmaceutical products on labels next to the trademark of all basic medicines appearing on the National Health List. This measure was designed to benefit Mexican consumers; information on the content of specific medicines will enable consumers to choose more easily between brands. This requirement has gradually become the practice of many companies, and shortly all manufacturers of products on the list are expected to abide by this requirement.

(b) The implementation of a program aimed at streamlining product presentation and eliminating some dangerous products whose production had been discontinued, for health reasons, in other countries.

(c) The requirement that all pharmaceutical companies manufacturing basic drugs have a balanced trade account.

(d) The requirement that drug manufacturing companies spend 4 per cent of their gross sales of intermediate products on research and development.

A package of incentives was also adopted for the purpose of promoting investment in new plants, import substitution of basic drugs, and research and development activities. Last but not least, a new price authorization scheme was established to provide companies operating under high rates of inflation with greater financial security.

One of the most outstanding achievements in this area is that Mexico is now manufacturing twenty-three new active substances that were previously imported, and efforts to initiate the production of an additional thirty-seven during the 1986-88 period are in a very advanced stage. Most of these projects were started by national companies, although an increasing number of international companies are participating. These efforts will result in an increase in domestic production of raw materials from 40 per cent in 1982 to 63 per cent in 1988. The pharmaceutical industry's trade deficit, which in 1983 reached $200 million, has been reduced to $100 million as a result of import-substitution and export-promotion programs. It is our hope that, by the end of the decade, this sector will have a balanced trade account.

In addition, two years ago the Mexican government initiated a very ambitious program to induce pharmaceutical firms to undertake research and development activities. The Ministry of Commerce and Industrial Development—in coordination with the Health Ministry, the National Council of Science and Technology, the Mexican Social Security Institute (IMSS), and various universities and research institutes—sponsored and promoted several projects among the national pharmaceutical companies, focusing primarily on the development of production processes for basic drugs whose international patents have expired. This is essentially a policy of import substitution. Recently, selective efforts also have been made to promote original research and development, particularly in the field of biotechnology.

Finally, it should be mentioned that negotiations are under way between the Mexican government and the National Chamber of the Chemical-Pharmaceutical Industry to start a Basic Medicines Program that would make available to consumers about sixty popular, over-the-counter products at low prices. The main lines of action have been pursued thus far with considerable success—despite a depressed market, scarce financial resources, and inflation rates higher than those anticipated.

The Development of the Mexican Electronics Industry

The electronics industry has received special attention in Mexico because of its strategic role in the new industrial technological revolution. Until 1982, the electronics industry in Mexico was characterized by a large trade deficit, lagging competitiveness, low levels of Mexican investment, and very limited research and development activity. Since then, government policy has stimulated the emergence of a new electronics industry. Special guidelines have been developed to promote (a) new investments in international-scale plants, (b) domestic integration of the electronics sector, (c) more efficient and competitive levels of production, and (d) balanced trade accounts. In addition, electronics manufacturers in Mexico must now spend 5 per cent of their income on research and development activities, either for their own development purposes or for those of their suppliers.

The following developments illustrate progress that has been made in this sector thus far:

(a) In 1982, electronics imports were twenty times higher than exports; by 1985, imports were only four times higher than exports. More recently, on account of trade liberalization, the rate is five to one; nevertheless, in specific areas such as computers, the rate is only three to one.

(b) Mexico is building up a very important electronics sector, particularly in computer equipment and telecommunications. With the participation of both domestic and foreign firms, production capacity is rapidly adjusting to international scale and standards.

(c) All companies in the computer and telecommunications sectors have now established important research and development or supplier development programs. Industrial reconversion efforts are expected to start soon in the radio and television industries and in other consumer electronics industries. Because of the important domestic market for these goods, the high level of employment their production provides, and their export potential, making them internationally competitive will be important in helping Mexico to achieve its industrial development objectives.

The changes in this sector are profound and substantial. Results have not, however, totally fulfilled initial expectations and goals—again largely because of the depression that has prevailed in most markets since 1982, huge financial constraints, and adverse investment conditions, often accompanied by protected international markets.

We believe that the achievements attained so far constitute clear signals of the type of industrial policy that can and should be implemented in selected strategic industries. For this reason the Mexican government, together with representatives of Mexican industry, is studying policy packages aimed at further developing competitive sectors and reshaping those with fundamental structural problems.

The three sectoral policies described have significant regulatory content, as well as important promotional aspects. In the future, the Mexican government expects to take similar action in industrial sectors where such regulatory measures have not been deemed necessary.

We consider that in most sectors, if development is to be stimulated, some deregulation has to take place to promote a more creative climate for growth and profit from existing investment, production, and export opportunities.

During 1986, additional programs have been put into place to promote further development in the petrochemical industry and greater competitiveness, creativity, and export orientation in the textile, apparel, shoe, home appliance, and automobile components industries, as well as in selected segments of the food and capital goods industries. With these goals in mind, the Ministry of Commerce has been undertaking studies and consultations with Mexican industry and shall proceed as necessary to consult labor unions and other concerned groups. The Mexican government will offer a general framework of industrial and foreign trade policies that will include the gradual reduction of protection levels, tax incentives, and financial and technological supports. Participating firms will in turn need to commit themselves to specific investment, employment, and productivity targets designed to benefit domestic consumers and to promote exports. Such programs will be the product of the mobilization of the firms' own resources, with the support of already established tax incentives, national commercial bank credits, and—if necessary—credit lines that we hope to have available from both public and private international financial sources, as well as greater foreign investment.

The Role of Technological Change in Mexico's Development Strategy

In the early 1970s, in keeping with the needs of Mexican society, the Mexican government first stressed the need to develop a technological base in order to attain self-sustained, steady industrial growth. Specifically, legal and administrative instruments[1] were implemented with the objectives of (a) formulating a coherent scientific and technological policy, (b) building a technological infrastructure, (c) developing human resources, (d) promoting research and development activities, and (e) strengthening the capacity of Mexican industry to bargain for, select, and assimilate foreign technology. However, as in the cases of many other developing countries—particularly those of Latin America—prevailing policies and market conditions only allowed for an improvement in the process of importing technology and for modest advancement in the development of local technological capacity. Both the macroeconomic and industrial policies continued to stimulate the import of technology—facilitated by our proximity to the United States—and produced a protected industrial environment that encouraged neither competition nor local efforts to develop technology.

Nevertheless, a remarkable increase in political commitment to scientific and technological development did allow us to allocate increasing financial resources to this sector and to create an important network of institutions, mechanisms, and fiscal and financial incentives for the promotion of technological development.[2]

By 1982, it was evident not only that the world economy had changed significantly—due mainly to technological developments—but also that the majority of countries were improving their levels of efficiency and competitiveness through national technology strategies. It was also clear that, due to conditions prevailing in the previous decade, Mexican firms had not taken advantage of the opportunity to advance industrial and technological restructuring that had been created by the rapid and substantial growth of the Mexican and world economies. The 1982 crisis caught most of industry off guard: On the one hand, the international technological frontier had shifted substantially; and on the other, modernization, adjustment, or conversion processes had to be undertaken in order to cope with external competition under strong financial constraints and a shrinking domestic market. Within this context, it became clear that those few companies that had adopted modern technologies—particularly those that had developed their own technological capacities to select, adapt, and create technology, as well as to face change—were more successful in overcoming short-term problems.

In recent years, Mexico's entrepreneurs have become increasingly aware that technology is a fundamental factor in their ability to overcome the crisis, as industrial and trade policy forces them to face increasing competition and as the threat of a more open economy becomes a reality, underlined by Mexico's membership in the GATT.

Mexico will continue, through medium- and long-term sectoral policies, to support technological development and industrial restructuring as the most viable means of confronting the changing conditions of the world economy and achieving self-sustained growth. The present and the future belong to countries that create their own comparative advantage—by assimilating the best from abroad, but also by themselves adapting and generating new technologies and products. The evolution of the world economy and the experience of many countries show that economic and technological performance cannot be based solely on the old concept of comparative advantage, which was in turn founded on the relative abundance of various resources. This traditional economic principle, partially disproved by the effects of the internationalization of industrial production and the much deteriorated "terms of trade" of recent times, now competes with a new version of the concept—one that is founded on a country's ability to develop national technologies and adjust to changing international conditions.

Future competitiveness will surely depend on a more equitable inter-national environment—and especially on developing-country willing-ness to undertake technological and industrial development.

Notes

[1] The creation of the National Council of Science and Technology (CONACYT) in 1970, the Law to Regulate Licensing Agreements of 1973, and the Law of Inventions and Trademarks of 1975.

[2] These institutions and instruments have produced a healthy effect on the more advanced entrepreneurs, who at an early stage understood the role of technology in import substitution, competition, and exports. As a result, important research and development efforts have begun in a spontaneous manner.

Chapter 3

U.S. Macroeconomic Strategy and the Advanced Developing Countries

James K. Galbraith

U.S. Macroeconomic Strategy

The relationship between any large, open, advanced, diversified consumer economy and a smaller neighbor must turn in part on the state of demand in the former country for goods produced by the latter. And so it is especially between the United States and Mexico. The United States accounts for two-thirds of Mexico's total trade, including half of its petroleum exports and virtually all of its non-petroleum exports.[1] Mexican exports to the United States alone account for about 7 per cent of Mexico's GNP.

Two factors determine short-run demand for imported goods in the United States. The first of these is the state of demand in the United States itself. A high rate of growth, capacity utilization, employment, and consumption in the United States means a high level of demand for goods in general, including imports. The second factor is the exchange rate, which helps to determine the competitiveness of U.S. industry at any level of demand. In particular, it strongly influences whether (at the margin) U.S. orders for new manufactured goods will be lodged primarily with foreign or domestic sources.

The Permanent Deficit and Domestic Demand

The state of demand in the United States is the product of large, complex, and uncertain forces, including, among other things, the actions of the fiscal and monetary authorities. Prediction of the behavior of the authorities probably constitutes the greatest single calculable risk facing the forecaster. Among other influences on U.S. demand, some, such as external supply shocks or fluctuations in business confidence, are impossible to predict reliably, while others, such as the growth of desired consumption expenditure, are relatively well behaved and hence not problematic.

President Reagan's tenure may have simplified the problem of predicting what the U.S. fiscal authorities will do. With the 1981–83 staged income tax rate reductions, followed by the introduction of tax indexing in 1985, the (nominal) deficit no longer tends to fall with strong growth or inflation. Correspondingly, the political agenda no longer includes the periodic tax reductions or expenditure increases that used to be necessary merely to prevent fiscal policy from becoming overly restrictive. Instead, to keep fiscal stimulus from getting out of hand, tax increases and expenditure cuts are now the behavioral norm. Yet with great effort each year, the best that so far seems achievable is a standstill—keeping the budget deficit as a share of GNP from rising.

This stalemate, should it persist, would imply that deficits will remain high, and so the stimulus imparted to demand by the fiscal behavior of the U.S. government will remain strong. The Gramm-Rudman-Hollings law of course raises the question: Will it persist? Gramm-Rudman clearly was enacted in response to the perception of stalemate. However, there is as yet no sign that Congress and the President are prepared to agree to any of the four possible substantive resolutions of the stalemate: (a) large tax increases, (b) large cuts in spending, including entitlements, (c) toleration of the automatic spending cuts provided for under the law, or (d) any combination of the above. What incentive have they to do so, when all the alternatives are more immediately painful than the deficits themselves?

The Exchange Rate as Incomes Policy

In these circumstances, the monetary authorities are nervous and careful. They wish, as always, to forestall inflation without, if possible, inducing a recession and the political reaction that would follow. The Federal Reserve has been pursuing lower interest rates and sustained growth, but in a hesitant way that has kept the dollar's decline "soft" and its level high relative to what would be required for trade balance.

To clear up a misconception, as of April 1987, the dollar remains overvalued—despite a substantial drop from peak values with respect to the yen, deutschemark, and other major currencies. The reason is that currencies of the newly industrialized countries with which the United States conducts an increasing share of trade have fallen with the dollar against these currencies. Thus dollar depreciation has put substantial pressure on Europe and Japan to reflate, but we are as yet experiencing neither the trade benefits nor the inflation consequences normally associated with devaluation.

Can the high dollar exchange rate last? Here the record of seers and pundits is not good. The rise in the dollar after 1980 was unforeseen. Attempts to forecast an expected drop failed regularly from 1981 until 1985, and attempts to delimit in advance the extent and pace of the dollar's regress once it got underway in 1985–86 have not been notably better.

One problem with such attempts is the assumption (shared by most, at least until the September 1985 Plaza Hotel accords on lowering the dollar) that the monetary authorities are essentially passive in exchange rate determination—that the underlying forces well up from patterns of preference and expectation in the markets. But one might ask instead: Has the high dollar been functional? Do policymaking authorities have reasons—good or bad—for preferring one course for the dollar exchange rate over another? Given a change in circumstances, will they react to forestall (or, under other circumstances, to cause) a change in the dollar's exchange value? If so, there may be a predictable element in the dollar's behavior that is not clearly incorporated in the market-based predictive models.

Without doubt, the distinguishing feature of the middle phase of the present economic expansion has been the failure of inflation to accelerate. Though some controversies persist, it is by now widely agreed that the high dollar bears the chief responsibility. The channels of pressure on U.S. costs run through direct price competition from foreign products, through the higher profitability of out-sourcing components, through the continuing depression of export industries and their wages, and probably also through a heightened awareness by American workers of the foreign wage levels with which they must compete. The importance and persistence of these channels has become apparent with the passage of time, as continued domestic growth has made competing explanations for price stability (such as the high unemployment rate or workers' fear of a tough anti-labor response from the administration) increasingly less persuasive.

One need not believe that the high dollar was planned in advance for these effects—only that, once events unfolded, the effects were recognized, if not by the econometricians, then at least by the more intuitive thinkers in the upper reaches of the Federal Reserve. There is ample evidence in business press commentary, not to mention congressional testimony in April 1987 by Chairman Volcker himself, that, given the deficits, a further sharp reduction in the dollar's international value would indeed be seen by top policymakers as courting the risk of returning inflation. Such fears can be overruled if the dollar goes too high—as it did in early 1985—or if the stability of U.S. banking is threatened, but in normal times they may well account for a strong aversion to allowing the dollar to slide low enough to reestablish equilibrium in the U.S. current account.

Thus, in effect, the high dollar has been the incomes policy that the Reagan administration forswore on ideological grounds upon taking office. Like an incomes policy, it helps to reconcile—temporarily—high consumption standards with low rates of price and wage increase. As such, it is a politically necessary complement to the permanent deficit; together, the two frame the macroeconomic legacy of the Reagan administration.

Qualifications

Stephen Marris and others have denounced this policy mix on the grounds that (a) it cannot be sustained, and (b) the longer change is delayed, the more severe the eventual costs—including a disagreeable choice between very high inflation and a severe credit crunch.[3]

The question here, however, is not whether attempting to sustain the high-deficit, high-dollar policy mix is a bad idea (indisputably, it is), but whether this course is likely to prove the most expedient of the available political choices in the years immediately ahead. My own view is that the party can indeed continue for quite a long time—perhaps through the end of the decade or longer.

In the medium term, certain circumstances—a recession, a banking crisis—would be required to force the policy mix away from its present configuration. Should a severe banking crisis begin to materialize, efforts to avert it could quickly take on an epic scale. A further large, autonomous decline in the trade balance *could* bring on a recession and that *could,* in turn, prompt a desperate effort to revive investment and exports with easier money and a lower dollar. As the U.S. national debt rises, investors *could* hit a point of portfolio saturation, leading to a one-time dollar depreciation. But these are remote and, on the evidence, even implausible scenarios. On the other side, an inflation crisis set off by a shock of some kind is possible—but this would generate an emergency tightening, driving up the dollar on the one hand and deepening the trade and budget deficits on the other.

The policy mix cannot, of course, continue forever. By 1990, with the net external debt close to one trillion dollars, and the interest on it nearly $100 billion per year, the burden of real interest payments to foreigners could begin to become a political issue as the next political generation begins to rebel against decisions made for it by the present one. We may then face the Marris choice, or we may yet decide to defer it again through more borrowing, until the net external debt reaches $2 or $3 trillion. Eventually, U.S. monetary policy may become more open than it appears to be today to a devaluation/reinflation "solution," with its attendant destabilizing politics. The later this occurs, the more aggravated the form it will take. Still, there is no obvious reason why wisdom and foresight alone will cause us to alter course before this situation arrives.

The Structure of U.S. Production, Trade, and Protection

The advanced developing countries, or their private entrepreneurs, do not base their long-range plans for expansion of export industry solely on a forecast of the expected future strength of demand from a major market country. They must also anticipate the pattern of comparative advantage, not omitting attention to the expected pattern of protection. For these purposes, an understanding of industrial trends and of the politics of protection within the prospective market is helpful.

Considerable controversy surrounds the issue of U.S. industrial trends. This short discussion attempts only to suggest that the macroeconomic strategy discussed above may have consequences for future trends in the U.S. industrial structure. A first set of issues concerns the size of the U.S. traded-goods sector as a whole; a second concerns its composition.

Size of Industry

It is obvious that a high-demand, high-dollar strategy increases the share of domestic services and imported tradeables in consumption, at the expense of domestically produced tradeable goods. Thus, in the expansion taking place since the end of 1982, the ratio of imports to GNP has risen 2.7 percentage points,[4] while new domestic service-sector jobs have outnumbered new manufacturing jobs by roughly eleven to one.[5]

The underlying economic process is straightforward. Recessions cause factories to close and companies to go out of existence. Often, the capacity they represent—whether out-of-date or simply too expensive to maintain under the conditions—is abandoned, once and for all. It disappears from the capital stock and must later be replaced by new investment if total manufacturing employment is to be restored.[6] But normal new investment is *also* curtailed during a recession. Hence, subsequent new investment at customary rates does not fully restore the capital stock, on which manufacturing's share in employment depends. The deeper and longer the recession, the greater is the drop in the share of manufacturing in subsequent total employment. Service providers do not disappear so easily, of course, for they and their capital (mostly human) are inseparable. The storefront vacated in the slump is reoccupied in the upturn.

In the expansion, total spending is restored quickly—almost as soon as investment activities pick up. At that point, however, the remaining capital stock cannot produce as much as before. Before new domestic manufacturing output comes on line, there is a lag during which the marginal new capacity and least-cost sources may be abroad—especially if the Japanese, among others, have not curtailed their own investment in the same period. Thus, in the immediate aftermath of recession, imports rise sharply. This increases the profitability of overseas suppliers, causing them to increase their investment, and so permanently changing the patterns of trade.

Hence recessions have the effect of permanently reducing the base of manufacturing employment unless extraordinary public efforts are made to boost manufacturing investment in the recovery and so restore the capital stock to its former level and growth path.[7]

After a recession, therefore, the pattern of investment and the expansion path of the economy will differ permanently from what they would have been had the recession not occurred. Contractionary macroeconomic policies are the cause of the phenomenon, as Robert Lawrence and others have argued. But standard expansionary macroeconomic policies taken after the slump do not restore the *status quo ante*. Depending on the policy mix, demand expansion can lead to a currency depreciation and inflation together with trade balance (as in 1976–79), or to a high dollar and price stability accompanied by a trade deficit and a debt explosion (as from 1983 to the present).[8]

Trends in Structure

With respect to the composition of tradeables output, it is now widely agreed that industrial adjustment in the United States, in reponse to the stimulus of changing patterns of demand, is comparatively rapid.[9] Profitability patterns within the U.S. manufacturing sector have been cyclical: One strong swing occurred in the six years before 1979, and a second strong swing in a different direction has taken place since then. I will argue that the direction of profitability has hinged on whether a company is *inward-looking* or *outward-looking,* as defined below, with particularly strong implications for the future position of high-technology industry in the United States.[10]

After the oil shocks of 1973, the United States came around quickly. Oil imports fell, while agricultural and capital goods exports soared. During the expansion from 1976 through 1979, U.S. trade, aided by a sharply falling exchange rate, remained in balance; and U.S. manufacturing—even if smaller after the mid-decade recession than it could have been—held its own in world markets. This was accomplished without the state apparatus of an explicit industrial policy that became so visible in Europe and Japan during this period. It seems that the United States, lacking nationalized industries and a tradition of administrative guidance, was if anything less rigid in its practices and better placed to take quick advantage of post-oil-shock opportunites than its major industrial-country competitors.

In the early 1980s, the rapid growth of advanced-technology industries slowed abruptly. As of early 1987, computers remain in the doldrums, as do capital goods exports, while aerospace is down, the energy business faces depression—not to mention the severe crisis in farming. At the same time, the maligned "middle-tech" automotive industry is back on its feet, reporting high sales, decent if streamlined employment, and good profits. Similar patterns apply through much of industry. Middle-tech is thriving; "high-tech" is in the dumps.

What caused the reversal? In part, the answer is inherent in the phenomenon itself: No speculative surge ever gets by without a subsequent shakeout. This is particularly true for the innovation-intensive industries that depend heavily on speculative finance in the venture-capital markets. Some solid technological gains are made in such surges to be sure, but they are nearly always smaller that we are led to believe. Moreover, the susceptibility of high-tech to speculative bubbles has surely increased in recent decades, as enthusiastic private venture-capital finance has displaced the plodding government as a source of finance.

Fundamentally, though, the return of middle-technology consumer goods to center stage reflects the already discussed changes in macro-strategy. This is not at all difficult to understand; indeed, every high-tech company is aware of it. Still, the *general* susceptibility of advanced technology to changed macroeconomic conditions seems to have been widely overlooked in recent policy discussions.

For purposes of evaluating the effects of exchange rate changes on profitability, we can divide all manufacturing companies into two generic types. In one category, place all those companies whose share of imports in all costs (including capital costs) is greater than the share of exports in all sales. Call these *inward-looking* with respect to the United States. In the other category, place all companies in the reverse position, and call them *outward-looking*. Allowing for cases of exact balance, this is an exhaustive classification for producers of traded goods. In the United States, inward-looking companies would include virtually all large consumer-goods manufacturing concerns, as well as foreign-based firms selling to the United States. Outward-looking companies would include enterprises in our major exporting industries: aerospace, agriculture, armaments, and so on down the list.

It is perfectly obvious that the low dollar and rising external demand helped outward-looking companies in the mid–1970s—that this was a prime source of the U.S. success in world markets through 1979. It can then be no surprise that the high dollar and rising internal demand have since had the opposite effect. What is less remarked on, and more peculiar to the U.S. position in the world, is that the outward-looking companies of the United States are generally higher-technology than the inward-looking companies. The reason is that while the United States is the world's premier consumer market, it is only a small part of the world's capital goods market. The sheer size of the U.S. economy makes it able to support a wide range of domestic enterprise and much foreign activity as well, fully exhausting all the scale and other economies that may exist in the production of consumer goods. Thus it is possible for a consumer-goods company, whether based in the United States or, say, Mexico, to focus exclusively on a small niche of the U.S. consumer-goods market; indeed, thousands of such enterprises exist all over the world. They are of course "inward-looking," as seen from the United States.

The situation with respect to U.S. internal investment-goods absorption is very different. Investment purchases constitute less than a fifth of GNP, and are both extremely diverse as to type and highly exacting as to standards. Economies of volume production and learning curves are not exhausted by the scale of the domestic market for such goods. Hence, as a rule, U.S. firms in investment-goods industries must compete in global markets if they are to remain competitive even at home—something that, say, General Motors or Whirlpool Appliances is not obliged to do. Thus investment-goods industries located within the United States tend to be "outward-looking." It is often the case (aerospace, computers, farm equipment, roadbuilding equipment) that a single U.S. firm maintains a highly prominent, if not dominant, position in an entire major area of investment goods over the entire globe.

It is investment goods that embody advanced technology. The consumer, in contrast to the offshore oil wildcatter or to Singapore Airlines, is a purchaser of low- and middle-technology goods.[11] Consumers do not buy exotic technologies because they cannot manage them. By the time an exotic technology has been packaged for mass consumption it is, virtually by definition, no longer exotic. The high-tech in the personal computer or the compact disc is nothing compared to the high-tech in the semiconductor or laser manufacturing process.

Thus the boom among outward-looking companies through 1979 corresponded to a boom in advanced-technology production. It stemmed from a demand surge that went well beyond internal markets, abetted by the flexibility of U.S. capital markets and the relatively low value of the dollar. The marginal high-tech markets overseas, in turn, kept U.S. technology industries on their technological frontiers; technically, U.S. aircraft, computers, microprocessors, and others remained second to none. Correspondingly, as these external markets for civilian high-technology capital goods have slumped—due to the high dollar and the Latin American depression—the world position of U.S. investment-goods firms has started to erode. At the same time, continuing growth in the peripheral economies of East Asia has provided expanding opportunities for the capital-goods producers of Japan, who have begun to position themselves for a wide-ranging challenge to U.S. dominance in this sphere.

In short, the rapid favorable adjustment of which the U.S. economy proved capable in the 1970s seems to work in reverse as well. It will be some time, of course, before the full effects of the declining U.S. relative position on the outward-looking, investment-goods, technological frontier are felt in a crisis of those industries with respect to their internal markets. But where an industry stands at the apex of an outward-looking chain (in farm equipment, for example) some signs of crisis have already appeared. These will multiply as time goes on. It is not clear, moreover, at what point the damage becomes irreversible by the simple device of ending the high-dollar exchange rate regime and substituting an internal incomes policy. In the high-technology sectors, once comparative advantage is lost, it may not be readily regained.

Implications for Advanced Developing Countries

If these views are roughly right, what are the implications of these U.S. realities for the investment decisions of ADCs seeking to make the most of trade possibilities with the United States? The most likely scenario is that the administration will continue to trade the fate of the outward-looking sector for relative price stability at home and that both present macroeconomic strategy and the consequent industrial trends persist. The main implication for the ADCs is that U.S. demand for consumer goods will continue to grow at its recent real rate of 5 per cent or thereabout, for as long as financial conditions permit. Moreover, for a time, much of this growth at the margin will be displaced to imports. Rapid import growth will therefore probably continue, even though the arithmetic of GNP shares dictates that eventually the growth rate of imports must converge with that of demand as a whole.

From the discussion of macroeconomic trends for all traded goods, there is an additional implication. Should a recession occur, import demand will of course drop sharply for a short time. But then it will resume even more quickly than before. Every cyclical contraction in the U.S. economy will produce a further *permanent* reduction in manufacturing employment as a share of total employment, with a corresponding increase in the propensity to import in the subsequent expansion. This process can continue as long as the United States has international credit and manufacturing employment to lose.

The decline in the U.S. technology position dictated by Reaganomics might suggest an opening for some ADCs in those advanced production niches. If the dollar remains high, it should be easy to underprice U.S. high-tech exporters—if not in direct sales to the United States, then at least in third markets. Korean automobiles can go to the United States, but Brazilian airplanes can go to Korea. Such prospects, however, are severely limited by the superior position that other developed countries will hold in the third-country markets for investment goods. The United States will lose its technology sectors mostly to Europe and Japan, not to the ADCs.

For the ADCs, the prime opportunity is to cater to the U.S. demand for consumer goods. We can now examine alternative means of taking advantage of this opportunity: the creation of autonomous national exporting industries on the one hand, and the integration of national factors of production into foreign manufacturing operations on the other. I shall argue that, for a country dependent on trade with the United States for manufacturing export growth, the first route is all but foreclosed. Patterns of protection are one part of the reason; the debt crisis accounts for the other part. Together, they provide strong incentives for ADCs in Mexico's position to develop close forms of association with the business enterprises of the potential market country.

The Patterns of Protection

The manufactured exports of *developing* nations almost by definition tend to be less technologically advanced than their manufactured imports. Advanced developing countries do not export advanced capital goods because they do not have a comparative advantage in such goods.

In the present situation, traditional low-technology industries provide an apparent source of opportunity for export expansion to U.S. markets. One route to expanding such exports without borrowing is to use existing capital equipment more intensively—indeed, to the point of virtual breakdown. A second is to divert goods away from production for domestic consumption. In response to the crisis, both strategies are in use. But both are limited by the threat and the experience of trade protection.

As the ADCs realize, most of the justifications of protection against ADC goods asserted on grounds of "unfairness" to U.S. producers are superficial. I will argue that ADC behavior, fair or unfair, is largely beside the point. Rather, low-technology ADC goods are especially vulnerable to U.S. protection because of their relatively *low* importance in the U.S. structure of production. That is, effective protection arises with higher probability against goods whose U.S. supply prices are irrelevant to U.S. wage levels and the risks of a renewed wage-price spiral.

A considerable literature on the types, intensities, and risks of trade protection—summarized and refined by William Cline—stresses the importance of non-tariff barriers (NTBs) as opposed to tariffs and seeks to analyze the factors determining whether an NTB will be imposed on a product or category of products.[12] Cline's best estimates for the United States suggest that the probability of an NTB depends on two factors: the degree of import penetration in the product category and the relative size of the industry in the U.S. labor force. That is, protection falls on large, labor-intensive industries with a high (and presumably rising) import share. The key examples where NTBs actually exist are: meat; dairy; sugar; confectionery; textiles and apparel; footwear; iron and steel; radio, television, and communications equipment; shipbuilding; and motor vehicles.

In comparison and mild contrast, the key sectors in which NTBs would be expected from Cline's forecasting equations are: textiles and apparel; leather products; footwear; pottery, earthenware, and china; radio, television, and communications equipment; motor vehicles; watches and clocks; and sporting goods. Thus there are few major sectors where NTBs are expected that do not have them. Cline's estimates, taken in conjunction with estimates of the growth of demand in various sectors, lead to the conclusion that new protection is unlikely to emerge in the United States except in a few small sectors where import penetration will come to threaten the eradication of an industry. The big players who need protection already have it. Recent flurries of trade legislation, up to and including the 1987 semiconductor sanctions against Japan, have not invalidated Cline's conclusions.

Moreover, these raw results actually overstate the degree of effective restriction on trade, since in some cases binding NTBs may exist without preventing a high growth rate of imports. Elsewhere in the analysis, Cline cites World Bank estimates for 1978–1990 showing expected growth rates for exports from the developing to the industrialized world to be 14.2 per cent for iron and steel; 16.5 per cent for machinery, electrical machinery, and transport equipment; and 15.4 per cent for "professional goods"—despite extensive protection in at least the first two of these sectors. Expected growth rates in the other main protected sectors are much lower: food products and beverages (3.9 per cent), tobacco (2.2 per cent), textiles (4.8 per cent) and apparel (5.9 per cent), and nonferrous metals (3.8 per cent).[13]

A general pattern emerges here that is consistent with Cline's basic results and also dovetails with the above discussion of U.S. macroeconomic strategy. Let us allow for three basic cases:

(1) *fully protected sectors,* in which protection exists and rates of import growth are low;

(2) *quasi-protected sectors,* in which protection exists, yet rates of import growth are high; and

(3) *sectors without any protection.*

We must first distinguish between cases where protection is desired and where it is not, and then (among those cases where it is desired) between cases where it is opposed and where it is not.

For purposes of analyzing the desire for protection, we may define inward-and outward-looking *industries* in a manner analogous to our earlier discussion of firms. An inward-looking industry is one whose fraction of imports in U.S. sales exceeds its fraction of exports in U.S. production; an outward-looking industry is one in the converse situation.[14]

As a rule, pressure for protection arises in inward-looking industries alone. Outward-looking industries clearly have more to lose than to gain from protection; their efforts to secure favorable governmental treatment on trade issues invariably have to do with subsidizing exports or opening foreign markets rather than with closing our own. Thus outward-looking industries fall altogether under case three above.

The issue that may turn on macroeconomic strategy is: Which of the inward-looking industries whose U.S. components desire full protection get it?

In autos and steel, the quest for full protection is fraught with controversy. In the case of steel, there are the industrial consumers who seek access to the cheapest sources of steel (as of oil, in these days of pressure for an oil import fee). Perhaps more important, in both cases there is the exceptional (relative) power of labor and salience of the collective bargaining process. Wage discipline in these industries does carry weight with the economy at large, and it would assuredly be undermined by full protection. The government's strategy of cost stabilization through the high dollar would be gravely threatened. Surely it is not an accident that the most outspoken voices against full protection in these sectors are those (for example, the Federal Reserve) with anti-inflation responsibility.

Full protection in tobacco, textiles, cheese, meat, and shoes raises the price of those goods to the U.S. consumer, and hence of course the profitability and size of the domestic industry, but it has no serious spillover effect on the general level of wages. The industries concerned are not the hot spots of U.S. labor relations. Is it possible, then, that— other conditions (such as those specified by Cline) being favorable— full protection exists in these sectors simply because there are few significant organized political forces to oppose it?

If so, lack of desire for protection rules it out for advanced-technology (outward-looking) industry. Conflict with macroeconomic strategy rules out full protection for mass-consumption, middle-technology industry. Full protection persists only for the lowest technology, inward-looking branches of industry without wage leadership traditions. Footwear and apparel as well as sugar and cheese are restricted because, from the government's standpoint, these concessions are politically profitable and economically inexpensive. But specialty steels and semiconductors and automobiles, in large if not completely unlimited numbers, continue to come in.

Demand and exchange rate conditions thus set up a strong pull for imports, while technological requirements and the credit crisis channel ADC producers toward outputs requiring mainly indigenous resources. But protection then acts as a damper to keep the flows small in these low- and low-middle-technology sectors. Agriculture and foodstuffs and traditional manufactures—tomatoes and tortillas and toy balloons—continue to flow northward and to provoke the usual fights. But because they are subject to fairly full protection, they are not the areas of most promising export growth.

What is left? Clearly, the window of opportunity is a small one. Moving through it depends on finding an unprotected, bankable niche. Such a niche indeed exists in the middle-technology, unprotected, consumer-goods sector—but the means of expanding production in this area are problematic. And that brings us to finance and to the entailed questions of autonomy and integration in the development of exportable manufactures.

The Supply of Finance

From 1973 through 1982, patterns of economic growth and development around the world were both fueled and disrupted by the extraordinary financial consequences of the rise of OPEC. Initially, OPEC's financial surpluses flowed to the great U.S., European, and Japanese commercial banks. Seeking employment in the advanced industrial world, they found none, owing to the cautious, anti-inflationary macroeconomic policies everywhere in effect at that time. Hence the surpluses flowed to the advanced developing countries, feeding a burst of growth, development, and capital flight in certain of these countries.

The affected ADCs were receiving resources more rapidly than they could absorb them—and incurring interest obligations that in real terms they could not meet. *A priori*, it was not irrational that they should do so; over and above the temptations of graft and capital flight, access to money meant a higher living standard and increased current imports, while historically real interest burdens have fallen with growth, inflation, and future inward financial flows. But then war (in the Falklands and the Persian Gulf), world recession, and OPEC's collapse dried up the petrodollars. Disinflation in the OECD countries meant that the real burden of contractual interest suddenly became vastly higher—instead of sharply lower—than the borrowers had planned. It could not go on, and the debt crisis began—with Mexico in August 1982.

Since then, we have had periods of hope, when new accords between major creditors, their banks, and the IMF were announced, and periods of disillusionment, when each such negotiation was followed by a request for another. The initial cajolery about short-run, cash-flow difficulties and the rest has ceased. So have the cathartic prognoses of the left. It is now accepted, as it was not in 1982, that the debt crisis is here for the long haul.

Until recent rumblings from Brazil, the pattern appeared well established. No large country had yet dared to default outright on its debt. On the other hand, none would pay more than the minimum required to keep alive the fiction of debt servicing and the minimum was falling. Bankers, for their part, will not lend new monies for any purpose except to roll over interest and principal due. A small, irregular increment in official assistance, with a reserve available for crises, has oiled the wheels of this very creaky machine. A tenuous equilibrium of endless negotiation has existed, seemingly unbreakable on either side because of the risks of formal default on the one hand and the impossibility of segregating new credits from old obligations on the other.

In this context, "success" had come to mean the avoidance of a catastrophic breakdown in communications, in negotiations, in order. This is not great success, but even success of this type is costly. Not every financial institution can indefinitely roll its interest due into new lending. Assuming it is not playing the same game with all borrowers simultaneously, its developing-country debt share will rise—and at some point, for some institutions, the share of "unpayable" developing-country debt in the portfolio becomes too large. The arrival of a banking crisis may well be a random event; the timing, location, and the victim institution will depend on a host of other factors, such as the mix of other loans in the particular bank's portfolio. But a climate in which crises of the Continental Illinois type are an endemic risk is not a good one for the resumption of new lending to the ADCs.

A return to the good old days—the fabled but elusive "return to creditworthiness" of central bank rhetoric—is therefore not likely to occur from any course of action that deeply indebted ADCs can take on their own. Nor, to state the obvious, is it likely that there will develop the political will in the United States or elsewhere to restore the creditworthiness of the ADCs by assuming and reducing or eliminating the debt. In short, we are back to the impasse and international financial intransigence of the post-World War I period, mitigated only by a much stronger desire on the part of U.S. authorities to avert a system-wide payments and financial crisis. Ultimately, though perhaps not for a while, a legitimating natural disaster (such as the disastrous earthquake or the drop in oil prices experienced by Mexico) or an internal political upheaval in some major country, followed by outright *de facto* default, seems the most likely outcome.

The continuing debt crisis implies, of course, grave difficulties for the creation of new middle-technology, exportable, consumer-goods industries in developing countries, which, above all, require foreign capital and foreign production equipment. Capital and equipment both come from the industrialized world, and (in the present crisis) the goods are not available without the finance. One cannot produce Japanese cars in Mexico without assistance from the Japanese. Because of the debt crisis, the requisite finance capital is not to be had from commercial banks. Hence advanced investment goods can no longer be passed to the ownership of ADCs on the scale that became common in the 1970s. A principal path toward developed status has been blocked.

The debt crisis does not, however, mean that no capital goods or other imports bought on credit can flow into Mexico and the other ADCs. It means that the price of credit is interdependence: The borrower of record for such operations will no longer be a government or national company of the ADC; hence, control will rest with a "creditworthy" entity from the industrialized world. It will be up to the ADCs to accept or reject such partnerships and the type of industrial development that goes with them.

In manufacturing, the most effective export strategy may be one that independence-minded ADCs and the U.S. labor movement will both bitterly resent: investment in middle-technology goods, under the wing of advanced-country businesses—the *maquila* model writ large. In other words, subcontracting, joint production, and the expansion of direct investment by multinational corporations will provide a borrower who can obtain credit and capital equipment with a standard product in the middle-technology range where demand growth is high, and—if the company in question is a U.S. (or Japanese or European) corporation—a buyer with some of the clout required to assure entry into the U.S. market. These arrangements involve advanced-country intermediation and control at most steps of the investment and production process. They imply profit-sharing with the industrial world, at best. And they are consistent with U.S. strategy for wage discipline, since the ADC workers thereby employed compete directly with their higher-paid counterparts in the United States.

For the multinational corporations, the attractions are obvious: low wages and a bargaining position on all the details of ADC operations that is stronger than it has been in decades. But the attractions are not unlimited, since all these conditions could change overnight in a political upheaval. Multinational corporations are therefore likely to move first into operations that require a low mix of heavy capital investment: the maquila model again.

Conclusions

If they wish to stay in the game as its rules are presently written, Mexico and other ADCs in a similar position must face a prolonged travail. Their debt demands domestic austerity sufficient to run export surpluses and to keep up minimal payments on the debt, borrowing with debtors' leverage the sums required to meet interest and rolling over principal. All autonomous routes to their development of exports meet with obstacles: Advanced investment goods are not an area of comparative advantage; low-technology traditional manufactures face protection; and the advanced capital equipment required to meet the fastest growing unprotected sectors of export demand in most cases can neither be generated internally nor purchased with internal finance.

Political strains in the ADCs will no doubt increase as governments face choices among the remaining options and make the bitter compromises necessary to realize such economic opportunities as are presented by the current structural situation. The rationality of even attempting to do so—given the increasing misery of the people, the bleak prospects, the underlying trade surplus and the apparent high economic return to a simple default on intermediate-term bank debt—will surely come under increasing question.

All of this sharply contrasts with the situation of a few years ago—when advanced capital goods exports from the United States were flowing to the ADCs and laying the foundation for their own, autonomous, fully integrated final-goods-producing networks. Then, the future resembled a future in which national governments might enthusiastically believe. Now, the future once again resembles the uninspiring past. Today, the ADCs are caught between the devil of the debt crisis and the deep sea of protection in their efforts to match resources to the opportunities that U.S. policies are creating.

Notes

[1] The author wishes to thank Jose Casar, William Cline, William Darity, Norman Glickman, Walt Rostow, Lance Taylor, Cathryn Thorup, and Sidney Weintraub for comments without associating them with responsibility for the views expressed.

[2] Before the 1986 fall in price, petroleum accounted (in dollars) for about 70 per cent of Mexico's exports overall, but for only one-half of its exports to the United States.

[3] Stephen Marris, *Deficits and the Dollar: The World Economy at Risk* (Washington, D.C.: Institute for International Economics, 1985)

[4] From 11.4 per cent in 1982 to 14.1 per cent in 1986, when measured in 1982 dollars. In nominal terms, the rise is smaller because dollar appreciation has depressed the price deflator for imports, which in fact fell 8 per cent over this period, including a sharp drop due to falling oil prices in 1986.

[5] Over seven million new service jobs, compared with about 625,000 net new manufacturing jobs, have been created since 1982.

[6] Evsey Domar called attention to this phenomenon in 1946; see his "Capital Expansion, Rate of Growth, and Employment," *Econometrica*, Vol. 14, 1946, pp. 137–147.

[7] Some argue that this process is at heart not supply- but demand- and technology-driven; that the decline in manufacturing employment over time can be attributed to changes in technology and to changing patterns of demand as incomes rise. Clearly, though, recessions *are* the precipitating events. Drops in manufacturing employment since 1950 have occurred in 1954, 1958, 1961, 1970–1, 1975, 1980–1, and 1982–3, and in no other years. Service sectors (wholesale and retail trade, finance, government, and

services proper) do not show this pattern. It is difficult to see why either a shift of demand toward services due to income elasticity or a shift of technology toward more efficient methods would occur in periods when income and investment are falling—and never when they are going up.

⁸ Another question is: Why should we care? De-industrialization skeptics rightly point out that the story told above seems to apply only to *employment*; the share of manufacturing *output* (valued in constant dollars) in the value of all output did not change materially in the thirty-two years after 1950. (The current or nominal dollar share of manufacturing output in total output did fall, from 29 to 20 per cent, but this, given the constant real share, is due to faster productivity growth and falling relative prices in the manufacturing sector. (See Robert Lawrence, *Can America Compete?* Washington, D.C.: Brookings Institution, 1984, p. 18). Yet these facts provide no basis for concluding, as the skeptics tend to do, that all came out for the best. A fall in manufacturing supply *relative to what might have been* does seem to have occurred. That is, in the absence of periodic recessions, there would have occurred a normal process of continuing *industrialization*: a *rise* in the real volume of manufactures compared to real GNP (and a larger fall in their relative price) together with (perhaps) constancy (rather than decline) of the share of nominal spending on manufactures in nominal GNP. Would we have been better off with a higher real share of manufactures? Yes, for two reasons. First, manufacturing is inherently the entry point of major technological innovation in social and economic life; the larger is investment in this sector the larger is the domain over which innovations will diffuse, and the larger the gross productivity gain. For this reason, other things equal, industrializing societies tend to get richer faster over time than those in the reverse situation. Second, durable manufactured goods embody wealth, yielding a stream of benefits over time; their diffusion across the population, at ever lower relative prices, is a major source of the cumulative rise in living standards. Fundamentally, there is just no reason to suppose that our particular history of induced or accidental recessions has produced a desired or "optimal" balance of manufacturing and service activity.

⁹ On this, see for example the survey provided in R.D. Norton "Industrial Policy and the American Renewal," *Journal of Economic Literature*, Vol. 24, No. 1 (March 1986), pp. 1–40.

¹⁰ I find this distinction more useful than traditional alternatives: import-competing vs. exporting, or capital- vs. labor-intensive.

¹¹ Economists have no rigorous definition of high-tech and a rather casual attitude toward what it comprises. However, a little reflection is telling. VCRs and PCs and digital watches may seem high-tech to laymen, but the tasks involved in assembling them—once the semiconductors have been made—surely do not seem exotic to engineers.

¹² See William Cline, *Exports of Manufactures From Developing Countries* (Washington, D.C.: The Brookings Institution, 1984).

¹³ Leather products, footwear, wood products, paper products, printing and rubber products, plastics, pottery, glass, and non-metallic minerals are intermediate cases, with expected growth of 9.4 per cent annually in each case, but it is hard to know whether these groupings conceal substantial internal variation. See Cline, op. cit., p. 89.

¹⁴ Thus steel as a whole is an inward-looking industry, even though U.S. steel firms may neither import materials nor export final product.

Chapter 4

Prospects for the U.S.-Mexican Relationship in the Motor Vehicle Sector

James P. Womack

After a decade of uncertainty engendered by two energy shocks, the motor vehicle industry in the 1980s has reasserted itself as the world's "industry of industries."[1] As a result, a host of developing countries—including Korea, Taiwan, Malaysia, Brazil, and Yugoslavia as well as Mexico—have concluded that a major stake in this sector is still essential to advanced economic development. These countries are formulating plans not only for rapidly increasing domestic motor vehicle production, but for large-scale entry into export markets.[2]

In the case of Mexico, a dramatic shift to a surplus in motor vehicle trade has just been achieved after decades of substantial deficits. Moreover, exports of finished vehicles and parts are likely to grow rapidly in the years immediately ahead. In the dismal economic landscape uncovered by receding oil prices, Mexico's motor vehicle sector is now rightly considered by Mexican economic planners as one of the best hopes for advancing the country's industrial infrastructure while managing its foreign debt.

However, Mexico and the other developing countries are devising plans at a time of rapid change in the motor industry's core technologies and methods of production organization and during a period of intense competition among the established producing regions. As a result, the most labor-intensive elements of motor vehicle production—those traditionally thought most suitable for transfer to developing countries—are under competitive attack from robotic assembly technologies, simplified product designs, and new approaches to production management. This concerted attack is driven with ever greater intensity by the struggle among Japanese, U.S., and European producers to gain (or regain) competitive superiority in the United States and Europe.

This chapter is concerned specifically with the U.S.-Mexican relationship in the motor vehicle sector over the remainder of this century in light of these new developments in manufacturing technology, production management, and world competition that are profoundly changing the logic of industrial development. Before suggesting changes in the current relationship that may benefit all parties involved, it is necessary to sketch the trajectory of technological and organizational advance in the worldwide motor vehicle industry and to review as well the evolution of the U.S.-Mexican automotive relationship.

The Trajectory of the World Motor Vehicle Industry

In our recent work at the Massachusetts Institute of Technology on the future of the world motor vehicle industry,[3] we found that the industry has advanced through three "transformations" and now stands on the verge of a fourth. These transformations have involved combinations of new technological capabilities, new patterns of social organization, and new competitive strategies in the international marketplace to seize the advantages inherent in new technology and social organization. Because these transformations have in each case altered industrial relationships between countries worldwide, they merit a brief summary.

The First Transformation

The motor vehicle industry was born around 1885 in France and Germany, and producers there led the world industry for some twenty-five years. However, the European producers emphasized technical virtuosity in the design of low-volume products—often custom-built for the well-to-do—and this inherently limited the growth and economic importance of the industry. In the period around World War I, Henry Ford and Alfred Sloan (of General Motors) in the United States engineered the first major transformation of the industry from custom building to true mass production. The perfection of the assembly line, in combination with new products explicitly designed for mass production, accounted for half of the breakthrough. The other half involved rationalization of shop-floor social organization through the minute division of labor (now commonly called "Fordism") and the development of management and marketing techniques capable of guiding the vast enterprises that mass production made possible (the contribution of Sloan). These new techniques changed the fundamental character of the industry. Numerous small firms building low-volume luxury vehicles and concentrated in Central Europe gave way to the familiar handful of mass-marketing giants—General Motors, Ford, and Chrysler—located in the Midwest of the United States.

These innovations strongly tipped the competitive balance in favor of U.S.-based manufacturing, and the U.S. juggernaut might well have concentrated practically all of the world industry in Detroit. This did not happen because of thoroughgoing trade protection on a country-by-country basis in Europe. However, the small scale of individual European markets in the interwar period gave no basis for more than a holding operation until the 1950s. At that point, the combination of an integrated European marketplace and a thorough mastery of U.S. mass-production techniques permitted a challenge to U.S. dominance in the industry.

The Second Transformation

The key element in the European challenge—the second transformation in the history of the motor vehicle industry—was the broad diversity in product offerings. These were in part the accidental result of national producers being restricted to their home markets by trade barriers over a lengthy period and having to develop specialized products for very different road conditions, tax structures, income distribution, and tastes in each country. This diversity of products was frequently cited by U.S. observers as evidence of the immaturity of the European industry. With time and market integration, they hypothesized, these producers would surely converge on "standard"-size products in the same way the U.S. industry had. Instead, buyer preferences in both the United States and Europe went in the opposite direction. European producers, with their diversity of products, gained a lasting advantage over those in the United States, first (in the 1960s) in the economy-car segments and today in the luxury-car segments of the industry.

The Third Transformation

A U.S.-European "duopoly" in the world motor industry was the temporary result of this transformation, but it was upset after 1973 by the Japanese, who touched off a third transformation. The key items in the Japanese armory were a new system of social organization based on the concept of groups and a new production philosophy based on the twin concepts of zero inventories and perfect quality.[4] Nearly fifty years after the initial breakthrough, these innovations finally achieved the full productivity potential inherent in Ford's mass-assembly technology.

The Japanese group approach is based on the simple premise that groups are more productive than isolated individuals (whether these are individual companies, or divisions of companies, or workers), provided there is a spirit of mutual obligation and two-way information flow among group members. Thus the Japanese have developed conglomerate groups—for example Mitsubishi, Sumitomo, Mitsui, and DKB. The members have extensive equity cross-holdings—sufficient, in fact, to protect against the threat of foreign-held majority shares—but are more like equals than building blocks in a hierarchy. At the next level down, they have perfected assembler-supplier groups, such as Toyota Group and Nissan Group, that comprise several hundred companies with extensive equity cross-holdings and arrangements for sharing work and tools in the manufacture of a given range of products. Within these assembler-supplier groups the Japanese have utilized product development teams for new products. Finally, at the level of actual production, they have developed work groups on the shop floor.

At all of these levels, the degree of shared skills and knowledge is much higher than would typically be the case in a Ford/Sloan-style industrial system. For example, in the shop-floor work groups, each member learns to do all of the tasks performed by the group, and tasks are rotated. Simple planning tasks are assigned to the group as well, along with responsibility for quality control and for identifying means of improving the work process. Similarly, in product planning and design, where no individual can hope to master every skill needed, development teams are formed to include from the outset a representative of every essential skill—market assessment, product design, product engineering, production process engineering, and plant operations. Because many of the necessary skills are in the supplier firms rather than in the assembler company, these teams involve close collaboration not only among individual workers but among many companies.

By contrast, the Ford/Sloan system tends to train both blue collar and professional workers in very narrowly specialized tasks and to treat the overall production process sequentially—generally without adequate thought for the interconnections between steps. Marketing specialists hand a product concept to the product engineers, who hand it over to the production engineers, who deliver it to the factory staff, either in the company's manufacturing divisions or in an independent supplier firm. Finally, on the shop floor, assembly workers and machine tenders have narrowly defined and unchanging tasks, while quality control, parts ordering, and process improvements are delegated to other narrowly skilled specialists.

The alienating consequence of this approach on the shop floor has long been known, but narrow skilling and task definitions for engineers, financial experts, marketing staffs, and general managers, as well as rigid task demarcations between assemblers and suppliers, are now also increasingly understood to be the source of severe organizational dysfunctions.

The Japanese group approach provides advantages at every level of world competition. The conglomerate groups provide enormous financial resources to weather market downturns and incorrect product decisions. In addition, the equity cross-holders continuously check on the management of each member firm in a manner that often seems more rigorous and informed than that of Western-style boards of directors. At the next level, the assembler-supplier groups yield remarkable savings in the amount of capital and manpower needed to produce motor vehicles because many redundant steps can be eliminated, planning can be more flexible, and group resources can be shared. The product development teams are able to bring products to market more quickly than their Western competitors and with many fewer manufactured defects caused by design and engineering errors. Finally, the shop-floor groups have achieved remarkable efficiency in work force utilization by eliminating many unnecessary steps; such groups seem to foster a feeling of involvement in decision-making that enhances employee dedication.

Equally important for the Japanese is their production philosophy. By concentrating most manufacturing steps very near the point of final assembly and producing parts only as needed (that is, "just in time"), the system dramatically reduces both inventories and defective parts. By concentrating the production system on the goal of perfection and defect *prevention*—rather than on defect detection and an acceptable level of rectification—the system yields complex, mass-produced products of unmatched accuracy while actually reducing costs.

As a result of these advances, the Japanese producers in the early 1980s were on average able to produce a vehicle of given specification and very high accuracy (often labeled "quality") in only half the labor hours (including management and design hours) averaged by U.S. producers. Even more remarkable—and a point still commonly missed in popular treatments of the Japanese phenomenon—this was in a period when the production hardware in both countries was practically identical. In essence, the Japanese achievement lay in taking very traditional manufacturing hardware and extracting its full productivity potential—not through speedups or low wages, but by shaping and implementing a new system of social organization.[5]

A final element in the Japanese achievement has been the design of a market strategy to take advantage of the reduced development times and costs permitted by their social organization. To the exasperation of U.S. and European producers, they have reduced model life from 8-10 years to 4-6 years and may reduce it further still. They have also reduced the time needed to move a new model from concept to initial production—from five to about three-and-one-half years. In addition, because of the flexibility of their production system, they have seized a former European advantage by developing new products for smaller market niches and are doing this without paying a large penalty in scale economies. This permits remarkably dynamic responses to changing market conditions.[6]

Responses to the Third Transformation

The short-term U.S. and European response to the Japanese challenge was similar to the European response to the U.S. challenge of the 1920s: protection of domestic markets. The main difference was that this time it was done through quotas rather than tariffs because quotas could be labeled "voluntary" and slipped around the prohibitions on country-specific tariffs in the General Agreement on Tariffs and Trade (GATT). However, there is now a very dramatic process under way of diffusing Japanese practice abroad—much as U.S. practice was diffused in Europe in the 1920s. The means include copying of Japanese innovations by Western producers, collaborations involving Japanese and Western partners, such as Toyota-GM, Chrysler-Mitsubishi, and BL-Honda, and, increasingly, direct investment in the United States and Europe by Japanese assembler firms and parts suppliers.

Initial experiences at the new Honda, Toyota-GM, and Nissan facilities in the United States make it clear that best practice can and will be transplanted. For example, the Honda plant in Marysville, Ohio, is assembling cars with only about 60 per cent of the labor hours required to accomplish the same tasks at a typical General Motors plant in the United States. Honda also has a very low number of delivered defects compared with the average of the Big Three—Ford, General Motors, and Chrysler—although it relies upon relatively conventional process machinery. Thus practically all of Honda's productivity and quality advantage, based on social organization rather than on enhanced technology per se, has been shifted 7,000 miles to a totally new cultural and social milieu.[7] The key question, therefore, is not whether the U.S. auto industry will be revitalized, but whether traditional domestic producers can introduce new techniques rapidly enough—burdened as they are with sunk investments and outdated social systems—to avoid losing much of the market to Japanese producers with new plants in the heartland of the United States.

Although the prospect of a Japanese-dominated North American motor vehicle industry is startling, it should be clear that this is a real possibility within the next twenty years. Four Japanese-owned or managed assembly plants are now operating in the United States and Canada, and six more are under construction. More than two million units of Japanese assembly capacity will therefore be in place in North

America by 1990, at a direct investment cost exceeding $5 billion (Table 1). The scale of this enterprise comes into focus when one realizes that, in less than eight years, a new Japanese-U.S. motor industry will have emerged with nearly four times the assembly capacity of the entire Mexican motor vehicle sector.

In addition, 129 Japanese-owned components plants were already operating or were being built in the United States as of mid-1987.[8] This is only the beginning of a flood likely to sweep over the continent in the next few years due to the strengthening of the yen, the components needs of the ten new Japanese assembly plants, and Japanese concerns about an extension of trade restraints to cover parts as well as finished units. This means that the entire motor vehicle industry in the United States and Canada will be rebuilt before the end of the century. The process may create opportunities for the Mexican motor vehicle industry, but the pace of change is likely to be very rapid; many of the most important decisions on the location of assembly plants and the relocation of parts plants will be made in the next few years.

The Fourth Transformation

In 1980, as we began our work in the MIT Auto Program, we thought the Japanese challenge might provide a major opening for developing countries in the production of parts and finished motor vehicles. On the basis of the traditional concepts of the product cycle, we assumed that the real Japanese advantage lay in low wages. The logical response of threatened producers in the United States and Europe would involve relocating production of a large portion of their output to lower-labor-cost countries with relatively advanced industrial infrastructure— countries such as Korea, Taiwan, or Brazil. Mexico in particular seemed destined to benefit as the low-wage production site closest to Detroit. Eventually, we reasoned, the Japanese would also be forced to source parts and even whole vehicles in the developing countries, and a fourth transformation of the industry would be at hand in which motor vehicle production would become the specialty of a number of the newly industrializing nations.

Four years later, we concluded that the industry is indeed on the verge of a fourth transformation—but not the one we had expected.[9] We now believe that new design and process technologies, in combination with organizational innovations, will transform the motor vehicle industry before the end of the century. The key consequence, for the present discussion, is that any "natural" tendency for the industry to relocate production destined for developed-country markets to the developing countries will be greatly attenuated.[10]

There is no mystery about this fourth transformation, although its precise trajectory is not yet clear.[11] A plethora of new electronic tech-

Table 1. New Japanese-Owned or Managed Assembly Plants

Plants in Operation (June 1987)	Location	Capacity
NUMMI (GM-Toyota joint venture)	Fremont, California	250,000
Honda of America Mfg. Inc.	Marysville, Ohio	360,000
Honda of Canada Mfg. Inc.	Alliston, Ontario	80,000
Nissan Motor Company	Smyrna, Tennessee	240,000
TOTAL		930,000

Plants Under Construction	Location	Capacity
Diamond-Star Inc. (Chrysler-Mitsubishi joint venture)	Bloomington, Illinois	240,000
Toyota Motor Company	Georgetown, Kentucky	250,000
Mazda Motor Company	Flat Rock, Michigan	300,000
Toyota Motor Company	Cambridge, Ontario	50,000
Subaru-Isuzu (joint venture)	West Lafayette, Indiana	200,000
Suzuki-GM (joint venture)	Ingersoll, Ontario	200,000
TOTAL		1,240,000

Source: MIT International Motor Vehicle Program data base.

nologies and materials—developed outside the auto industry but now ready for absorption—are fundamentally altering the production system and the product by reducing labor intensity while improving quality. Microprocessor-driven, computer-aided design systems (CAD) are eliminating the drafting room as they reduce product development times. Microprocessor-driven robots for painting and welding are already in their third generation and will soon be joined by machinery for automated final assembly. A new generation of automated and flexible machining systems is removing the direct labor content from the fabrication and assembly of engines, transmissions, and electric motors while greatly expanding the flexibility of the previous generation of dedicated automation, which was able to handle only one type of product. New nonferrous materials—notably reinforced plastics—will simplify production and extend product life. At the same time, vehicle construction principles will be extensively modified through modularization of the many vehicle systems (such as suspension, braking, steering, climate control) to permit full use of these design and manufacturing tools.

These new technologies and materials could have a profound effect even if the social organization of the production system were not to change greatly. In the combination most likely—rapid technical advance accompanied by rapid organizational change to fully diffuse Japanese practice worldwide—the amount of unskilled and semi-skilled labor needed in auto production will fall dramatically even as the demand for highly skilled workers and advanced social organization rises. The MIT Auto Program's final report estimates that between 1979 and 2000, auto production in the developed countries will increase by about 30 per cent even as the total amount of labor employed in the sector falls by 40 per cent.[12]

Over the long term, these tendencies do not play to the strengths of the newly industrializing countries if their objective is to capture large amounts of manufacturing activity from the developed countries by using low wages as the prime lure. (There are, however, significant *short-term* opportunities for a number of low-wage countries such as Mexico because many of the new technologies are some years away from perfection, and beleaguered producers in the United States and Europe need immediate help with cost reduction. Similarly, Japanese producers fleeing the rising yen are moving their most labor-intensive activities to developing countries, including the Mexican *maquila* zone.)

However, on the positive side, the new technologies, along with new systems of human organization, could permit an explosion of productivity and wealth creation for domestic consumption in newly industrializing countries even if they do not become major exporters. How best to attain and implement these advances is the key policy question facing developing countries over the longer term. This brings us at last to the question of the implications of technological and organizational change in this industry for the U.S.-Mexican relationship.

The Evolution of the U.S.-Mexican Relationship in the Motor Vehicle Sector

For several decades now, the U.S.-Mexican relationship in motor vehicles has been a four-way affair involving the U.S. and Mexican governments, U.S.-based assemblers (General Motors, Ford, and Chrysler), and, increasingly, Mexican-owned parts makers. The objectives of all of these participants have not necessarily changed over time, but the bargains struck between them have shifted because circumstances and bargaining strengths have altered, often quite outside their direct control.[13]

Specifically, prospects for rapid market growth in Mexico and slowing market growth in the United States gradually increased the desire of the U.S. multinational corporations to secure a strong, long-term position in Mexico. Recently the U.S. multinational assemblers have shown a strong interest in Mexican sourcing of the most labor-intensive components (for example, seat covers and wiring harnesses). These changing perceptions on the part of the multinationals have increased their willingness to bargain with the Mexican government, whose desire to build an advanced industry has been a constant, but whose leverage over the multinationals has varied with domestic economic prospects and U.S. receptiveness to export-promotion strategies. Finally, shifting perceptions of Mexican stability and credit-worthiness—and the broader international competitive situation of the American auto industry—have affected U.S. government receptiveness to Mexican government initiatives in the auto sector.

We can see this process proceeding through three phases, and perhaps soon into a fourth. In the long period from the beginning of the auto age until 1962, motor vehicles in Mexico were for the most part imported, with only modest amounts of local manufacturing—this being almost entirely final assembly initiated to offset shipping costs and tariffs. Local content was below 20 per cent.

By 1962, Mexican industrialization had reached the point where government officials were convinced that development of a domestic auto industry was both feasible and essential. The Mexican economic miracle of the early postwar period—based on manufacturing of light consumer goods—was beginning to taper off, and government planners recognized that motorization of the Mexican economy without a domestic motor industry would quickly create an unsupportable trade imbalance.

The U.S.-Mexican relationship entered a new phase with the Mexican government's decision in favor of the vigorous pursuit of import substitution. Prohibitions on the import of new and used vehicles and a local-content requirement of 60 per cent for each vehicle produced in Mexico marked an effort to capture for Mexico those parts of motor vehicle manufacture—for example, major mechanical components—that were thought to aid most directly the technical advance of Mexican industry. The policy acknowledged the dominance of the multinationals at the assembler level and continued to permit 100-per-cent foreign ownership, but endeavored to extract higher levels of Mexican manufacturing effort by using the lure of access to a protected domestic market with greater growth potential than the mature U.S. market.

In addition, the parts sector was preserved for Mexican initiatives through: a) a requirement that a substantial fraction of the local content be bought from Mexican parts suppliers, and b) a restriction of foreign equity holdings in these components firms to 40 per cent.

While the government's objective was to convert Mexico into a major motor vehicle manufacturer with a stable or declining motor sector trade deficit, the chosen policy instruments had a number of weaknesses. In particular, the small size of the domestic market dictated a small number of firms, both in major parts and in final assembly, if minimum-scale economies were to be achieved. However, a large number of firms, backed by their home governments, wanted market access, and in the end eight final assemblers set up operations in a total market of only about 100,000 units. In addition, most assemblers tried to cover the market with a range of products. As a result, Mexican production runs were remarkably low and consumer prices of comparable products (despite much lower labor costs) considerably higher than in the United States.

In addition, the Mexican government's leverage on the multinational assemblers to increase local content was limited. When the companies failed to achieve their content targets—as they routinely did in the early years of the import-substitution program—the government had two powerful but impossible alternatives: to shut companies down, with widespread job losses, or to nationalize them, creating a furor with their home-country governments. The only feasible alternative was much weaker. It involved continual government prodding—through, for example, the adjustment of production quotas, price controls, import permits, corporate taxes—whereby the level of Mexican content did increase, but at a rate much slower than the government wished. In addition, the level of technology transfer, particularly into the Mexican-owned supplier firms, was very modest. After a period of adjustment, however, the relationship was only minimally conflictual because the multinationals and the domestic parts makers were satisfied with their protected market. Equally important, U.S. domestic interests were not threatened, since despite the Mexican government's best efforts, the Mexican automotive trade balance with the United States was consistently negative.

As the size of Mexico's oil reserves became known in the 1970s, and as oil prices boomed and the economy began to accelerate, the Mexican government realized that a key element in the relationship had changed: The prospects for domestic market growth were suddenly very large and the multinationals could be pushed much harder. Export promotion and trade balancing, rather than simple import substitution, emerged as a feasible strategy—as the price of continuing multinational access to one of the world's key growth markets.

The 1972 Auto Decree was the initial move in this direction, with modest export targets, but the major breakthrough came in the 1977 Auto Decree, which set the industry firmly on this new path and brought the U.S.-Mexican relationship into a third phase. Under the terms of the 1977 Decree, each final assembler was required to balance its automotive trade within a few years. This logically would balance overall automotive trade as well. Strict limits were also set on new foreign-owned investments not dedicated to export production. At the same time, however, the local-content level to be met by every vehicle produced in Mexico was raised, and the decree retained many other restrictions on producer activities (for example, prohibitions on vertical integration downward into the domestically owned parts business)—making the total package quite different from the U.S.-Canada Auto Pact, which also utilizes assembler trade balancing.

In the early 1980s, to meet Mexico's trade balancing requirements, all six of the multinational assemblers operating in Mexico (GM, Ford, Chrysler, Volkswagen, Renault, and Nissan) constructed large engine plants geared primarily for export. These were the first state-of-the-art auto manufacturing facilities built in Mexico. In addition, for reasons of world competition unrelated to the 1977 Decree, U.S. firms set up a number of light manufacturing plants (for seat covers, trim, wiring harnesses, and minor mechanical parts) in maquila zones along the U.S.-Mexican border, with output earmarked for U.S. assembly plants. These were one element of the U.S. industry's short-term response to the Japanese challenge.

Due to the long lead times necessary to bring major plants on line and the boom in the Mexican economy through 1981, the short-run results of the 1977 Auto Decree were the opposite of what had been expected: Through 1981, the Mexican trade balance in autos steadily worsened, as the boom in domestic vehicle production and sales—where the average vehicle produced contained more than 40-per-cent imported parts—caused imports to rise much faster than exports.

Since 1982, this trend has been dramatically reversed. The economic crisis has greatly reduced domestic demand, thereby reducing parts imports. (It should be noted that every vehicle produced in Mexico still consists of 30- to 40-per-cent imported parts.) In addition, Chrysler and General Motors have decided to utilize their substantial excess capacity in Mexico to assemble products for the U.S. market (where a booming auto market after 1984 created a shortage of assembly capacity). Exports of fully furnished units assembled in central Mexico was 35,000 in 1986 and could easily grow to 125,000 by 1989 if demand continues strong in the United States.[14] As a consequence, the Mexican motor vehicle industry ran a substantial worldwide trade surplus (about $500 million) for the first time in 1985. More significant, the completion of a number of additional facilities whose output is earmarked for the United States[15] promises to shift U.S.-Mexican motor vehicle trade from its current balance to a large Mexican surplus in the years just ahead, even if the Mexican domestic market makes a strong recovery (Table 2).

Table 2. U.S.-Mexican Trade in Motor Vehicles and Parts, 1965-1985 ($ millions)

Year	Mexican Imports from the United States	Mexican Exports to the United States	Balance
1965	159	0.1	−159
1970	195	18.0	−188
1975	528	136.0	−392
1980	1,067	245.0	−822
1981	1,900	460.0	−1,440
1982	1,240	619.0	−621
1983	886	1,000.0	+114
1984	1,580	1,450.0	−130
1985	2,180	2,000.0	−180

Source: Motor Vehicle Manufacturers Association of the United States, tabulated from U.S. Bureau of the Census data from customs forms FD 410 and IM 146.

Thus Mexican economic planners can look with some satisfaction at their work of the past twenty-five years, which has created a major motor vehicle industry with steadily and now rapidly growing exports. In addition, Mexico is now making a dramatic transition toward producing finished automobiles for export to compete in the United States with products from Japan. If it is successful, this will dramatically change the current external view of Mexican industry as an adequate producer of domestic consumer goods but hardly a serious competitor against the best developed-country products (Table 3).

Table 3. The Growth of Mexican Production and Export of Finished Vehicles, 1965-1985 (thousands of units and percentages)

Year	Automobile Production	Commercial Vehicle Production	Total Production	Exports as a Percentage Production
1965	46	21	67	*%
1970	137	56	193	*
1975	237	119	356	*
1980	303	187	490	3.7
1981	355	242	597	2.3
1982	301	171	473	3.4
1983	207	78	285	7.7
1984	232	112	344	9.9
1985	247	151	398	14.6

* = Less than 0.1 per cent.
   Source: Asociación Mexicana de la Industria Automotriz, as reported in Motor Vehicle Manufacturers Association of the United States, *World Motor Vehicle Data,* various years.

What may become a problem, however, is that Mexico's success in turn may change the attitude of the U.S. government, ushering in a fourth phase in U.S.-Mexican relations. Mexican policy in the auto sector has long relied on import restraints, investment restrictions, local-content requirements, and export requirements that run counter to U.S. liberal trade ideologies. However, as long as Mexican policy allowed a role for U.S.-based multinational producers and did not threaten U.S.-based production, there was no protest. Now, Mexican auto trade with the United States is likely to swing sharply positive at a time when the U.S.-based motor vehicle industry is on the defensive, the overall U.S. trade balance is ever more negative, and Mexico is newly vulnerable to criticism of its industrial promotion policies in its negotiations as a GATT member. Moreover, in light of the debt crisis Mexico has an urgent need to spur its motor vehicle industry to achieve even greater export flows, which logically would also go to the United States.

If Mexico were the only U.S. trade partner suddenly improving its trading position in the motor vehicle sector, the problem would surely be modest. Indeed, with the additional factor of the Mexican foreign debt, there would be no problem at all. U.S. lenders would welcome the prospect of dollar flows from merchandise trade going to debt repayment, and the transnational producers would be satisfied with their long-term prospects in a protected market. Current prospects, however, are of course very different: Within the next few years, a tremendous surge of finished unit imports and motor vehicle parts will arrive in the United States. Finished unit imports will continue to increase from independent companies in Yugoslavia and Korea; from multinational subsidiaries in Brazil, Korea, and Taiwan, as well as Mexico; and from the European-based producers of luxury vehicles. Parts shipments from many of these same countries will dramatically increase, and Japanese producers will bring in enormous volumes of parts to supply their final assembly plants in the United States. As a result, the U.S. motor vehicle trade deficit, already a staggering $55 billion in 1986, could easily increase by 50 per cent in the next three to four years. Remarkably, this can happen even if Japanese finished unit shipments to the United States do not rise above the current "voluntary" limit of 2.4 million vehicles per year.

This flood of imports into the United States is not, however, the result of rapidly emerging competitiveness in the motor vehicle sector in all of these countries. In large part it is due instead to a combination of weak currencies in the developing countries; limits on Japanese finished units, which divert Japanese assembly to third countries, including Mexico; and export incentives from developing-country governments desperate to gain foreign exchange for debt repayment. The trend does, however, seem certain to force the U.S. government to take a much more aggressive stance on imports, and this in turn may affect Mexican access to the U.S. market.

This is particularly the case because the multinational position on Mexican auto exports is not necessarily to Mexico's advantage in the upcoming trade debates. The U.S.- and European-based multinationals with operations in Mexico—GM, Ford, Chrysler, Renault, and Volkswagen—are all under the strongest pressure to improve their production systems to better compete with the Japanese. If Mexican-sourced parts and finished units were lowest cost and/or highest quality, there would be a groundswell of interest from producers to add Mexican production capacity and eliminate U.S. capacity. To date, however, the reverse has generally been the case. For a few particularly labor-intensive components (wiring harnesses and seat covers) and for items that are both energy-intensive and bulky to ship (springs), Mexico is the lowest-cost source for U.S. producers. *This*—rather than government policy—is the reason for the extraordinary growth of *maquiladoras* in the auto sector. However, the rush to build maquiladoras will soon be over. For more complex parts, Mexico is not competitive with Korea, Taiwan, and other locales in East Asia, where somewhat higher wages and shipping costs are offset by higher productivity and a better reputation for product quality and reliability of delivery.

In addition, prospects for rapid market growth in Mexico—historically the main incentive for multinationals to increase their commitment to heavy manufacturing in central Mexico—are now much more remote. Given the debt crisis and the likelihood of a long-term slump in the world oil market, it could easily be a decade before the Mexican domestic market surpasses its 1981 peak. Thus, rather than a synergistic combination of rapid market growth and low cost, Mexican manufacturing investments (apart from maquiladora plants) present a problem for Western multinationals. As indicated by Renault's recent actions in closing its auto assembly plant and offering its new, highly automated engine plant for sale at a fraction of its cost, there are limits beyond which a beleaguered producer cannot go—no matter how great the long-term growth prospects in a market.

For the advancing Japanese assemblers, on the other hand, Mexico hardly exists. While Mazda has offered Ford considerable technical assistance on the new Hermosillo plant and a number of the supplier affiliates of Japanese assemblers are establishing maquiladora plants, no Japanese assembler has made a major commitment in Mexico since Nissan did in 1967. Moreover, this is no easy way for additional Japanese firms to set up production in Mexico under the terms of the 1983 Auto Decree. Unless they are willing to export practically all of their output to the United States, they must immediately achieve 60-percent local content and restrict themselves to a single product line. While these latter stipulations may sound trivial to those unfamiliar with the industry, to industry executives they mean establishing engine, transmission, and components plants at a cost of more than $1 billion before an assembly plant can produce a single car. Only Nissan, a Japanese producer now encountering serious competitive problems both in Japan and abroad, is directly participating in the Mexican motor vehicle industry. Moreover, there is no obvious way for additional Japanese firms to participate at the assembler level under the terms of Mexico's most recent (1983) Auto Decree, which seeks to increase scale economies by reducing the range of products produced in Mexico.

Thus the recent Mexican export success in engines and assembled vehicles, based largely on government policy rather than on a change in fundamental competitiveness, may soon produce a U.S. reaction, moving the U.S.-Mexican relationship into a fourth phase. As a prologue to discussing this phase, it is essential to clarify the key industrial dynamics produced by the recent transformations in the world motor industry.

Technological and Organizational Factors in the Fourth Phase of the U.S.-Mexican Relationship

The third and fourth transformations of the world motor vehicle industry have changed its development and locational logic. The key aspects of the new industrial logic are summarized below.

1. The amount of manual and semi-skilled labor needed in motor vehicle production will now fall rapidly. The long-term future of the maquila industry is therefore threatened both by automation of assembly operations and by the redesign of products to eliminate the most labor-intensive parts.[16] These technological trends are not just a problem for the maquiladoras. Prospects for additional export-oriented plants in the Mexican interior justified on the basis of cheap labor are not bright.

2. The strong tendency in production geography will be to fabricate as many parts of a vehicle as possible near the point of final assembly. This permits dramatic reductions in in-process inventories through the use of "just-in-time" parts production as well as dramatic improvements in quality. All across the world we may therefore expect to see the creation of Toyota City types of complexes such as the already announced Buick City and Saturn projects. The "world car" assembled at a number of points using parts manufactured at high-volume plants spread around the globe is now a vision of the past. A scenario of rapid growth in fabrication of complex parts in Mexico for assembly in Detroit is therefore obsolete. "Just in time" increasingly means a few hours rather than several days for delivery.

3. The day of the "passive," arms-length supplier simply bidding on specifications handed out by assemblers is also past. Suppliers will need to take responsibility for designing and engineering parts as well as guaranteeing quality and keeping inventories to a minimum. The level of cooperation between suppliers, assemblers, and manufacturers of production process machinery will also increase greatly—or all three will fail individually. This will be a particular challenge for the Mexican parts makers, whose technology and production organization have historically been very weak and whose relations with foreign-owned assemblers have been distant and conflictual.

4. U.S. multinationals no longer lead the world motor vehicle industry. In the area of organizational expertise, they lag badly behind the Japanese, who are further perfecting the techniques they developed to launch the third transformation. In fourth-transformation innovations in product and process technology, the Japanese are now moving

from parity with the Americans into the lead. Thus any U.S.-Mexican bargains on the next phase of their motor vehicle relationship must centrally involve the Japanese. To pursue a new relationship that ignores or excludes them—for example, through some sort of bilateral "auto pact" restricted to U.S.- and Mexican-owned firms—could in the long term weaken both the Mexican and U.S. motor industries.

5. Scale economies in the motor industry for individual products are now falling, due to the ability to produce many variants of an engine, a transmission, or an electric motor with the same flexible and highly automated machinery. For example, the new FIAT engine plant for the FIRE family of engines uses no direct labor either in the fabrication of parts or in final assembly and can change its output mix instantaneously. However, the minimum scale for competitive manufacture of major mechanical items and for the assembly of finished vehicles is still in the annual range of a quarter-million to a half-million units. The Mexican industry still lags badly in achieving the production scale needed to run even a Ford/Sloan, first-transformation motor vehicle industry. (The 1983 Auto Decree, which dramatically reduces the number of models a producer may assemble, would be a major step ahead if it did not at the same time worsen other scale problems by raising the local-content level for each model.)

6. The day of building motor vehicle plants as massive job generators is over. Any attempt to build or sustain plants with "appropriate technology" (i.e., simple machinery and large amounts of manual labor) will guarantee failure in world competition. The challenge instead is to move toward highly efficient plants producing low-cost and high-quality products that are affordable domestically and internationally competitive in quality. This does not mean the immediate introduction of robots at every work station in Mexican assembly plants and lavish spending on other types of "high-tech." Rather, it means an insistence on state-of-the-art social organization throughout the plant and use of the latest technology where this is essential to high quality, notably in welding and painting.[17] Nevertheless, assembly plants that used to employ 6,000 or more workers will now employ 2,500 or fewer, while engine and major mechanical plants will be much more highly automated and will have very low employment totals. A country such as Mexico, which needs to increase both employment and exports in its motor sector, would therefore be wise to insist on best-practice plants and to seek employment gains by increasing production volume rather than by increasing the number of worker hours per unit of output.

These key facets of the new industrial logic are essential background for thinking about the bargains to be struck in the next phase of the U.S.-Mexican relationship.

Proposals for Advancing the Relationship

The U.S.-Mexican relationship in motor vehicles has involved a succession of bargains among the four key parties—the U.S. and Mexican governments, the U.S.-based multinational assemblers, and the Mexican-owned parts makers. Future bargains will need to involve a fifth party as well: the Japanese-based multinationals, including the parts makers in their industrial groups. Successful future bargains may be defined as ones that advance the interests of each party—or at least make no party worse off. Are there opportunities in the current situation for a new and successful bargain—for a positive-sum fourth phase in the U.S.-Mexican relationship? The answer can perhaps be found in examining the interests and circumstances of each of the parties:

The *Mexican government* needs to boost exports in the motor sector—perhaps its most promising means of dealing with the debt crisis. There is also an obvious need to reduce the cost of motor vehicles in the *domestic* market, in order to increase the industry's production volume and employment. In addition, strengthening the Mexican-owned parts sector remains a high priority on the domestic political agenda.

The *U.S. government* urgently wishes to enhance the competitiveness of its domestic industry through improved efficiency and quality. Otherwise, this and future U.S. administrations will face unpalatable choices between much more encompassing trade management or a staggering trade deficit in motor vehicles that requires further weakening of the dollar. However, the United States also has grave concerns about Mexico's stability and its ability to repay its U.S.-held debts. Thus a successful, export-oriented motor vehicle industry in Mexico—provided it does not further weaken the U.S.-based industry—is highly desirable.[18]

The *U.S.-based multinationals* badly need to improve efficiency and quality in order to regain their competitive edge. To the extent that Mexican production can aid in this effort, it will be expanded. However, under current Mexican regulations, which require very high levels of local content for all products manufactured south of the maquila zones, new investments are likely to occur mostly in these zones. The current spurt of assembly activity in the Mexican interior is only a short-term strategy by Detroit to utilize excess capacity in the severely depressed Mexican industry in order to overcome short-term capacity constraints in the United States. New investment for these activities is very modest; Detroit also assigns a low priority to any major new investment designed to secure a strong position in a large, high-growth market of the future. The U.S.-based multinationals have more pressing problems and fear that market growth in Mexico is a decade or more away.

The *Mexican-owned parts makers* need a strong Mexican assembler industry if they are to have a market for their output; they also need to increase their technology level and degree of cooperation with the assemblers to make a dynamic Mexican industry possible.

The *Japanese multinationals* wish to gain access to new markets and are now willing to undertake major manufacturing investments within those markets to do so. They know from recent experience in the United States that, by implementing their new approaches to production management, they can greatly undercut the production costs of competitors already producing in those markets. However, the Japanese assemblers are also increasingly thinking about coordinating their worldwide manufacturing systems, and the Mexican focus on rigid local-content requirements thus far has made Mexico a less attractive production site than many others.

A number of bargains may be possible on the basis of this set of interests. While the exact details of any bargain are the proper business of government officials, industry executives, and bankers, it may be useful to suggest here the broad outlines of a potential bargain that seems more promising than others in light of the technological and organizational trends in the world motor industry.

Such a bargain would involve the creation of a U.S.-Mexico motor vehicle pact—or, even better, a U.S.-Mexico-Canada motor vehicle pact, which, however, would incorporate more safeguards for Mexico than the U.S.-Canada Auto Pact has provided for Canada. Final assemblers qualifying for participation in this pact would enjoy open trade in motor vehicle products between the United States and Mexico. To qualify for participation in the pact, however, motor vehicle assemblers would agree to achieve and maintain a substantial Mexican surplus in their U.S.-Mexican auto trade.[19] In addition, participating producers might agree that a given minimum fraction of the value added in their Mexican production would consist of high-value-added activities (e.g., the manufacture of complex mechanical components and engineering research and development activities[20]) and that a minimum fraction of their local value added would be obtained from Mexican-owned companies. In return, participating producers would be exempted from the existing local-content rule. In addition, participating assemblers would be allowed to bargain among themselves on their high-value-added obligations and their obligations to purchase components from Mexican-owned companies.

What would this arrangement mean in practice? Assembler A (a mythical but typical company, regardless of nationality) is now prohibited from exporting units manufactured in the United States and Canada to Mexico. Assembler A's production for sale in Mexico is restricted to two body styles using a common set of major mechanical parts also made in Mexico; the local content of each body style must exceed 65 per cent. In addition, assembler A is permitted to assemble a vehicle with 30-per-cent Mexican local content—but only on condition that all of the output will be exported. Finally, assembler A must keep its imports and exports to and from Mexico in balance (which it does by exporting a large number of engines to the United States); and it must obtain 40 per cent of its Mexican value added through the purchase of components from majority-Mexican-owned suppliers.

Under the proposed motor vehicle pact, assembler A would be able to sell any of its U.S. or Canadian production in Mexico, provided the vehicles met some agreed minimum level of U.S. and Canadian value added. Assembler A would not be subject to any local-content requirement on any vehicle produced in Mexico—again, provided that the vehicle met an agreed minimum standard of value added. Indeed, assembler A would be under no obligation to produce any whole vehicles in Mexico; a large surplus in engine exports, for example, would guarantee the right to bring in a whole range of finished units. The arrangements could be even more flexible: If assembler A chose to establish a series of high-value-added export plants in Mexico, it could bargain with assembler B to allow this assembler to conduct nothing but low-value-added activities in Mexico, provided their combined production achieved the minimum level of high value added. Similarly, if assembler A obtained a very large fraction of its Mexican value added from Mexican-owned suppliers, it could join forces with assembler B, having a much lower fraction of its value added from Mexican-owned companies—provided their combined value added achieves the target level.

Supposing for the moment that such a motor vehicle pact could be negotiated, what would be the logical consequence for the Mexican motor vehicle industry? Based on the arguments presented earlier in this chapter about technological and organizational trends in the world motor vehicle industry, it would likely be as follows:

Participating assemblers with substantial existing investments (e.g., General Motors, Ford, and Chrysler) would revamp their production systems to produce, largely for export, a single model of car or truck at very high volume and to produce a large fraction of the value added in that vehicle at the point of final assembly. This arrangement would at last get the Mexican industry over the scale-economies and geographic-fragmentation hurdles that have for so long hurt its international competitiveness.

Those assemblers agreeing to participate who lack existing investments (notably the Japanese producers with major manufacturing operations in the United States) could proceed initially by building a major export-oriented plant for high-value-added components. By sending most or all of the output of this plant to the United States, they could in turn sell in Mexico any of the vehicles they produce in the

United States (provided they met an agreed minimum level of U.S. and Canadian value added). In the longer run, they would probably begin to imitate the U.S. Big Three by building an assembly plant and other major mechanicals plants alongside the initial components plants to reproduce the whole vehicle at the point of final assembly.

Finally, the Mexican motor vehicle industry as a whole would, as a matter of pre-agreement, run a substantial trade surplus with the United States.

But why should any of the five key participants in a new U.S.-Mexican bargain in the motor vehicle sector—the Mexican government, the U.S. government, the U.S.-based multinationals, the Mexican-owned components suppliers, and the Japanese multinationals—favor such a Mexican vehicle pact? The pact would be in their respective interests for the following reasons:

The *U.S. government* will soon have to choose some form of additional trade management to deal with the deluge of motor vehicles and parts headed for the United States. While trade management is unpalatable to the current administration, the President has set a precedent with the Voluntary Restraint Agreement on Japanese imports, and it seems likely that quota agreements with many additional countries will soon be necessary to head off domestic demand for much more comprehensive trade protection.

Additional bilateral trade agreements will necessarily involve prioritizing U.S. relationships with the many trading partners contributing to the growing deficit in the U.S. motor vehicle account. In this circumstance, why not negotiate a motor vehicle pact that can be hailed as "trade liberalization" with Mexico—the country whose domestic economy and political stability are most important to U.S. financial and security interests? In combination with restraints on other trading partners judged less important on these criteria, an increase in Mexican imports to the United States could be accommodated even while the overall motor vehicle trade deficit were being reduced.

The *Mexican government* faces precisely the opposite problem: In the absence of Mexican initiatives on a motor vehicle pact, mounting concern in the United States about the U.S. trade deficit may lead to very adverse treatment of Mexican imports into the United States. A motor vehicle pact could also dramatically advance many of the government's objectives for the motor vehicle sector: increased scale, increased production of high-value-added items, more assemblers (including Japanese assemblers), and increased competition (which under present rules means reduced scale).[21]

The *U.S.-based multinational assemblers* would be able to rationalize and integrate their total U.S., Canadian, and Mexican operations—an idea they have championed for decades. Their Mexican plants, when operated at appropriate scale, would have dramatically reduced manufacturing costs.

The *Japanese multinational assemblers* face a need to move many of their activities offshore to escape both the high yen and U.S. quotas. In addition, they would like to participate in the Mexican domestic market, where they hope they can achieve the same success against the U.S. multinationals as they have in the United States. They have many choices, of course, as to where they relocate production from Japan, but a motor vehicle pact along these proposed lines would greatly enhance the appeal of Mexico as a site since free access of Mexican-produced vehicles to the United States would be guaranteed to qualifying assemblers.

The *Mexican-owned components companies* are a special case. As noted earlier, they need a healthy Mexican assembler industry to be healthy themselves—and this would be their primary reason for favoring a motor vehicle pact. For them, however, a pact would present many problems of transition. They would need to increase their scale to world scale, and many workers would need to be relocated to be near the revamped, final-assembly plants. In addition, these firms would need to work much more closely with assemblers than they have in the past, and they would need to develop their own design, engineering, quality assurance, and inventory minimization programs. To do this, they would need extensive financial help that can only come from foreign sources. (The proposed World Bank restructuring loan for the Mexican components industry is one obvious source of new foreign financing.) They would also need extensive technical and organizational assistance that can only come from foreign components firms—either through licensing or, preferably, through joint ventures. (This would be particularly critical for working with the Japanese assemblers, who delegate much greater responsibility to their suppliers. The current wave of joint ventures in the United States between U.S. and Japanese components firms is a tacit acknowledgment that arms-length supplier relations of the traditional U.S. variety are simply unworkable with Japanese assemblers.) To ensure that organizational know-how and technology are in fact transferred through these arrangements, the Mexican government would need to greatly increase its expertise in the motor vehicle sector to act as an effective judge of proposed licenses and joint ventures.

Without doubt this is a complex bargain, and many difficult negotiations would be needed to arrange it. Yet the logic of world industrial development points in the direction of such a new bargain. It points this way so powerfully that a fourth phase in the U.S.-Mexican relationship—based on other principles or on a desire to maintain the status quo—is likely to prove a negative-sum bargain for all parties involved. The current situation also calls for striking a new bargain sooner rather than later; key decisions are being made daily about the restructuring of the U.S. and Canadian motor industries. These decisions present opportunities for both the United States and Mexico to strengthen their domestic industries through prudent integration, but the moment for truly major decisions and changes in direction will soon be over.

Notes

[1] The phrase "industry of industries" was originally used by Peter Drucker to describe the role of the textile industry in the mid-nineteenth century world economy and the importance of the motor vehicle industry in the mid-twentieth century. See *The Concept of the Corporation*(New York: New American Library, 1964). Despite a recent challenge from electronics and computers as we approach the end of this century, the title still belongs to the motor vehicle industry. Indeed, the motor vehicle industry is rapidly becoming the leading end user of microprocessors and other types of electronics.

[2] The motor vehicle industry includes finished cars, trucks, trailers, buses—and their component parts. The common tendency is to equate motor vehicles with automobiles, but in Mexico this would leave out a third of the industry's output in units and probably half of its output in sales value.

[3] "A Century of Transformations," Chapter 2 in Alan Altshuler, Martin Anderson, Daniel Jones, Daniel Roos, and James Womack, *The Future of the Automobile* (Cambridge: MIT Press, 1984).

[4] For explanations of the Japanese group approach at the conglomerate and assembler-supplier levels, see Michael Cusumano, *The Japanese Automobile Industry* (Cambridge: Harvard University Press, 1985). For an explanation of the Japanese work groups at the shop-floor level, see Richard Schoenberger, *Japanese Manufacturing Techniques* (New York: McGraw-Hill, 1982).

[5] For a thorough review of these points, see "The Competitive Balance," Chapter 7 in *The Future of the Automobile, op. cit.*

[6] For a provocative analysis of the flexibility of the Japanese system of production organization and its consequences for differentiation of motor vehicle products, see David Friedman, "Beyond the Age of Ford: The Strategic Basis of the Japanese Success in Automobiles," in John Zysman and Laura Tyson, eds., *American Industry in International Competition*(Ithaca: Cornell University Press, 1983), pp. 350-90.

[7] This assessment is based on recent plant tours by the author and on interviews with Japanese and U.S. auto executives about the initial results of Japanese direct investment in the United States. Note the term "assembling"; Japanese plants are manufacturing only 30 per cent of each vehicle in the United States—the rest being parts from Japan.

[8] For a full listing of Japanese direct investments in the United States, see "Japan's Expanding U.S. Manufacturing Presence: 1985 Update," in *Japan Economic Report*, No.13A, Japan Economic Institute, April 4, 1986.

[9] "The Future Shape of the World Auto Industry," Chapter 8 in *The Future of the Automobile, op. cit.*

[10] This logic is developed in greater detail in James P. Womack and Daniel T. Jones, "Developing Countries and the Future of the Automobile Industry," *World Development*, Vol. 13, No. 3 (1985), pp. 393-407.

[11] For a full discussion of the potential paths of development, see "Technological Opportunities for Adaptation," Chapter 4 in *The Future of the Automobile, op. cit.*

[12] See "Labor Relations and Employment Adjustment," Chapter 9 in *The Future of the Automobile, op. cit.*, for additional estimates of employment declines and changes in needed skills.

[13] For what will surely be the definitive study of the U.S.-Mexican relationship in the motor vehicle sector from 1962 through 1983, see Douglas C. Bennett and Kenneth E. Sharpe, *Transnational Corporations Versus the State: The Political Economy of the Mexican Auto Industry* (Princeton: Princeton University Press, 1985).

¹⁴ These were not the first complete vehicles to be exported from Mexico. Pickup trucks were exported to a few developing countries from the early 1970s, while Volkswagen sent Beetles to Europe after the German parent shifted to the Rabbit/Golf model in 1974. For a period in the mid-1970s, Volkswagen also sent its Safari model to the United States (where it was marketed as the Thing, a fair moniker for an open-bodied vehicle that was neither car nor truck). However, these vehicles were either in unique market niches (the Beetle and the Safari) or were destined for developing countries under special trading arrangements. None was intended to compete head-on in developed-country markets with products from the developed countries. The export of Chrysler K Cars to the United States beginning in 1985 was therefore an extremely important step for the Mexican industry.

¹⁵ Ford has just commenced shipments from its new 130,000-unit Hermosillo assembly plant. While a small fraction of these cars were originally earmarked for the Mexican internal market, they are assembled largely from imported Japanese parts and are now too expensive for domestic buyers. Thus they may all be sent to the United States. In addition, Chrysler will add P and J models to the K cars already being exported, and General Motors will export A bodies. Finished unit exports to the United States could rise to 250,000 units by 1989 if the U.S. market continues to be very strong.

¹⁶ It may avoid confusion to stress that we are concerned here with the long term. Without question, *maquiladora* plants will continue to proliferate for some years to come. Until recently, this was largely U.S. investment; soon it may be largely Japanese. Without doubt, Mexico will benefit from these plants, particularly those under Japanese management, which introduce best-practice production organization (see "Plants in Mexico Help Japan Sell to U.S.," in the *New York Times,* May 26, 1987, pp. D1, D6, for a report on the impact of the initial Japanese investments). The problem being stressed here is simply that they do not build a foundation for the future, since the labor-intensive activities they perform will disappear over time. Thus, rather like steel, the maquila operations are likely to be a "sunset" industry in the 1990s.

¹⁷ The new Ford plant at Hermosillo has followed just this approach. Ford has relied on Mazda, its Japanese affiliate, to lay out the plant, select the process machinery, and teach the Mazda system of production organization to all plant personnel. Initial indications, based on a recent plant tour by researchers in the MIT International Motor Vehicle Program, are that the plant has been remarkably successful in transplanting Japanese best-practice to northern Mexico.

¹⁸ This, it should be clear, is not an impossible qualification. For example, if production for sale in the United States were relocated from Japan to Mexico, the effect on the U.S. industry would be neutral, while the effect on the Mexican industry would be positive. The effect on the Japanese could be positive as well—if a commitment to Mexican production provided Mexican market access.

¹⁹ Alternatively, they might agree to maintain their value added in Mexican manufacturing at a certain level (say 1.4 times) their Mexican domestic sales. This is the type of formula used in the U.S.-Canada Auto Pact.

²⁰ A requirement that substantial engineering and development work be done in Mexico is particularly important for the future of the Mexican industry. In an age of satellite communications and computerized engineering data bases, it should be possible—if the Mexican government develops sufficient knowledge about the industry to negotiate effectively—to build a world-class engineering component into the Mexican industry.

²¹ The importance of increasing the level of domestic competition within Mexico can hardly be overemphasized. Even the Japanese will take the opportunity to relax if given a protected market. A case in point is the Nissan plant at Cuernevaca, Morelos, compared with the plant at Smyrna, Tennessee. The former is a typical developing-country branch plant set up to adapt to local practice. As such, it breaks little new ground in either technology or production management compared with General Motors, Ford, Chrysler, and the other Mexican producers. The Smyrna plant, by contrast, is designed to compete head-on with other Japanese imports and American products; it employs the most sophisticated organizational systems Nissan can bring to bear, and it is able to produce vehicles at a cost far below the U.S. average even though its wage rate is nearly the same as Detroit's.

Chapter 5

Automated Manufacturing and Offshore Assembly in Mexico

Susan Walsh Sanderson

Direct labor is becoming less important in the overall cost of many manufactured goods, and the increased use of computer-aided design and manufacturing (CAD/CAM) and robotics may erode the comparative advantage that low-wage regions currently hold for some important categories of manufacturing. This is particularly a problem for those developing countries which, like Mexico, have relied on offshore assembly for jobs and revenues but have not been able to compete as independent producers of world-class goods for export.

During the 1960s and 1970s, U.S. and European firms responded to increased foreign competition by moving the most labor-intensive phases of production to low-wage regions in the developing world. Today some two million people worldwide are employed in offshore assembly operations with an annual output of $15 billion. Eleven developing countries account for 75-80 per cent of world offshore assembly output, primarily in the production of electronics goods.[1] From 1982 to 1985, imports entering the United States under tariff items 806.30 and 807.00 (imports containing U.S.-made components) increased by 67 per cent—from $18.3 billion to $30.5 billion. In 1985, these imports accounted for 8.9 per cent of total U.S. imports.[2] Most 806.30 and 807.00 imports from developed countries contain only a small proportion of U.S. parts (e.g., catalytic converters installed on automobiles to meet U.S. air quality standards). Imports from developing countries, by contrast, include a high proportion of parts made in the United States. Reliance on offshore assembly has varied greatly among sectors, with three industries—automobiles, electrical and electronics products, and apparel—responsible for most of it. In 1982, five groups of products made up three-quarters of the value of all imports brought in under tariff items 806.30 and 807.00: motor vehicles and parts (46 per cent), semiconductors (17 per cent), television receivers and parts (5 per cent), office machines and parts (4 per cent), and clothing (4 per cent).[3]

By 1985, however, changes in technology—as well as the increased use of these tariff items by developed countries such as Japan and West Germany to export automobiles and trucks that contain U.S.-made components and parts—resulted in a shift in the major products imported under items 806.30 and 807.00; motor vehicles accounted for 57 per cent of the value of imports in these two categories; office machines and parts, 6 per cent; semiconductors, 4 per cent; and piston-type engines and parts, 3 per cent.[4] Manufacturing firms are undergoing changes in methods and organization that have the potential for altering co-production relationships between developed and developing countries.

The automobile and the electrical and electronics industries have been among the first to adopt these new process technologies. Although the Japanese are working on applications of CAD/CAM and robotics in the apparel industry, there have been no significant effects on this industry to date. Much more dramatic have been process innovations such as surface mount technology (SMT) and new assembly techniques in the electrical and electronics industries. Electrical and electronics manufacturing is of primary importance to many developing countries, as it accounts for more than 60 per cent of all offshore assembly activity worldwide and two-thirds of offshore assembly activity in Mexico. The total value of all electrical and electronics goods exported from Mexico to the United States was nearly $3.8 billion in 1985.[5]

Mexico, with more than 735 in-bond assembly plants (*maquiladoras*) employing some 200,000 workers at the end of 1985,[6] is particularly vulnerable to manufacturing changes in the United States. U.S companies have traditionally dominated Mexico's assembly industry, although more recently Japan, Holland, Sweden, and Finland have established new plants there. Because Mexico generally has not been competitive in the world market for manufactured goods, offshore assembly plays a dominant role in Mexico's manufactured exports and is second only to oil as a source of foreign exchange. In 1985, 97 per cent of Mexico's machinery and equipment exports to the United States—goods worth $3.8 billion—were produced in Mexico's in-bond plants.[7] About two-thirds of the *maquila* exports were electronic and television parts and communications equipment.

This chapter, focusing on the electrical and electronics industry, explores the potential impact of automated manufacturing technologies on offshore assembly in Mexico and the policy implications of these changes for Mexico and the United States.

Trends in Offshore Electrical and Electronics Assembly

The future of offshore production, used primarily by European and U.S.-based manufacturers, will be determined in part by the ability of the companies of these developed countries to compete with those of Japan and the East Asian newly industrializing countries (NICs). During the 1960s and 1970s, offshore assembly helped bridge the wage gap between industrial and developing countries, but offshore assembly has not been sufficient to stave off competition.

Mexico's manufactured exports are still inextricably linked to U.S. manufacturing. In 1984, 94 per cent of all electronics goods exported from Mexico were brought into the United States under tariff item 807.00, indicating that they were assembled of U.S. parts (see Table 1); by 1985, this proportion had risen to 97 per cent. This contrasts markedly with Asian countries such as Singapore, less than half of whose exports of electrical and electronics goods are assembled abroad from U.S. parts. Moreover, offshore production in Mexico is far more labor-intensive and includes fewer domestic inputs—aside from direct labor—than in Singapore. To capture the difference between assembly in Singapore and in Mexico, we devised a crude measure of productivity based on the dutiable value per worker. Workers in Singapore's offshore electrical and electronics assembly industry produced fifteen times more revenue in 1984—or $2,211 per worker compared to $166 per worker in Mexico.[8] While this measure does not allow us to separate out the effects of automation from greater domestic content, it does demonstrate that Singapore is significantly less dependent than is Mexico on U.S. inputs and that linkage to Mexico's domestic production is virtually nonexistent.

Because Mexico's maquiladoras contribute fewer raw or semi-finished materials to the assembly process, they are less likely to be able to withstand technological changes in the manufacturing process that would reduce the need for low-skilled labor. Moreover, they are not in a position to take advantage of shifting cost factors—such as the high dollar, or high U.S. interest rates—that may give an advantage to goods manufactured abroad. Manufactured goods, whether wholly produced in the United States or assembled abroad of U.S. parts, have been adversely affected by the overvalued dollar, and countries that depend exclusively on the assembly of U.S. goods will feel the brunt of the decline in U.S. competitiveness. Reliance on U.S. manufacturers

Table 1. Value of U.S. Imports from Mexico, 1984
(customs value basis, U.S. $ thousands and percentages)

Product Category	Total Imports	807.00 Imports	807.00 Imports as % of Total in Category
Animal and vegetable products	$1,715,377	$ 57	—
Wood, paper, and printed matter	271,201	97,271	36
Textiles and textile products	322,493	214,768	67
Chemicals and related products	8,379,728	3	—
Non-metal and chemical products	354,963	11,735	3
Metals and metal products	5,553,083	4,069,861	73
Electrical and electronics products	(3,247,113)	(3,039,024)	93
Miscellaneous products	557,928	351,160	63
Total, all categories	17,154,774	4,744,855	28%

Source: Calculated by the author from data provided by the U.S. Department of Commerce, 1986.

makes Mexico vulnerable both to technological change and marketplace shifts affecting the position of U.S. firms relative to their competitors.

Figure 1 illustrates the extent to which U.S. parts are assembled abroad, by using a cluster analysis of forty selected electrical and electronics products plotted along two dimensions: U.S. parts assembled offshore as a percentage of total imports, and total imports as a percentage of domestic consumption in 1983. Many of the semiconductors used in the United States are wholly manufactured abroad. Of those made from U.S. parts, about 80 per cent of the assembly is carried out offshore. In contrast, the final assembly of household appliances by and large still takes place in the United States, although many of the components are made abroad. In an intermediate category are passive electronic components, such as resistors and capacitors, with about 40 per cent of U.S. domestic consumption assembled offshore from U.S. parts. In marked contrast, the vast majority of smaller consumer electrical and electronics products—such as radios, phonographs, and tape recorders—are imported. About one-third to one-half of U.S. domestic consumption of televisions, calculators, and communications equipment already has been lost to imports. But the United States is holding its own in major appliances (mostly because

Figure 1. Forty Selected Electronic and Electrical Products—Illustrating Extent to which U.S. Parts Are Assembled Abroad

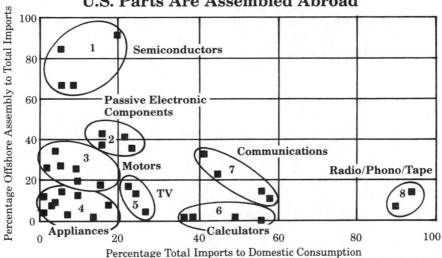

Note: This scattergram shows forty electronic and electrical products assembled abroad by U.S. firms in 1984. Each black square represents a single product. (It should be noted that a high percentage of U.S. semiconductors are assembled offshore, although imports of the four types in this analysis represent a relatively small share of the U.S. market.)

Source: Susan Walsh Sanderson, "American Industry *Can* Go Home Again," *Across the Board,* February 1986.

transportation costs are high), in some passive electronic components, and in semiconductors. As the recent outcries of many beleaguered U.S. semiconductor firms attest, however, the U.S. lead in both the design and manufacture of chips is seriously threatened.

In just twenty years the United States has gone from being the world's major producer of consumer electrical and electronics goods to being a major consumer of products made elsewhere, even though many of the products were invented in the United States and U.S. firms still hold patents on the principal developments. This has occurred in cases where the technology is stable (toasters, for example), as well as where the technology is changing rapidly (semiconductors and computers). The Japanese and the Asian NICs are now able to offer a wide variety of low-cost, high-quality products that have not only replaced U.S. goods in overseas markets, but have penetrated U.S. domestic markets as well. This has happened despite the fact that many U.S. manufacturers have used the same low-cost labor in assembly.

Offshore assembly may have accentuated the tendency of U.S. manufacturers to pay single-minded attention to the development of new products, without attention to how those products would be manufactured. As the strength of Japanese manufacturing attests, this has proved to be a serious, if not fatal, mistake. U.S. manufacturers are now trying to catch up, but whether they will be able to regain lost markets in such consumer products as televisions, videocassette recorders, or even computers is still uncertain. It is not yet clear whether they will even try. The term "hollow corporation" has been used to describe the growing phenomenon of U.S. manufacturing firms that import goods made elsewhere rather than make the substantial investments necessary to compete in the production of the products themselves.

Firms that do not "opt out" of manufacturing altogether have two choices: to continue to use the same production techniques they have used in the past, including offshore assembly; or to organize their production more along the lines of Japanese firms—with greater attention to integrated design and manufacturing, automation, and "just-in-time" delivery of parts. One of the key questions concerning the future of offshore assembly is whether it can be effectively incorporated into the new systems of manufacturing organization and production.

Trends in Automation

In the United States, automobile firms were among the first to adopt state-of-the-art technology, which has enabled them to consolidate old factories, close obsolete ones, and upgrade parts and assembly plants.

In mid-1985, General Motors had some 4,240 programmable robots in operation; the company expects to have 10,000 in place by 1988, carrying out a variety of tasks, including assembly, machining, loading, spot and fusion welding, painting, and parts transfer.

The automakers have also already achieved cost savings by changing organizational practices. The proportion of salaried to hourly workers has been reduced, and inventories have been shaved. Improving the quality of electrical parts and electronic components has become a major focus. General Motors, for example, is moving toward getting many of its components from a single source and establishing long-term contracts with its parts suppliers in order to help them reduce unit costs. In exchange for a longer-term contract, and presumably a more stable relationship, GM has asked suppliers to reduce prices.

Some of these same changes have been going on in the electrical and electronics industries. Computer-aided manufacturing and some elements of the factory of the future can be seen in IBM's printer factory in Charlotte, North Carolina, and in its typewriter assembly plant in Lexington, Kentucky. General Electric's dishwasher plant in Louisville, Kentucky also exemplifies this trend. So does Xerox's ability to cut in half (in just two years) both the manufacturing costs and the time it takes to develop products in its mainstay copier business, while paring the number of quality problems by two-thirds. Xerox has spent about $100 million since 1980 to automate manufacturing and materials handling and expects to be able to continue to manufacture a substantial part of its machines in the United States and compete on a worldwide basis.

Some firms have moved assembly operations back to the United States. For example, by automating the welding of semiconductor chips, the Fairchild Semiconductor Corporation is able to conduct a portion of its chip assembly in South Portland, Maine, rather than manually in Southeast Asia. At Fairchild's Digital Products Division in South Portland, semiconductors are produced with the aid of a computerized design system and a high-volume, automated robotics assembly line. An automated warehouse and its computerized inventory-tracking system ensure on-time delivery.

Similarly, Priam Corporation, the San Jose-based maker of Winchester disc drives, spent more than $10 million on an advanced automated manufacturing plant, thus breaking with the industry trend of manufacturing disc drives offshore, primarily in Asia.[9]

Computer-aided manufacturing is changing the labor content and the locational choices that were dictated when manual techniques were necessary. In the automobile industry, robots have largely replaced welders and painters, reducing the required number of hourly laborers and making high-wage areas more competitive. New techniques are increasingly being used in assembly as well. In the electronics industry, for example, surface mount technology (SMT), which allows components to be attached directly to printed circuit boards rather than inserted through holes in the board, is making manual assembly obsolete. SMT is increasingly being used for resistors and capacitors as well as for integrated circuits. Philips, the European-based electrical and electronics giant, estimated that worldwide usage of SMT will more than double by the early 1990s. Board assembly was one of the activities that had moved abroad to lower-wage regions and has become one of the mainstays of assembly activity in many developing countries. In Mexico, for example, board assembly for U.S. manufacturers employs some 17,000 people.[10]

Technological Projections

This section describes the relative technological difficulty of automating various stages of manufacturing in electrical and electronics manufacturing. The estimates provided, based on the expert opinion of scientists at the Robotics Institute at Carnegie-Mellon University, indicate the progress of new process technology and the types of activities most likely to be affected first. As with any other projections of the future, there are many uncertainties. Actual rates of technological change and adoption of new technologies depend on macroeconomic factors as well as the competitive position of firms and their ability to make capital investments. Nevertheless, these projections are valid as indications of the order, if not the actual rates, of adoption of new technologies.

Table 2 shows estimates by robotic industry experts of current and projected levels of automation of electronics manufacturing in the United States. It is projected that 25 per cent of component fabrication and 20 per cent of printed circuit board fabrication and assembly are currently automated, and that it will take 5 to 7 years before 80 per cent will be automated. About 15 per cent of inspection and testing activities are already automated, and it is estimated that it will be another 10 years before 80 per cent is automated. The more difficult tasks to automate are wire harness assembly, sub-system assembly, and system assembly; it is expected to take 10 to 15 years to fully automate these activities.

Impact on Offshore Assembly in Mexico

Assessing the potential impact of automated manufacturing on employment is difficult. A 1981 study of prospective changes in manufacturing technology in the United States concluded that at least one million

Table 2. Current and Projected Levels of Automation of Electronics Manufacturing

Stage of Manufacturing	Current Automation	Years to 80% Automation
Component fabrication	25%	5
Printed circuit board fabrication	20	5
Board assembly	20	7
Sub-system assembly	0	15
Wire harness assembly	5	10
System assembly	0	15
Inspection and testing	15	10

Source: Projections based on author's interviews with experts in electrical engineering and computer science at The Robotics Institute, Carnegie-Mellon University, Pittsburgh, 1985.

manufacturing operative jobs are already within the domain of industrial robots and that the next generation of visual and tactile robots might affect about 2 million additional factory workers.[11] Studies of other industrialized countries indicate that the potential for replacement of jobs is equally dramatic. A recent study of the British textile industry indicated that several thousand jobs might be lost due to innovations in microelectronics alone; the authors found that automation of textile manufacturing in the United States could lead to a substantial loss of relatively low-paid jobs by 1990.[12] In the electronics industry, much of which is currently assembled offshore, there may be substantial reductions in the labor intensiveness of many processes in the near future.

The overall rate of adoption of the new technologies will depend upon a number of interrelated factors: the rate of technological development, the size of the firms in a given industry as it affects their ability to make the large capital investments necessary to automate, and macroeconomic variables within both the United States and developing countries.

How might these advances in process technology affect assembly operations in Mexico? In a recent study of the impact of automated manufacturing technologies on offshore assembly, my collegues and I at Carnegie-Mellon University developed unit-cost models for comparing manual offshore assembly with domestic automated and flexible assembly. These were combined with an assessment of the levels of offshore assembly in selected developing countries, along with projections of the future development of assembly technologies and their potential impact on the revenues and employment of Mexico and Singapore.[13]

Table 3 presents the total value of the top forty electrical and electronic exports from Mexico to the United States according to their stage of manufacturing process and the years it is expected to take for them to be automated to the 80-per-cent level.

About 45 per cent of the exports from Mexico are component fabrications and board assemblies—the two manufacturing processes projected to be automated within the next five years. Mexico has specialized in the production of passive components such as connectors and capacitors, which make up 70 per cent of Mexico's total component fabrication. The automation of sub-system and system assembly is far more complicated and costly and may not have any serious impact on offshore assembly before the end of the century. Currently, wiring sets, electrical motors, and generators make up almost 60 per cent of Mexico's sub-system assemblies. The assembly of electrical and electronic goods encompasses almost 100 different products, none of which represents more than 10 per cent of the total dollar volume.

Table 4 shows the U.S. dutiable value of electrical and electronic products imported under tariff code item 807.00—a fair approximation of the value of these assembly activities to Mexico—as well as the Mexican employment associated with each stage of manufacturing. About 30,000 workers and $450 million in revenues—or roughly 40 per cent of the revenues and employment that Mexico currently derives from offshore assembly—could be affected by new manufacturing technologies within the next half-decade if automation proceeds at the predicted rate. By the turn of the century, the balance of revenues and employment could be affected.

How quickly these new manufacturing technologies will be adopted depends not only on the availability of new technology, but also on a number of other macro- and microeconomic factors. It is to these factors that we will now turn our attention.

The Role of Technological and Economic Factors in the Diffusion of New Technologies

The United States and the European nations have been slower than Japan to adopt many new production and organizational innovations. The Japanese consumer industry is leading the way in the application of surface mount technology; European and U.S. firms lag behind because of the high cost of implementation in a single plant, (estimated to range between $200,000 and $2 million) and the lack of standards. Such high costs may leave many of the smaller companies in trouble; it

Table 3. Top 40 Electrical and Electronics Exports from Mexico to the United States, Value and Years Expected to Reach 80% Automation (U.S. $ thousands and percentages)

Stage of Manufacturing	Value (1984)	Percentage of Total Value (1984)	Years to 80% Automation
Component fabrication	$842,034	31.6%	5
Board assembly	$344,266	12.9	7
Sub-system assembly	$860,517	32.3	10–15
System assembly	$617,795	23.3	15
Total, all stages	$2,664,612	100.0%	

Source: Susan Walsh Sanderson, et al., "Impacts of Automated Manufacturing Technology on Offshore Assembly," (unpublished research report, Carnegie-Mellon University, Pittsburgh, 1985.)

Table 4. U.S. Dutiable Value and Mexican Employment Associated with U.S. Imports of Electrical and Electronic Products from Mexico, 1983 (U.S. $ thousands and percentages)

Stage of Manufacturing	Total	Dutiable Value	Percentage of Total Dutiable Value	Employment	Percentage of Total Mexican Employment
Component fabrication	$581,010	$199,226	18.2%	13,611	18.1%
Board assembly	360,821	249,818	22.8	17,070	22.7
Sub-system assembly	643,392	309,573	28.4	21,206	28.2
System assembly	532,606	339,542	31.1	23,237	30.9
Total, all stages	$2,117,829	$1,098,159	100.0%	75,124	100.0%

Source: Susan Walsh Sanderson, et al., "Impacts of Automated Manufacturing Technology on Offshore Assembly," (unpublished research report, Carnegie-Mellon University, Pittsburgh, 1985).

is no accident that most of the firms that have adopted automated production have been industry giants. It is generally believed that the United States is two years behind Japan in the applications of surface mount technology. The difficulties that U.S. firms are having in adopting the new technology are illustrative of the overall competitive advantage that the Japanese have been able to achieve in the production of semiconductors and consumer products. The Japanese have been building SMT into their commercial and commodity products.

The speed with which U.S. firms will adopt the new process technologies depends on organizational as well as technological innovations. The ability of Japanese companies to spread the costs and risks of new investment has given them a major competitive advantage, particularly in comparison to smaller U.S. firms that are neither vertically integrated nor have parent companies with deep pockets and a willingness to make the large investments needed. The inability of U.S. and European firms to spread the costs among their related companies has been a further obstacle to justifying the major capital investments essential for the effective adoption of these new technologies.

Key macroeconomic variables—especially exchange rates and interest rates—have a significant impact on production location decisions. Although the dollar has taken several plunges since 1973, it was high for much of the period between 1973 and 1985.[14] The effect of the overvalued dollar was to drive down the relative prices of foreign goods and to increase the tendency to purchase goods manufactured abroad. The $170-billion U.S. trade deficit in 1986—up 14 per cent from $148.5 billion in 1985—was in part the result of the overvalued dollar. Indeed, the dollar had been so high for so much of a decade that even the use of cheaper labor in offshore assembly was not sufficient to offset the significant cost advantages enjoyed by goods wholly manufactured abroad. The U.S. balance in manufactured products swung from a surplus of $17.4 billion in 1980 to a deficit of $107.4 billion in 1985. Imports remain high in 1987 despite the drastic decline in the value of the dollar relative to the yen and other major currencies in recent months. This does not necessarily mean, however, that production will return to the United States, as many U.S. firms no longer manufacture electrical and electronic products.

In addition to the detrimental effects of a strong dollar on worldwide demand for U.S. manufactured goods, high interest rates tend to exacerbate this condition by driving exchange rates even higher. High U.S. interest rates, as reflected in U.S. bond and security markets, make investing in these financial markets attractive to foreigners. U.S. interest rates have been running as high as six percentage points above the comparable Japanese rates. This interest rate differential has, on the one hand, been responsible for one of the largest financial flows in history, with Japanese, European, and other foreign investors pouring billions into U.S. financial markets and helping to finance the U.S. budget deficit and keep U.S. interest rates from skyrocketing. But high interest rates are one of the reasons why U.S. manufacturers have such great difficulty in modernizing plants and competing in an increasingly competitive international market. High interest rates compress corporate planning horizons and increase the minimum acceptable rate of return on investment, making research and development and large-scale investment in new plant and equipment unattractive. By the same token, an unstable dollar, either undervalued or overvalued, makes long-term investment untenable by shifting cost advantages and changing patterns of demand.

Policy Implications

Advanced developing countries such as Mexico that have not yet been able to produce a wide variety of goods at world-class quality and cost face a serious dilemma. If U.S. firms continue to automate—as they surely must if they are to keep pace with the Japanese—then Mexico will suffer the direct loss of jobs and revenues associated with the products automated. Right now, manual assembly is the least-cost alternative but, for a wide variety of products, automated techniques are rapidly gaining ground. Flexible automation offers some profound advantages and, as the Japanese have already demonstrated, can lead to greatly reduced costs and the production of higher-quality goods. But automated techniques also reduce the need for certain groups of unskilled and semi-skilled workers. While offshore assembly activities will continue to provide some jobs and revenues for developing countries for some time to come, their overall significance to the future economies of developed and developing countries is likely to be small. Instead of becoming the dominant production pattern, as some have predicted, co-production activities may be marginalized and left to a few small producers who lack the capital and technical resources to automate.

If developing countries fail to keep pace with new manufacturing technologies, they risk falling even further behind and, in the absence of stringent protectionist policies, they will lose domestic and export markets to more efficient competitors. But automating their own manufacturing facilities requires substantial capital and expertise and may alter labor force requirements. It is important to recognize that the industries of the future will have different staffing and manpower requirements than did the factories of the past, and that they may *not* be significant generators of employment. Nevertheless, they may be important sources of revenue and may provide for the domestic production of goods. Thus, attempts to attract automated factories may be a

very viable long-term strategy. Selling this strategy may prove difficult, however; the hardship and suffering of unemployed and underemployed workers is real, and the temptation to impose protectionist
policies in an effort to create or retain jobs is great.

In past decades, the key stimulants to Mexico's high growth rate
have been public sector investment and, more recently, increased export revenues generated from oil and easy access to international
capital markets. With the 1982 economic crisis that culminated with
the nationalization of Mexico's banks (and many other enterprises
previously in the private sector), and with the 1982 sharp devaluation
of the peso, the level of international investment in Mexico slowed
substantially. Several rounds of peso devaluation were successful in
cooling off the nearly 100-per-cent inflation to more acceptable levels,
but the ensuing decline in imports of primary and secondary goods led
to a virtual halt in production and a collapse of many enterprises and
development projects.

For part of 1982 and most of 1983, Mexico suffered a *negative*
growth rate. Only since the beginning of 1984 has the economy begun
to adjust to these changes and shown some signs of revival—only to be
slammed again by the precipitous drop in the price of oil. But Mexico is
saddled with a $95-billion foreign debt, an increasingly overvalued
peso, falling currency reserves, and a climbing budget deficit, in addition to high inflation and unemployment. It was hoped that new exchange control policies would have a positive impact on the direct
foreign investment outlook as the Mexican government pursued international investors with more tangible incentives such as 100-per-cent
foreign ownership and capital investment and employment incentives.
However, direct foreign investment for 1983 was estimated to be about
$11.5 billion, and the influx of foreign capital during the first three
months of 1984 was only $29.5 million—about one-tenth the amount
for the same period in 1983 and comparable to levels of foreign investment in the 1950s, when Mexico's economy was much smaller.

Without a substantial influx of new capital and technology, and
with increasing numbers of young workers entering the labor force and
competing for a limited number of positions, Mexico's economic future
is bleak. Moreover, changes in technology may mean that even fewer
relatively well-paid manufacturing jobs will be available for the very
large number of aspiring workers expected to make up Mexico's future
labor force. It will be difficult to match the skills needed for the
factories and workplaces of the future with the current levels of education of the population.

As the 1986 plunge in the price of oil has dramatically demonstrated, the combination of Mexico's tremendous foreign debt, coupled
with the most recent crash in the price of oil, makes it unlikely that
Mexico will be able to pay off its debt even with the most aggressive

and successful export strategy. Moreover, the drop in oil revenues constrains government action and will necessitate further cuts in spending.

Mexico's government has recently launched a major effort to cut spending by closing some of its less efficient businesses. One of the first casualties was Fundidora de Monterrey, an obsolete, state-owned steel plant in Monterrey employing 11,000 people. This move came at a particularly difficult time for Mexican workers, as they have lost one-third of their purchasing power since 1982. Just how much reallocation of resources Mexico will be able to undertake and still maintain political stability is as yet unclear.

Several times in the past, Mexico has embarked on a path toward greater trade liberalization, only to revert to measures providing traditional privileges to protected domestic industries. Import substitution is a policy deeply rooted in the strength of the political and economic forces allied to it, as well as in the ideology, history, and rhetoric of Mexico's ruling party. But the world has changed substantially, and it is no longer possible for domestic policies to succeed if they impair rather than enhance the country's competitive position.

Those developing countries that have not already been able to achieve independent production capabilities face competition from the successful newly industrializing countries (NICs) as well as from Europe, the United States, and Japan. Moreover, they are attempting to compete primarily on the basis of low-cost labor in the production of goods that will have reduced requirements for low-skilled labor as a result of automation. In the long run, it is doubtful that low-skilled labor will be sufficient to provide a competitive advantage in an increasingly sophisticated global marketplace.

In the past, most national economies and national markets were independent of one another, and the subsidiaries of multinational companies functioned as autonomous units, with operations and product lines specific to the host country. This fitted well into the policies of many developing countries such as Mexico that granted access to local markets in exchange for domestic production and then protected these firms from competition. But the era of largely independent national markets is fading fast, and firms that have been operating in protected markets are unable to compete effectively with their more efficient counterparts. It will be exceedingly difficult for many of these firms to survive in an era of more open competition.

Mexico: Japan's Gate to the U.S. Market?

Is there a way for Mexico to take advantage of these changes in manufacturing organization and technologies and become a partner of U.S., European, or even Japanese firms in the factories of the future?

The Japanese have been forerunners in the implementation of new manufacturing technologies, and it is useful to follow their activities as they attempt to transfer their patterns of organization and manufacturing to the United States. Japan's direct foreign investment in this country as of 1984 was estimated to be $14.8 billion. According to the most recent Japan External Trade Organization (JETRO) survey, the Japanese already have 545 Japanese-affiliated manufacturers employing 66,000 U.S. workers in production in the United States as of March 1985.[15]

Large final assemblers in the automobile and electrical and electronics industries in Japan have been able to produce low-cost, high-quality products through superior organizational strategies. They have been able to do so largely because of the coordinated production networks, highly automated final assembly, and the predominance of "obligated relational contracting," which together have provided low-cost, high-quality parts.

Ronald Dore described the Japanese system of relational contracting in talking about the textile industry, but the pattern of organization applies more broadly to Japanese industry as a whole. According to Dore, there are three good things about relational contracting between enterprises. First, the relative security of such relations encourages investment in supplier firms. Second, the relationship of trust and mutual dependency speeds the flow of information, making it easier for news of impending changes in final consumer markets as well as technological innovations to pass up and down the chain. Third, a by-product of the system is a general emphasis on quality.[16]

Foremost among the concerns mentioned by respondents in a survey of 238 Japanese-owned manufacturing facilities in the United States were problems related to procurement of local supplies. These Japanese firms mentioned five major problems involved with reliance on local sources of supply in the United States.

(1) Unstable quality of parts;
(2) A high percentage of U.S.-made parts that barely pass inspection compared to the much higher quality assurance achieved by Japanese parts makers;
(3) Delays in delivery;
(4) A lack of bargaining power with suppliers, making it difficult to get concessions on prices and delivery dates; and
(5) Higher inventories than the companies would like to hold, due to higher costs for smaller lots and unreliable delivery schedules.

Could Mexico increase its role in—and benefits from—Japanese parts production and final assembly for the U.S. market? To date there are about a dozen plants run by several Japanese companies manufacturing products for the U.S. market in Mexico. Four of the Japanese giant electrical companies already have plants or intend to open plants in Mexico in the near future. For example, Hitachi plans to build TV chassis and cabinets in Tijuana. Sony Corporation, which opened a TV plant in Tijuana last year, intends to triple capacity in 1986. Sanyo Electric is doubling the size of its seven-year-old plant that makes small refrigerators and electric fans. Matsushita Electrical Industrial plans to employ 1,400 Mexicans at a Tijuana TV plant—four times the employment at its U.S. facility.[17] Much of the current investment of Japanese firms in Mexico (like that of U.S. firms in the maquila industry) involves the assembly of Japanese parts with little inclusion of Mexican domestic content. If Japanese firms continue to restrict their investment to the assembly of Japanese parts, they will have little impact on Mexico's economic development. And if this is the case, Mexico will be risking trade frictions with the United States by supplying parts for Japanese firms in the United States.

How and where products are assembled is starting to have increased significance for politicians and government officials, as Japanese and U.S. firms struggle over turf in the production of all sorts of products. Take, for example, the dispute between Japanese and U.S. semiconductor manufacturers over alleged Japanese price-cutting that was argued in October 1986 before the International Trade Administration. Spokesmen for Hitachi, Mitsubishi, and the Nippon Electric Company claimed that U.S. companies assemble their products in Malaysia, Singapore, Hong Kong, the Philippines, and other "cheap-labor" nations in Latin America and Asia, while many Japanese firms assemble their products in the United States. They argued that more than half of the value of each chip is added in assembly, that U.S. chips assembled in Asia should be considered imports, while Japanese chips assembled in the United States should be considered U.S. domestic products. The Semiconductor Industry Association maintained that producing the chip, not the casing or packaging, is the costly core of the business, and that it is the location of the fabrication plant that should determine the nationality of the chip.

Further complications are being introduced by the growing number of joint ventures between European, Japanese, and U.S. firms. It is becoming increasingly difficult to determine the national origin of a single product, much less a whole product line. What is the appropriate criterion? Is it the point of final assembly? the proportion of value of its component parts? or some other measure? It is as yet unclear whether the increasingly tangled web of linkages between firms of different nationalities as well as the more traditional co-production activities characteristic of U.S. and European electrical and electronics manufacturing will diffuse demands for protectionist measures.

If Mexico forms production alliances based on new manufacturing processes and patterns of organization with Japanese, U.S., or European manufacturers, and if these are to make any real difference for long-term Mexican economic development, it will be essential to link them to domestic suppliers and production. Right now there is little incentive for domestic producers to improve either the quality or the cost of their goods because they operate in a protected market.

Although protection of Japanese infant industry is often cited as evidence that similar measures can work in developing countries, there are many reasons to believe that this is not the case. Some profound cultural and historical reasons figure in the success of these measures in Japan's case, and these may be difficult or impossible to reproduce in other countries. Ronald Dore has noted the factors that have proved very important in the Japanese case are stability and trust in contractual relationships and a high regard for quality. The problem is that these factors are lacking in the Mexican context—as well as the United States, for that matter—and that protection therefore tends to lead to even greater inefficiencies. How to protect infant industries while at the same time creating firms capable of manufacturing world-class goods for export is still the subject of much anguished debate in both developed and developing countries.

Focus on Training Engineers and Acquiring Strategic Inputs

One of the principal impacts of computer-aided design and manufacturing (CAD/CAM) and robotics is to reduce the importance of low-cost labor in the production process and to increase the significance of skilled scientific and technical personnel. One of the keys to Japan's success in manufacturing has been its large number of highly trained engineers who specialize in applying new technologies to the manufacturing process itself. Manufacturing firms in the United States are trying to make up for their single-minded attention to new product design and insufficient concern about how that product could be manufactured in the most efficient and economical way. The best engineering schools in the country have launched new programs in computer-aided design and manufacturing. Mexico, as well as other developing countries, will have to follow suit and train engineers and computer scientists in design and manufacturing.

In Mexico, insufficient attention has been paid to the education and training of engineers and scientists, particularly in comparison to the large numbers of lawyers and doctors who graduate each year from Mexican universities. Many Mexicans receive advanced training in the United States, but those in fields such as computer science and electrical engineering tend to remain there. Many factors contribute to the brain drain: the cultural similarities and proximity of Mexico and the

United States, Mexico's current economic hardships and lack of employment opportunities, Mexican disillusionment with the near-term economic situation, and the debased Mexican currency. Some serious efforts nevertheless will have to be made by Mexico to train and retain its scientists and engineers, particularly in disciplines related to design and engineering, if Mexican industries are to attain status as world-class producers in an increasingly competitive global marketplace. The Asian NICs have been very successful in training engineers and encouraging students to return, and the availability of highly trained engineers has been a major drawing card for recent foreign investment in Taiwan, Hong Kong, Korea, and South Korea.

Equally important will be the opening up of markets to goods such as semiconductors, controllers, microprocessors, and computers—goods that now form the basis for the production of everything from automobile parts to consumer electronics. Reserving these products for domestic producers in a protected market at a time when prices are falling dramatically and innovations are occurring at an extremely rapid rate is the equivalent of wearing concrete boots in a race with fleet-footed competitors. Every effort should be made—whether through outright purchase or domestic manufacture—to make these products available for domestic production. It is probably more important to Mexico's long-term future that manufacturers have an opportunity to incorporate the best available technology and components into the final products rather than antiquated technology and outmoded parts.

The Asian NICs were able to "bootstrap" their development by production sharing—that is, by using their labor-cost advantage to become subcontractors to multinational companies from both Japan and the United States. They were able to move from supplying only low-cost labor to the extensive use of domestic sources of processed materials. They learned by using, doing, and copying; by taking advantage of market niches; and by making large capital investments when they deemed it expedient—and by sometimes losing on the gamble, at least in the short run, as the costly foray of South Korea's Hyundai Group into semiconductor manufacturing demonstrates. Moreover, Mexico's rivals in Southeast Asia have been much less concerned with the national origins of the technologies and components that form the basis of their highly competitive products.

To be successful as an exporter, Mexico will have to pay a great deal of attention to identifying new process technologies, products, and designs that can provide the basis for developing a niche in an increasingly competitive global marketplace. A precondition for long-term growth will be to create a favorable investment climate for both domestic as well as foreign manufacturers.

Conclusions

Curiously, Mexico and the United States confront a similar dilemma, but on vastly different scales and with different resources and skills to bring to bear on the problem. Burdened with high deficits, they must both meet the challenge of an increasingly competitive world. And, in different degrees, they must deal with industries that have lost competitiveness, in part because of macroeconomic factors such as overvalued currencies and high interest rates, but also because those industries have failed to make the necessary long-term investments in modernizing production techniques and facilities. The resultant losses in market share to lower-cost and higher-quality producers, and the accompanying job and revenue losses, have prompted cries to curb trade and enact a rash of protectionist legislation ranging from the imposition of tariffs to import quotas.

In the Mexican case, government incentives and subsidies will not be enough to attract new enterprises; such measures are no substitute for a stable political and economic climate when it comes to attracting foreign investment. In the short run, much-needed foreign investment may be impossible to obtain, as bankers and industrialists have long memories, and Mexico already has a massive foreign debt and an uncertain economic future. In the U.S. case, trade restrictions will do little to foster a favorable macroeconomic environment so necessary for encouraging investment in the new technologies that are essential for the long-term viability of any enterprise. For Mexico, the challenge will be to develop policies that promote sufficient exports to finance long-term development. In the short run it may be impossible to export enough to finance imports and service the massive foreign debt, and mechanisms for reducing the debt burden will have to be found. Just how to create conditions that foster economic growth and development is the major policy challenge of the decade.

Notes

[1] Anthony Edwards, "How to Make Offshore Assembly Pay," *Economist Intelligence Unit*, Serial Report No. 171, 1984.

[2] United States International Trade Commission, *Imports Under Items 806.30 and 807.00 of the Tariff Schedules of the United States, 1982–1985*, USITC Publication 1920, December 1986, p. ix.

[3] USITC, *Imports Under Items 806.30 and 807.00 of the Tariff Schedules of the United States, 1980-1983*, USITC Publication 1688, April 1985.

[4] Robert Ayres and Steven Miller, *The Impacts of Robotics on the Workforce and Workplace* (unpublished technical report, Carnegie-Mellon University, June 1981).

[5] USITC, *The Impact of Increased United States-Mexico Trade on Southwest Border Development*, USITC Publication 1915, November 1986, p. xviii.

[6] Ibid., p. xv.

[7] Ibid., p. xviii.

[8] Calculated from employment and earnings data based on the maquila survey conducted by the Secretariat of Commerce and Industrial Development in Mexico and from the Economic Survey of Singapore, issued by the Singapore Ministry of Trade and Industry.

[9] John Kerr, "Priam Stays Onshore with Automated Factory," *Electronics Business*, July 10, 1984, pp. 236–238.

[10] Susan Sanderson, "Impacts of Automated Manufacturing Technology on Offshore Assembly," (unpublished research report, Carnegie-Mellon University, June 1986).

[11] Ayres and Miller, op. cit.

[12] H. Rush and Kurt Hoffman, *Microelectronics and Clothing: The Impact of Technical Change on Global Industry*, (Geneva: International Labor Organization, 1985).

[13] Susan Sanderson, Gregory Williams, Timothy Ballenger, and Brian J.L. Berry, "Impacts of Computer-Aided Manufacturing and Robotics on Offshore Assembly and Future Manufacturing Locations," in *Regional Studies*, Vol. 21.2, pp. 131–42.

[14] The dollar has been on a roller-coaster ride since 1973. It rose from 1973 to 1976, then plummeted, then rose again until early 1980, plummeted again, then rose sharply in the second quarter of 1981 and remained high through much of 1985. In September 1985, the dollar plunged, reaching a record post-World War II low in spring 1986.

[15] JETRO (Japan External Trade Organization), *Handy Facts On U.S.-Japan Trade* (New York: 1986).

[16] Ronald Dore, "Goodwill and the Spirit of Market Capitalism," *Journal of Sociology*, Volume XXXIV, No. 4, 1983.

[17] *Business Week*, April 21, 1986.

Chapter 6

Technology and Employment Along the U.S.-Mexican Border

M. Patricia Fernández Kelly

In less than two decades, the U.S.-Mexican border has become a setting for government-sponsored economic policies with a distinctly international flavor. With the launching of its *maquila* program in 1965 and its consolidation after 1972, Mexico joined more than fifty other developing countries hosting export-processing zones (EPZs) and competing for foreign investments in light manufacturing.[1] In a relatively short period of time, the maquila program has resulted in over 1,000 assembly plants and over 300,000 jobs, mostly in the assembly of electronics, garments, and other labor-intensive products for export. General Electric, RCA, NCR, American Hospital Supply, Texas Instruments, General Motors, and United Technologies are among the hundreds of companies resorting to maquila operations. As a result, Mexico ranks first among the developing countries performing assembly work for U.S.-based multinational firms.[2]

The maquila program has greatly benefited from customs and tax incentives on both sides of the border. For example, Article 807.00 of the U.S. Customs Code allows for the temporary export of components, raw materials, and machinery to foreign countries for the purpose of assembly. Finished or semi-finished products manufactured in this manner may be returned to the United States duty free. The same goods are taxed only on "value added," calculated on the basis of the cost of producing abroad. In the case of labor-intensive operations like garments and semiconductors, value added is largely a function of wages paid to workers. As a consequence, since the early 1960s, customs provisions like Article 807.00 have provided a rational foundation for the movement of assembly operations from advanced industrial countries to low-wage areas in developing countries, principally in Asia and Latin America. In 1983, the total Article 807.00 value from assembly work performed in Mexican *maquiladoras* for U.S. firms was $3.7 billion, representing 82 per cent of the value of all manufactured exports from that country.[3]

The importance of the maquila program is further demonstrated by the fact that for approximately ten years it has been the fastest growing sector of the Mexican economy, surpassing the rates of expansion of oil production and tourism. By the end of 1985, maquila industry had moved ahead of tourism as a source of revenue for the Mexican government—an impressive feat for a program once considered to have limited scope. Mexican public officials now consider this form of industrialization a key aspect of their country's development strategy.

Although there have been favorable appraisals, the maquila program from its inception has also raised sensitive, substantive concerns focused primarily on the extent of maquila impact in three areas:

(1) Can maquiladoras become vehicles for technology transfer and labor upgrading?
(2) Does a predominantly female labor force distort patterns of employment in the area?
(3) Do maquila operations threaten the very notion of "integrated national development" by thrusting Third World countries into competition with one another as providers of increasingly cheaper labor?

The purpose of this essay is to examine these questions and to suggest implications for economic policy along the U.S.-Mexican border. The focus is on the electronics industry, which, together with garment manufacture, spearheaded the movement of production from advanced industrial countries to foreign, low-wage areas of the world.

Advanced Technology and Industrial Development Along the U.S.-Mexican Border

Although their significance today is considerable, maquila operations had modest beginnings. In 1964, the U.S. Congress terminated the "bracero program," a bilateral arrangement with Mexico (in effect since 1942) permitting Mexican agricultural workers—most of them male—to be employed legally in the United States. As a result of this action, Mexican government officials faced heightened unemployment among agricultural workers and incidents of social unrest along the border. They turned to exportable manufactures as an expedient solution for creating jobs and diminishing popular frustration. After a portentous tour of Asian industrial zones in the spring of 1965, Octaviano Campos Salas, then Minister of Industry and Commerce, described the fusion of foreign investment and domestic labor as a path leading to Mexico's future competitiveness on an international scale.[4] In his view, the country could reach a new stage of development by offering multinational corporations similar or better conditions for assembly than those available in Asia.

Since then, still other factors have been recognized to add to the lure of the Mexican border as a site for industrial activity. Among them is the area's proximity to markets, headquarters, and distribution facilities situated in the United States, where most of the largest companies and investors are based. By 1970, the Mexican government had developed and made available an incentives package designed to encourage investment in export manufacturing. The plan was expanded in 1972[5] and slightly modified in subsequent years.[6] Its net effect was to extend to maquila operations privileges that were not extended to national industries.

Although Mexican government policy was an important factor in promoting industrialization along the border, it was not first in the series of events that made possible the expansion of the maquiladoras. In the 1960s, long before incentives were officially granted, several U.S.-based companies had already entered into informal agreements with local entrepreneurs in border cities. Thus the latter became brokers between foreign investors and the Mexican government. Some of them went so far as to provide the needed infrastructure. For example, in Ciudad Juárez, Chihuahua, one of the largest concentrations of maquiladoras, the wealthy Bermudez family shifted investments away from capital-intensive agriculture by transforming cotton fields into industrial parks. They, and other enterprising members of the local elite, were at the forefront of a trend that changed the fate of border cities in less than a decade.

From the preceding sketch it is apparent that the growth of the maquila industry originally depended on the partnership between foreign investors and local businessmen. It was only later that the Mexican government intervened to sanction and legitimize the program. Therefore, the government's role was *not* the planning and implementation of a coherent development strategy, but a reactive course of endorsing—after the fact—a phenomenon previously made possible by strong international pressures.

Mexican officials soon saw maquila operations not only as a mechanism for job creation, but also as part of a strategy for technology transfer and the upgrading of workers' skills. This has been a key point in the official agenda since 1974. Businessmen and managers similarly believed that the plants would bring about an industrial revolution along the U.S.-Mexican border, and their expectations were not without foundation.

Maquiladoras are part of an international reorganization of production that has fostered the proliferation of export-processing zones in less developed countries. Like most EPZs in the world, the maquila program is primarily dedicated to the assembly of electrical and electronics components, followed by that of garments and other light manufactures. By 1984, 417 plants (60 per cent of all maquiladoras) and close to 130,000 workers (65 per cent of the maquila work force) were participating in electrical and electronics assembly.[7] It is not surprising then, given the "high tech" image of the electrical/electronics industry, that many Mexicans saw it as a vehicle for technology transfer of vital interest to national industry. There was hope that these companies, which had unleashed the age of advanced technology in the United States, would also extend it beyond the U.S. southern border.

The limitations of maquila operations as channels for technology transfer were not explored until Jorge Bustamante issued his pioneering critique in 1975.[8] In particular, the document stressed the fact that maquiladoras are by and large centers for intensive manual labor with no emphasis on research and development, design, and marketing. While it is true that most plants of this kind require some specialized personnel—mostly engineers, technicians, mechanics, and mid-level managers—the vast majority of jobs are in direct production; between 70 and 85 per cent of all jobs offered by maquiladoras are for assemblers.

Three other factors militate against maquila operations becoming centers for technological development:

First, maquiladoras are not "firms" in the conventional sense of the word. They can be better described as departments or subcontractors characterized by limited autonomy and dependence on companies headquartered in distant points like New York or Dallas. Partly for the same reason, maquiladora managers lack incentives to develop independent technological know-how; nor do they need to apply existing expertise in creative or original ways. Instead, the competitiveness of the maquiladoras lies in their ability to produce steadily, intensively, and at low cost for parent firms.

Second, through the special legislation mentioned earlier, the maquila program was constituted as a privileged enclave with few (if any) links to national industry. Whatever expertise and technological know-how has accumulated in the plants has for the most part remained there. No stimuli exist to enable direct exchanges between maquiladoras and domestic firms. This cleavage is accentuated by the fact that a national industrial base is almost completely absent in areas where maquiladoras have flourished. The gap between the export processing plants and domestic production is demonstrated by the small proportion of local inputs in maquila assembly: In almost two decades of existence, maquiladoras have not absorbed more than 1.5 per cent of their total inputs in *domestic* components and raw materials.[9]

Third, the extension of advanced technology to maquila production is also constrained by structural factors operating on an international scale. It was foreign competition in standardized production, primarily competition from Japan, that forced many advanced industrial countries to seek alternative strategies aimed at retaining their comparative advantage in the world market. Indeed, the benefits derived from international wage differentials, as well as the need to reduce production costs and remain competitive in the international sphere, are mentioned most often by managers as reasons for starting operations in Asia and along the U.S.-Mexican border. Yet massive movements of capital from advanced industrial countries to Asia and Latin America would not have been possible without the application of advanced technology to production itself. This has had several paradoxical effects. Thanks to the availability of computers, firms headquartered in various U.S. locations can harmonize and control production in subsidiaries or subcontracted affiliates all over the world. Thanks also to the same sophisticated equipment, it is now possible to subdivide the labor process into increasingly minute and repetitive operations. This allows unskilled and semi-skilled workers in distant geographical areas to participate in the manufacture of even the most complex products. Maquila operations can best be understood in the context of this coexistence of centralized production with decentralized manufacturing.

Thus contrary to some optimistic forecasts in advanced industrial countries, "high-tech" is not eliminating manual labor; rather, it is reorganizing it on the basis of geographical and national considerations.[10] The separation between the design of technology (which generally takes place in advanced industrial countries) and the actual assembly of consumer products (which is increasingly being carried out in developing countries) is one of the consequences of the application of computer technology to manufacturing.

Decentralized production and the simplification of manufacturing operations afford investors in general, and managers in particular, four distinct advantages:

(1) Increased control over production, partly enhanced by the gap between design and assembly;

(2) Increased flexibility in hiring due to the new possibility of engaging in direct production many formerly unemployed or "unemployable" persons without specific training;

(3) Reduction in the length of on-the-job training periods resulting from the almost total replaceability of direct production workers; and

(4) Intensification of work and greater output through the implementation of high production quotas fulfilled by workers specializing in one or two operations.

These four advantages have political as well as economic aspects. The geographical separation between design and assembly strengthens employer control over workers in various locations, while the feasibility of subdividing complex production processes into unskilled operations justifies the search for cheap labor in developing countries.

The electronics industry has created the tools for enhancing—and has received the benefits of—this international rearrangement of production. Almost from its inception, electronics manufacturing has relied heavily on highly specialized research and development, while transferring assembly abroad—first to Asia, and then to Latin America. For example, in the early 1960s, Fairchild, one of the pioneers in the field, was one of the first companies to design and produce consumer electronics products in large volumes. It was also one of the first to move its assembly operations to South Korea (1962) and to Hong Kong (1964). This started a trend that still continues today.[11]

In electronics production as well as many other areas of industrial production, the race to improve existing technologies while at the same time lowering costs greatly limits the participation of developing countries in the process of technology transfer. This is particularly true when, as in the case of the maquiladora program, incentives for autonomous research and development are absent.

The technology gap separating production in advanced and developing countries has widened in the last five years as a result of the bifurcation of the electronics industry. On the one hand, the majority of large and small U.S.-based electronics manufacturers continue to produce relatively simple components with limited random-access memory, but with wide application in a variety of consumer products. The assembly of such components requires low levels of quality control, and they can also be easily and cheaply transported. Such factors render geographical distance inconsequential, making less developed areas in Asia and the U.S.-Mexican border attractive settings for their production. On the other hand, the electronics industry is experiencing a rise in capital-intensive production, including the formation of large corporations dedicated to the manufacture of fourth- and fifth-generation computer components, interactive graphic terminals, fiber optics-related products, a variety of software and applications systems, and equipment linked to bioengineering and artificial intelligence. In this sector, creativity is astonishing, but costly. Invention, discovery, and prototype fabrication require sizable investments in highly skilled personnel, heavy machinery, and quality control—as well as proximity to major universities and to specialized markets often linked to military and defense expenditures. As a result, regions in New York, California, Texas, and Florida are becoming preferred locations for this kind of production.[12]

Thus even the mobility of capital investments fostered by the availability of advanced technology has its limits. The type of production that is likely to continue to be carried out in the developing countries—in some parts of Asia, Latin America, and the Caribbean Basin—for the most part involves the relatively simpler, standardized components. The extent to which the U.S.-Mexican border will be thrust into further competition with Asian locations will be affected by the following three considerations:

1. It is important to remember that forecasts anticipate worldwide increases in demand for simpler electronics components through the end of the century. This suggests that locations such as the U.S.-Mexican border will continue to be favored for relatively simple assembly.[13]

2. Some Asian countries, particularly Hong Kong, South Korea, and Taiwan, have implemented economic policies relying on joint ventures, greater selectivity by type of industry, and enhancement of links to national firms. These policies are enhancing the eligibility of these countries for increased investment in intermediate electronics and machinery, which, in turn, will result in more profitable types of production.

3. The series of economic crises experienced by Mexico since 1982 have increased the country's "comparative advantage" as a source of inexpensive labor for world market production. This may cause alarm among those concerned about issues of national development. Nonetheless, the drop in wage rates following the devaluation of the peso has been seen as a distinct advantage by those wishing to start up new operations in Mexico—as evidenced by the rapid expansion of the maquila program in the last three years.

Thus what we are witnessing at present is not a loss of competitiveness of Mexico vis-à-vis Asia, but a further step in the reorganization of production and increased specialization of various parts of the world in certain types of manufacturing. This, too, places limits on the possibilities for technology transfer.

Finally, the constraints on technology transfer are also related to the hiring practices of maquiladoras and to the hiring of women as a preferred labor force.

Maquila Employment, Technology, and Women

An obvious fact about the maquiladoras is that they have never provided employment for those most deeply affected by the elimination of the bracero program. Instead, they precipitated the entrance of women, especially young and single women, into the work force. Until recently, 85 per cent of maquiladora workers were women between eighteen and twenty-five years old. Although the proportion of women has declined to about 70 per cent for reasons discussed below, maquiladoras continue to be a predominantly female industry.

The bracero and maquila programs are gender-specific labor allocation strategies linked by history and cultural circumstance. The case is all the more interesting given earlier government statements justifying sponsorship of maquila operations on the basis of their potential as creators of jobs for recently idled workers. Ironically, ten years after the implementation of the maquila industry, unemployment had increased by 3.8 per cent.[14]

What explains the coexistence of rising unemployment with rapid industrialization? Part of the answer lies in the employment practices of the plants: Maquiladora managers have from the beginning resorted to selective hiring policies.[15] In general, the plants have not created jobs for men, who customarily had been counted as members of the "traditional" work force. Rather, they have expanded the potential pool of available labor by recruiting "formerly unemployable" women—housewives, students, or others who had been counted as members of the economically inactive population. When these women are fired or lose their jobs as a result of plant closings, they are no longer classified as unemployable or economically inactive; instead, they became part of the "newly unemployed." These women have expanded the mass of workers without jobs even in the midst of accelerated industrialization.

In locations like Ciudad Juárez, women's wages are vital to the subsistence of their households. Because approximately 49 per cent of the population in that city is fourteen years of age or younger, the need to support children is a contributing factor precipitating women's search for jobs. Such compelling motives for seeking wage employment were expressed by a woman standing in line for a job interview at a maquiladora: "I am single. . . . But my sister Beatriz married when she was only fifteen. Now she is unmarried and has three children to support. All of us live with my parents. Beatriz and I are the oldest in the family, that's why we really have to get a job." These problems are exacerbated by the scarcity of jobs among men in general, and among men living with maquiladora workers in particular. Seventy-five per cent of the men (fathers, husbands, brothers, cousins, etc.) sharing households with women maquiladora workers in Ciudad Juárez are

either unemployed or underemployed.[16] The occupations most prevalent among these men were: unskilled construction worker, petty clerk,
laborer, and street vendor.

The meaning of these findings can only be appreciated when one
considers the web of personal relationships between men and women in
a context devoid of occupational alternatives. A glimpse of this was
offered by a forty-year-old woman whose two daughters were employed
at electronics plants: "Why do they have to work, my two daughters?
Because we are poor. With six children at home our need is great. Men
can't be trusted. Besides, there are few jobs for them in Ciudad Juárez.
You can be a 'parkero' like my husband and earn a little money, but . . .
we can't count on his contribution. Sometimes he gives me 'gasto'; most
of the time he doesn't. That's why my girls have to work."[17]

Maquiladora managers have not overlooked the advantages derived from the lack of occupational alternatives in Ciudad Juárez. The
results of almost one hundred personal interviews clearly indicate that
managers, wishing to be highly selective in the personnel they employ,
perceive high levels of unemployment and underemployment as an
asset. Both labor market conditions and familial needs prompt the
employment of women in the maquiladoras. The case of the Mexican
border shows that men's inability to find gainful employment can be a
strong precipitant of women's search for jobs. Gender also intervenes in
processes affecting wage formation.

It is important to remember that wages for direct production
workers in Asia—which has the largest concentration of export-processing plants—average only 35 cents an hour. In the last decade,
wages for maquiladora workers have fluctuated due to external pressures. For example, hourly wages in Ciudad Juárez in 1978 amounted
to approximately 58 cents, or $112 a month. By January 1982, that
sum had risen to almost $364. But by September of that year, after a
major currency devaluation, the same amount was equivalent to only
$156. Subsequent drops in the value of the peso have further reduced
purchasing power among maquiladora workers, as the price of basic
goods has risen.[18]

Following the logic underlying the maquila program, many industrial promoters and public officials in Mexico have welcomed the series
of peso devaluations since 1982 as measures that would make the
country more attractive for investment. To a large extent they were
right; the number of maquiladoras grew at a rate of 7.2 per cent after
1983, sharply contrasting with the 3.5-per-cent average growth rate of
the preceding decade.[19]

Nevertheless, currency devaluation also had a negative impact on
earnings. In 1978, the 58-cent hourly wages of maquiladora workers in
Ciudad Juárez already were five times smaller than the minimum
wage in the twin city of El Paso, Texas, only fifteen minutes away

across the border. In 1986, workers doing similar tasks in Ciudad Juárez are earning only 50 cents an hour, even though inflation rates have skyrocketed. Wages have dropped considerably since research began on the border industrialization program.[20]

These factors are rapidly transforming the options of working women and men, and thus the characteristics of the labor supply. At the same time that the number of assembly plants grew along the border and in other points in Mexico's interior, managers were puzzled by apparent labor shortages. The trend was significant enough to lead many companies to modify their hiring practices to some extent. Not only did they begin to incorporate women from age brackets or schooling levels that formerly had been considered unacceptable, but they also started employing very young men. In 1981, almost 90 per cent of those employed in the maquiladoras were women; at present, that figure hovers below 70 per cent.

The reasons for sudden labor shortages in a country characterized by high levels of unemployment and underemployment are not immediately evident. Some managers feel that the intense industrialization of the last decade and a half has exhausted the available labor pool, but employment and demographic statistics disprove this. Spokesmen for the industry also believe that automation in newly established maquiladoras is changing the composition of the labor force and, therefore, the definition of what constitutes a desirable employee. That may be partly true; nevertheless, unskilled and semi-skilled jobs still predominate in the maquila industry.

Is there a better explanation for the oddly persistent labor shortages? During a brief, exploratory research project conducted along the Tijuana-San Diego border in late 1983 and 1984, other factors were uncovered that help elucidate the phenomenon.[21] With escalating inflation rates and shrinking wages, many women *can no longer afford* to work in a maquiladora. In the past, the tediousness of manual labor and the harshness of working conditions were perceived by workers as the price one paid for the relative stability of employment and earnings that slightly surpassed subsistance requirements. Today that "cost-benefit" equation is changing dramatically. Rather than work in the maquiladoras, many women, especially those who support children, are choosing to cross the border illegally to seek jobs as maids or factory workers in the United States.[22]

The previous analysis underscores the importance of women's employment as a source of vital income for their households. For many years, working as an "operadora" (assembler) in a maquiladora was seen by outsiders as a way for young women to earn pocket money, but research has shown that women's earnings in the export-processing plants are by no means just supplementary. The need for women's wages is made all the more pressing by the prevailing rate of male unemployment and underemployment, which has increased since the maquiladoras were created. Despite the magnitude of these changes, minimal efforts have been made to improve the earnings of maquiladora workers. Two factors to a large extent explain this neglect:

First, because most of them are women, maquiladora workers continue to be considered supplementary wage earners rather than the main providers of households. Thus the fact that they are paid unusually low wages even for low-skilled occupations is not seen as a problem by government officials, legislators, and union leaders. Although this belief flies in the face of reality—maquiladora workers contribute most of their earnings to supply family needs—it attests to the resilience of gender mythology. The issue is compounded by women's own self-perceptions as individuals whose primary roles are those of daughters, wives, or mothers rather than workers.

Second, and perhaps more important, the very reasons why women are hired to perform repetitive, manual operations act against their capacity to organize and present their demands to employers. Managers generally share the opinion that women are particularly well suited to intensive manual work because of their dexterity, patience, reliability, and sense of responsibility; by contrast, they perceive men as less nimble, less trustworthy, and more volatile than women. In-depth interviews with a sample of 87 employers and almost 600 workers between 1978 and 1984 suggest that the rhetoric about feminine agility and responsibility often conceals attempts to control women at the workplace while at the same time reducing their options for collective political expression. Consider, as illustrations, the following two testimonies. The first is a typical remark by a superintendent of a major electronics plant in Ciudad Juárez: "We like to hire girls who don't have too much experience because they aren't spoiled. We shape them to our needs by appealing to their feminine sensibilities. Then you can trust they won't fly off the handle, making unrealistic demands or joining unions. We like to think of our company as a family where everyone knows their duties."

The second observation was offered by an unemployed man with ample experience as an illegal immigrant in Texas and Arizona. When asked whether he had considered looking for a job at an assembly plant, he responded: "Me, in a maquiladora? That's woman's work! And it's hard work at low pay. A man wouldn't stand for it. They hire girls because they think they won't give them any trouble. As for a man, he doesn't have to ask permission from his mother or his wife to cross the border. That's where the better jobs are."

The same factors that reduce women's participation in workers' organizations also militate against their potential for occupational mobility and participation in technology transfers. Three major barriers prevent women from gaining access to jobs requiring technical expertise. The first two are structural; the third underscores the impact on factory work of myths regarding the social roles of men and women.

First, the barriers to technological development discussed in the previous section are compounded by the organization of labor in the maquiladoras. Typically, the occupational hierarchy in such plants consists of a manager or two, a few engineers acting as superintendents or supervisors, a large number of "group leaders," and a vast majority of assemblers. In addition, maquiladoras generally have a clerical staff of secretaries, receptionists, and accountants; an auxiliary body of repairmen, mechanics, warehousemen, and transport operators; and a group of maintenance workers, janitors, and custodians.

Depending on their size and means, maquiladoras may include variants of these occupational categories. For example, in small subcontracted shops, assemblers may also be responsible for maintenance functions, or a secretary may act as an accountant. However, the basic occupational stratification of the plants does not vary significantly.

From this description it can be seen that jobs within the maquila hierarchy are clearly divided on the basis of sex, with supervisory and technical positions (above group leaders) predominantly filled by men. Ninety-nine per cent of all managers, 75 per cent of all personnel directors, and 87 per cent of all engineers are men. And, although no systematic research has been carried out on the subject, impressionistic evidence suggests that, in almost twenty years of maquila operations, the number of direct production workers able to climb to higher positions on the occupational ladder is insignificant. Beyond the mark of "group leader" or "quality controller," women are barred from access to most jobs. Even if such barriers didn't exist, the number of technical jobs available in the maquiladoras is tiny compared to the large number of openings in direct production. Consequently, most workers are confined to dead-end positions with little hope of upward mobility.

Second, a combination of factors has led maquiladora managers to recruit technically trained personnel from local universities and vocational centers rather than to train in-house production workers for technical positions. The belief that women (especially young, single women) are unable to handle machines and technical knowledge competently plays a role in such decisions. Nevertheless, gender prejudice is not the only factor to consider.

With few exceptions, local engineers, most of them young and inexperienced, are hired to serve primarily as supervisors. Of the fifty engineers working at maquiladoras and interviewed in Ciudad Juárez in 1983, forty-three responded that their functions were primarily administrative and supervisory, with little opportunity for enhancement of technological expertise.[23]

The reasons why technological research and development does not take place in the maquiladoras to any significant degree have been discussed. Given their structural limitations, maquiladoras are ill-suited to promote the advancement of technological knowledge, even among locally trained engineers. Instead, it seems that many engineers are hired to act as credible symbols of authority vis-à-vis production workers. Or, as a personnel director explained: "There aren't many lady engineers around. If there were, I wouldn't hesitate in hiring one. Of course, she would have to be very good, and she should be capable of inspiring respect—sometimes even a little fear. Men are generally better at doing that."

Finally, traditional perceptions regarding the "proper place" of men and women also play a role in limiting women's participation in technical fields. The very notion of femininity, as understood by a large number of people in places like Ciudad Juárez, is antithetical to the definition of technology. Machines are the product of crude rationality; women are supposed to be guided by emotion and sensitivity. Technology is cold and impersonal; women value warm and intimate relationships. It follows logically from this line of reasoning that anything having to do with technological matters is better suited to the male temperament. It comes as no surprise that women's participation in technology transfers is not an issue that reaches policymakers' agendas. This is true even in situations where women take part, on a day-to-day basis, in a process presumed to foster technological development. Such is the case of the maquiladoras.

Once formed, myths are surprisingly resistant to change, even in the midst of evidence that challenges their basic assumptions. Women who customarily handle printed boards, complicated wiring, integrated circuits, semiconductors, and computer terminals are among the first to question the motives that isolate them from technical knowledge. This is particularly true when they must solve assembly problems resulting from the incorrect application of blueprints designed in the company's home country. A woman who had been a group leader for several years reported having seen many instances where female assembly workers had been responsible for decisions affecting the application of specialized technology[24]: "You learn a lot when you are an assembler. At first, everything is new and you are intimidated by all the hardware. Gradually, you realize that terminals are just terminals, and capacitors are just capacitors; they are not magic wands but tools. . . . We used to get the blueprints from our parent firm in Bloomington, but in trying to use them, sometimes we would find all sorts of 'bugs.' The engineer would get desperate with all the wasted parts rejected by quality control. It was us, the girls in the assembly line, who knew the process best; the ones who had direct experience with the workings of a particular circuit or another. We would work for hours to solve a problem. Afterwards, the engineer would thank us and take the credit for what we had done. We were invisible behind our aprons, behind our conveyer belt."

Our research has shown that part of the task facing policymakers is to remove the barrier that keeps women invisible. They must seriously consider the contribution women could make if only their skills were acknowledged.

Future Policy

The basis of this analysis has been the premise that technology is neither an abstraction nor a factor independently acting on society. Rather, I have assumed that technology transfers are part of the political, economic, and ideological exchanges among individuals. The maquila program provides a good illustration of that proposition.

The internationalization of manufacturing, made possible in large part by advanced technology, has afforded corporations greater efficiency in production, more flexibility in hiring practices, and an important edge in their negotiations with labor. By moving assembly operations to the developing world while retaining control over design and technology in industrial countries, firms have diversified economic and political risks. Nevertheless, the same factors that provide distinct advantages to employers can translate into a weakening of workers in bringing about improvements in wages and terms of employment. Paradoxically, the same changes that account for the creation of sophisticated computer technology have also spun a web of international production fraught with dangers for wage earners.

Women maquiladora workers are part and parcel of this new world. As a result, their lives express many unresolved contradictions. To what extent can integrated national development be achieved through strategies like the maquila program, which open the country to foreign investment solely in exchange for cheap labor? Can maquiladoras be transformed into a viable path for the creation of better jobs, higher standards of living, and expanded occupational opportunities for women as well as men?

Positive responses to these questions depend on governmental policymaking in the future. Without deliberate planning, maquiladoras can only follow their logical *raison d'être*—that is, fulfilling the requirements of parent firms and lowering production costs by hiring the most vulnerable sector of the working population: women in less developed countries.

In spite of the problems outlined in this chapter, maquiladoras continue to be a vital source of earnings for hundreds of thousands of

Mexicans and their families. Therefore, the challenge does not concern the existence of the program itself. Rather, it is about the steps that might be taken to incorporate maquiladoras into a larger program for national development. Integrated planning should include an interest in growth, but it should also take into account measures designed to raise standards of living, purchasing power, and working conditions for the majority of plant employees.

Moreover, planning does not, as some would fear, have to result in the stifling of investment or economic activity. The following four measures illustrate potential benefits that planning could assure at minimal cost:

1. *"Backward Linkages" with Domestic Firms.* One of the major problems of maquila operations is their extreme isolation from the surrounding economy. The experience of countries like South Korea, Singapore, and Taiwan suggests that export processing can be most effective when linked with national firms providing services and secondary inputs.

The very definition of maquila production has prevented plants from absorbing domestically fabricated components. This trend could, however, be reduced in two ways: First, additional incentives and/or exemptions could be offered to foreign companies willing to purchase a portion of their components in Mexico. A feasibility study is needed to appraise the extent to which this would be cost-effective. Nevertheless, there is no reason to believe that this measure would raise the cost of production, especially if counterbalanced by additional tax exemptions. While this would reduce the amount of earnings directly received by the Mexican government, it would also stimulate further economic activity from which other revenues could be expected in the future.

Moreover, additional backward linkages could be created through the provision of services and manufactures having to do with the processing of waste and residues, transportation, and packaging. Such activities could be subcontracted to small Mexican firms benefiting from private and public loans. In sum, Mexico must outline and create the conditions to enhance the probability that the maquiladoras will absorb small but significant proportions of domestic materials and services.

2. *Training and Technological Development.* A similar strategy might be followed with respect to the transfer of simple types of technology for domestic production. A small number of maquiladoras might be awarded additional tax exemptions when becoming part of an experimental project aimed at establishing and equipping "sister" firms owned by local investors with simple technology for domestic production, consumption, and export. Some of the training could have an application in sectors not directly related to maquila production.

At present, maquiladoras have no incentive to maintain their work force for extended periods of time or to upgrade the skills of workers beyond the level of direct production. However, mechanisms could be created to transform maquiladoras into training centers. For example, instead of despairing about the scarcity of qualified personnel at the local level, companies could be encouraged to dedicate part of their resources to in-house training. As part of such a scheme, the Mexican government could provide workers with vouchers for on-the-job training. Firms accepting vouchers would qualify to have a portion of their training costs paid by the government. While this measure would require some additional investment, the benefits to both industry and domestic economic activity could be considerable.

3. *Selectivity by Industry.* Time after time, research has demonstrated that not all forms of industrial activity are beneficial to communities or nations. The maquila program is particularly inefficient in that it does not differentiate among various industrial activities and their impact on the community. Since fly-by-night garment operations have proved to have negative effects and few redeeming features, there is no reason to continue encouraging that type of investment. Additional taxes and stricter conditions should be imposed on companies wishing to invest in Mexico in industrial activities shown to have been deleterious in the past. On the other hand, companies in advanced sectors of technological development also willing to make a commitment to industrial activity in terms similar to the ones sketched here should be deserving of additional incentives.

4. *Promotion Programs.* Perhaps most important, the enormous human resource formed by the experience of tens of thousands of women who have been employed in maquiladoras should not go to waste. The business sector should be encouraged to promote a small number of qualified assemblers to positions of greater responsibility, including those requiring technical and supervisory skills.

There have been few instances of organizations catering to the experience and needs of women working in the maquiladoras. There is, however, one major and hopeful example. Since the early 1970s, the Centro de Orientación de la Mujer Obrera (COMO) in Ciudad Juárez has served as a reservoir of information too often ignored by promoters of the maquila industry and by government officials. In the course of its hazardous existence, COMO has implemented promotional programs and conducted research on the characteristics and lifestyle of maquiladora workers. The most significant lesson derived from this wealth of knowledge is that women who have worked in the plants desire an opportunity to make a lasting contribution to their families and communities. Centers such as COMO deserve serious consideration by the Mexican government and private industry. They could easily be transformed into training and counseling centers where workers could both obtain comprehensive information about their rights and responsibilities under Mexican law, and learn some of the skills that would enable them to compete for better jobs.

The history of the maquila program has been characterized by a laissez-faire attitude on the part of the government. The assumption has been that even the smallest demand made of foreign companies could result in the loss of investments, whose most important effect has been the creation of sorely needed jobs. As a result, there has not been a serious attempt to study ways of reconciling the need for vital economic activity derived from export manufacturing with the need to protect the interests of workers and communities. It is time to redress this limited approach to the maquila industry. The suggestions included here are neither unrealistic nor extreme. They merely support the statements of Mexican public officials that maquila operations should be an integral aspect of Mexico's strategy for development.

Notes

[1] See Joseph Grunwald and Kenneth Flamm, *The Global Factory, Foreign Assembly in International Trade* (Washington, D.C.: The Brookings Institution, 1985), pp. 68-85.

[2] Figures provided by the Dirección de la Industria Maquiladora y Estímulo a la Industria, Mexico, D.F., December 1984.

[3] Susan Walsh Sanderson, "Impacts of Automated Manufacturing Technologies on Mexico's Offshore Assembly," (paper presented at the Overseas Development Council conference on the impact of global technological change on U.S.-ADC relations, Racine, Wisconsin, November 1985).

[4] M. P. Fernández Kelly, *For We Are Sold, I and My People: Women and Industry in Mexico's Frontier* (Albany: State University of New York Press, 1983).

[5] The incentives granted to maquila operations included a) amendments to Article 23 of the Mexican Customs Code, allowing for the temporary entrance of foreign machinery, components, and materials, b) the waiving of foreign investment provisions, permitting up to 100-per-cent foreign control over industrial investments, and c) the purchase or lease of Mexican land for industrial purposes for up to 99 years through trusts entered with national banks. These and other incentives originally applied to a 12.5-mile border belt. Since 1972 they have been extended to the rest of the country, with the exception of three highly industrialized areas: Mexico City, Guadalajara, and Monterrey.

[6] Since 1983, maquiladoras have been allowed to sell up to 20 per cent of their production in Mexico's domestic market.

[7] Figures provided by the Dirección de la Industria Maquiladora y Estímulo a la Industria, Mexico, D.F., December 1984.

[8] Jorge Bustamante, "Maquiladoras: A New Face of International Capitalism on Mexico's Northern Frontier," in June Nash and M. P. Fernández Kelly, eds., *Women, Men, and the International Division of Labor* (Albany: State University of New York Press, 1983).

[9] Banco Nacional de México, *Distribución Sectorial de las Exportaciónes,* Vol. LX, No. 703 (June 1984).

[10] M. P. Fernández Kelly, "Contemporary Production and the New International Division of Labor," in Steven E. Sanderson, ed., *The Americas in the New International Division of Labor* (New York: Holmes and Meier, 1985). See also Harley Shaiken, *Work Transformed: Automation and Labor in the Computer Age* (New York: Holt, Rinehart and Winston, 1985).

[11] See D. O'Connor, "Changing Patterns of International Production in the Semiconductor Industry: The Role of Transnational Corporations," (paper prepared for the Conference on Microelectronics in Transition, University of California, Santa Cruz, May 1983). For a succinct history of the electronics industry, see L. Siegel, *Delicate Bonds: The Semiconductor Industry* (Mountain View, California: Pacific Studies Center, 1984).

[12] For a discussion of this point, see Manuel Castells, "Toward the Informational City? High Technology, Economic Change and Spatial Structure: Some Exploratory Hypotheses," Institute of Urban and Regional Development, Working Paper No. 430, University of California at Berkeley, 1985. See also M. P. Fernández Kelly and Anna M. García, "Invisible Amidst the Glitter: Hispanic Women in the Southern California Electronics Industry," in Ann Statham, Eleanor Miller, and Hans Mauksch, eds., *The Worth of Women's Work: A Qualitative Synthesis* (Albany: State University of New York Press, forthcoming).

[13] See A. Glasmeier, P. Hall, and A. R. Markusen, "Recent Evidence on High-Technology Industries' Spatial Tendencies: A Preliminary Investigation," Institute of Urban and Regional Development, Working Paper No. 417, University of California at Berkeley, 1984.

[14] See M. P. Fernández Kelly, *For We Are Sold,* op. cit.

[15] See V. Beechey, "Some Notes on Female Wage Labor in Capitalist Production," in *Capital and Class,* Vol. 3, 1977, pp. 45-66.

[16] M. P. Fernández Kelly, *For We Are Sold,* op. cit.

[17] A "parkero" is paid gratuities for parking cars at companies and public places. "Gasto" is an allowance from earnings given by men to their wives.

[18] Information provided by the Departamento de Investigación, Banco Nacional de México, December 1984 and August 1985.

[19] The period of austerity following the peso devaluation had resulted in a 40-percent drop in real wages by March of 1986. See Cathryn Thorup, "U.S. Relations with Mexico Tense," *Journal of Commerce,* March 24, 1986.

[20] See Vicki L. Ruiz and Susan Tiano, *Women on the U.S.-Mexico Border: Responses to Change* (Boston: Allen and Unwin, 1987), pp. 77-128.

[21] Exploratory research included unstructured interviews with ten company managers, twenty-five workers in various sectors, and twelve public officials, promoters, and union representatives.

[22] Supporting evidence of this is being collected as part of "A Collaborative Study of Hispanic Women in Garment and Electronics Industries." This project is being partly funded by the Ford Foundation's Program in Governance and Human Rights. Field work for the project is being conducted in Los Angeles, Orange, and San Diego Counties as part of the research agenda at the Center for U.S.-Mexican Studies, University of California, San Diego. See M. P. Fernández Kelly and Anna M. García, "The Making of an Underground Economy: Hispanic Women, Homework and the Advanced Capitalist State," in *Urban Anthropology,* 14 (1-3), 1986, pp. 59-90.

[23] This sample was not selected in a random manner. Nevertheless, the opinions expressed were frequently similar to those documented.

[24] That these experiences are not unusual is attested to by other authors' accounts. See in particular Shaiken's excellent description (op. cit.) of how workers intervene in the application of technology in the automobile industry.

Chapter 7

Biotechnology and Food: The Scope for Cooperation

Cassio Luiselli Fernández

Along with microelectronics and the invention of new materials, bio-technology has emerged as a field of profound technological innovation and impact. Although the early achievements in this field were relatively modest, the applications of biotechnology are likely to be increasingly significant in the remaining years of the century. Indeed, the impact of biotechnology—like that of microelectronics—will affect not only industry but many aspects of daily life.

Developments in biotechnology inevitably will affect relations between nation states, including those between the United States and Mexico. Biotechnology is an area in which the United States has an overwhelming worldwide advantage—perhaps more so than in any other realm of science, with the possible exception of certain military technologies or the production of software. Mexico, for its part, is relatively well endowed with the industrial and scientific infrastructure needed to exploit biotechnology and probably has an excellent chance of adopting and adapting biotechnologies fairly quickly. Major obstacles would arise only with technologies that need massive initial investment or large-scale operations to achieve economies of scale. On the whole, biotechnology could have an extremely positive impact on many areas of crucial interest to Mexico, including agriculture, food production and processing, and medical and health science. It is, in short, a field of strategic importance to Mexico's development that will have increasing relevance to bilateral ties between Mexico and the United States. Moreover, there is still time, if we act judiciously and intelligently, to make this field a showcase for compromise and cooperation rather than another example of North-South confrontation.

The new biotechnology[1] is an integral part of a more basic revolution in biology, which, with the advent of ecology as an autonomous and mature science and with the deciphering of the genetic code, has been transformed into one of the most promising and fascinating fields of human knowledge. Partly due to the newness of its many sub-fields and to the speed with which discoveries are being made, it is difficult to give the "new biotechnology" a definition that is precise and at the same time sufficiently inclusive. For the purposes of this analysis, however, the broad definition adopted by the U.N. Economic Commission for Latin America (ECLA) may be most useful: "Biotechnology is used to describe a range of techniques involving the application of biological agents—live organisms or their components—in the production of goods or services." The expression "genetic engineering" will be employed to refer specifically to the manipulation of genetic material.[2] While this definition is somewhat general, failing to make specific mention of such important branches as biomedical engineering, it does provide a basic point of reference.

This analysis will begin with a very brief review of the state of the art in biotechnology, with special emphasis on applications in the agricultural sector. It will also analyze the principal obstacles to developing biotechnology in Mexico with respect to both scientific experimentation and practical applications, particularly in the food industry.

Current State of the Industry

Biotechnology is experiencing a highly accelerated rate of development, but upon limited bases. Important products derived from the new biotechnologies—for example, interferon, insulin, and artificial sweeteners—are already on the international market. Undoubtedly their numbers and volume will continue to grow at a dizzying rate; many products that were only in the early stages of laboratory tests a few years ago are now beginning to bear fruit at the manufacturing stage. In effect, the time that intervenes between scientific discovery, technological development, and commercial marketing is being shortened to four or five years. Nevertheless, it must be acknowledged that the promises of biotechnology, although they appear to be growing with the passage of time, will not be realized as easily or quickly as was hoped not long ago. Research costs have turned out to be much higher than expected, and scientific advances are meeting with formidable obstacles relating to the premises and techniques of genetic engineering of complex organisms. Until this obstacle can be overcome—and at present a technological breakthrough is not on the immediate horizon—biotechnology will have to be developed within the important but limited framework of simple organisms.

In biotechnology, the United States is the leader by far in theoretical as well as in technological and industrial matters. Japan and the countries of the European Economic Community (EC) follow. In the Third World, only Brazil stands out; it has had a national program since 1981 and has successfully developed (at least technologically) an ambitious alcohol-for-petroleum substitution program. India, Argentina, and Mexico have made interesting advances, but these are only significant in local terms. Little is known about the status of the research and development of biotechnology in the socialist nations, although there are indications that advances there remain limited.

In the United States, while there is no explicit national biotechnology policy, there is a large body of decisions, regulations, and incentives that encourage—albeit in a disorderly fashion—the growth of biotechnology. It is the market stimulus and competition, however, that are driving the U.S. advances within this almost entirely private industry. Universities also have played a decisive role in the development of biotechnology in the United States—so much so that controversy and conflicts have arisen concerning their participation in the commercial development of biotechnology products.

In the last five years, a plethora of biotechnology companies has sprung up in the United States, most of which have succumbed to high research costs and intense competition. Some, however, have not only survived but have been consolidated, contributing to the maturity of the industry. CETUS, GENEX, and GENETECH are the most outstanding examples, but it is estimated that, in late 1984, some 250 firms dedicated exclusively to biotechnology were in existence. More recently, large chemical, petroleum, mineral, and pharmaceutical companies have been entering the field, resulting in a formidable industrial sector. It is impressive, for example, that very large, established firms have invested dramatic sums in the installation of biotechnology laboratories; two cases in point are Monsanto, which (in 1984) had invested $150 million, and DuPont, which had spent $85 million. Furthermore, the relationship between industry and universities creates an immense industrial nucleus with which foreign competition would be very difficult.

Possibly for these reasons, Japan has pursued a more cautious yet still active strategy. In Japan, it is the older chemical-pharmaceutical firms that have, in close cooperation with the government, invested in the development of biotechnology. The Japanese also have opted to associate with U.S. firms. The Europeans, for their part, have developed grandiose plans, and some large firms, notably in the Federal Republic of Germany, have become actively involved in the field by modernizing their equipment and making important investments.

Great Britain, whose mature chemical-pharmaceutical industry was nearing obsolescence, has created numerous autonomous small and medium-size companies that closely follow the U.S. model.

All of these facilities in the advanced industrial countries are strategically oriented toward the future. The market outlook for conventional products, industrial processes, and completely new products is excellent and is continually being revised.

Obstacles to the Industry's Development

Before turning to the issue of demand, a few remarks are fitting concerning the obstacles that the industry faces at this stage of its development. Four such obstacles can be identified, the first being the issue of safety and regulation. Initial doubts and exaggerations about the risk of epidemics from recombinant DNA have dissipated, but safety and regulatory problems remain, arising from the newness of the industrial processes and products of biotechnology. These problems not only hinder and raise the cost of development; they also inhibit investment. The creation of mechanisms of evaluation and oversight of the impact of these new technologies is needed, along with the establishment of *international* standards and regulations to govern the handling and transport of biological material.

A second obstacle concerns the need for the definition of products and the protection of patents. The United States recently took an important step in this direction by accepting the patenting of a microorganism transformed through genetic engineering. Similar events are beginning to take place in other developed countries. The forms and methods for registering patents vary considerably from country to country, and they act as barriers to the formation of an international system of industrial protection in biotechnology. Therefore, for the field to advance on a worldwide scale, there must be an international accord to harmonize patenting procedures. In this field Mexico must make an enormous effort to upgrade and update its outdated patent system.

The creation of a worldwide system should of course take into account the welfare and needs of all nations, including those of the Third World. It should not, as is often the case, favor only the interests of the richest countries and their multinational firms. Multilateral forums such as the U.N. Conference on Trade and Development (UNCTAD), the U.N. Industrial Development Organization (UNIDO), and the Food and Agriculture Organization (FAO) should contribute to the process—since the ownership of certain knowledge in this area should not be exclusively in private hands but should, on the contrary, be available to the universal public domain. Access to some techniques and products must be made available to poor countries. Naturally, it is not expected that this will be possible in the case of every product to come from biotechnology, but easy access could be granted for certain basic genetic materials used in agriculture. For all of these reasons, prompt advancement is urged in the crucial area of the definition of patents and the protection of industrial patent rights.

A third obstacle stems from the uncertainty that still exists over how soon biotechnology will make a major impact, and what its contribution and influence will be on lowering costs, raising productivity, and changing the workplace. Investment decisions, policy, and regulatory measures are all are affected by this uncertainty. This obstacle will be removed as empirical research advances to the manufacturing and finished-product stages. Meanwhile, attempts will proceed to anticipate and quantify—as much as possible—the expected impact of the different biotechnologies.

Finally, the fourth obstacle, which in a way is a corollary to the first three, refers to government policy. Difficulties arise from policy design—from the degree to which it is selective, and from the manner in which its priorities are set. Internationally, policies on this issue vary greatly, and the possibility of linking the processes and chains of production through a coherent coordinating mechanism remains distant. Regional, or even international, coordination of biotechnology policy is a subject of particular interest to developing nations, especially those of Latin America. If the need to compete were reduced within the region itself, Latin American countries could economize on resource use and help shape cooperative policies that are more complete and consistent internally, as well as better coordinated regionally and internationally.[3]

It should be noted that the principal difference between the official policies of the United States and Mexico is in the realm of patents—a field in which differences between developed and developing countries are common. Progress in the area of patents must be made through negotiation and requires, at least for Mexico, reliance on policy that includes a modern and realistic regulatory framework.

Demand Prospects

Let us now analyze the demand aspects of biotechnology. In spite of the obstacles just listed, practically all estimates of the potential market for biotechnology are optimistic. Those doubts that do exist concern the time periods projected for the commercialization of certain products. A study by the Javier Barros Sierra Foundation in Mexico demonstrates that by the year 2000, the world market for products of biotechnology will be more than $60 billion.[4] The following sectors are singled out: food and agriculture ($20 billion), energy ($16 billion), chemical products ($10 billion), and health ($9 billion). Needless to say, these figures are only approximate estimates for a highly dynamic field. They are useful inasmuch as they indicate the relative importance of the products, showing the agro-food sector at the forefront.

In the agricultural sector, important advances in simple and single-cell organisms are proceeding at a rapid pace. The progress in seeds, nitrogen fixers (although still far from being a reality), biological pest control methods, enzymes, amino acids (such as methionine and lysine), and other nutrients merits attention. However, other efforts involving the cultivation of cells to integrally improve plants and animals are still in the most preliminary stages. Images of protein-fortified super-cereals resistant to intense frost and drought, or clones of some genetically superior specimen of an animal, or super-tomatoes weighing many kilos definitely remain more within the realm of science fiction than that of the supermarket aisle.

In any case, it is clear that in the years between now and the turn of the century, the dynamics of biotechnology will be dominated by the United States and driven first by the appearance of new products and the shortening of time lags between discovery and commercial utilization; later by the positive impact on industrial productivity in affected sectors; and finally, by the consolidation and industrial reorganization of the market. In the process, the industry will have matured, becoming a pillar of the new industrialization. This scenario can be a starting point in assessing the prospects and outlook for Mexico in this field.

Mexico: A Base for Biotechnology?

Mexico is endowed with a number of important prerequisites for relatively rapid development of this new realm of technology. Some of Mexico's critical development needs could be usefully addressed by some of the above-mentioned technologies. In early 1984, ECLA and the Mexican Secretary of Public Works and Industrial Commerce consulted with members of the manufacturing private sector, the academic community, and various public sector offices in an effort to define the objectives, means, and instruments to develop a comprehensive biotechnology policy. The consultations made it clear that, in the medium term, biotechnology offers great hope for reducing the country's excessive dependence on food imports; for correcting some problems in the food and health sectors; and for advancements in the control of pollution. They also made it clear that Mexico lacks well-defined programs and policies, as well as some key elements in the industrial structure.

Furthermore, communication between the scientific and technological community and the industrial sector is very limited.

Mexico has a long and fairly successful history in traditional biotechnologies. In the production of beer, bread, liquor, and cheese, experience was gained that to some degree facilitated the adaptation of more modern (but still conventional) biotechnological industries—pharmaceuticals, agrochemicals, and food additives, among others. This prior experience of course does not guarantee that Mexico will be able to jump from its present base to effective use of the new biotechnologies founded on genetic engineering and recombinant DNA techniques. Nevertheless, by international standards, Mexico does have a mature and reasonably efficient traditional biotechnology industry that will be able to furnish some preliminary know-how and the supply mechanisms needed to embark upon the development of the new biotechnology.

A systematic appraisal of the Mexican research and development apparatus and of the creation of hard science in the field of biotechnology can be summarized as follows[5]: A promising infrastructure for the development of this field exists, but it remains disjointed and characterized by uneven development. As in some other areas with potential for technological development, there is a lack of structural support at the national level. The need for this support is pronounced in the areas of equipment, capital goods, industrial services, and coordination. Needless to say, budgets are small and frequently have been allotted without a clear sense of priority. Interesting advances have taken place, however, at the scientific level. At the time of the first forays into the new biotechnology, the two most important institutions of higher learning in Mexico, the National Autonomous University of Mexico (UNAM) and the National Polytechnic Institute (IPN), possessed a small team of first-rate—by world standards—young scientists. According to the Barros Sierra Foundation study, in Mexican laboratories today, projects are being developed by some five hundred researchers exclusively dedicated to the field of biotechnology (albeit broadly defined and concentrated in relatively simple and repetitive techniques). Furthermore, Mexico possesses five academic programs in the field—four at the master's level and one at the doctoral—and it is estimated that about one hundred professionals have acquired postgraduate degrees in biotechnology or closely related fields. Unfortunately, the journey from scientific research to the manufacture of a final product presents many challenges at each step along the way. In the Mexican case, the links grow progressively weaker in the passage from the lab to the factory. In its pilot programs, Mexico suffers from serious deficiencies and is unable to translate discoveries at the experimental stage into production on a truly industrial scale.

Table 1. Mexican University Research Centers with Adequate Physical Infrastructure and Trained Personnel

Center	Location	Research Focus
UNAM Genetic Engineering and Biotechnology Center	Cuernavaca, Morelos	Application of genetic engineering and biotechnology, health and food sectors
UNAM Research Center on Nitrogen Fixation	Cuernavaca, Morelos	Molecular biology and genetic engineering applied to plant cells
IPN Center for Research and Advanced Studies, Department of Biotechnology and Bioengineering	Mexico, D.F.	Fermentation and enzyme engineering
IPN Center for Research and Advanced Studies, Modern Plant Biology Unit	Guanajuato, Gto.	Seed conservation and preservation, genetic engineering applied to cells
UNAM Biomedical Research Institute	Mexico, D.F.	Industrial microbiology, fermentation, and enzyme engineering

Source: Rodolfo Quintero Ramírez, ed., *Perspectiva de la biotecnología en México* (Mexico: Javier Barros Sierra Foundation and CONACYT, 1985).

In summary, it can be said that, at the industrial level, Mexico uses virtually no indigenously developed technology. There are, however, encouraging examples of technological adaptation appropriate to Mexico's capacities and needs. A case in point is the parastatal company FERMEX, which has adapted foreign technology to produce lysine and other essential amino acids. Similar examples may be cited in the production of penicillin. Multinational firms predominate in the use of modern technologies, and they have their own methods of production and technological development that do not transfer easily to Mexican industry. However, some new biotechnology firms have been formed with Mexican capital and employees and are in a position to eventually develop techniques as sophisticated as those using recombinant DNA. Regrettably, the ties between these companies and either the industrial sector of the more traditional biotechnologies or the scientific community are quite tenuous. Moreover, there is still no package of fiscal and credit incentives to encourage the development of this nascent sector.

Potential Applications of Biotechnology in Mexico

Biotechnology nevertheless does offer Mexico some truly revolutionary possibilities for enhancing its capacity to meet some of its own critical development needs. The technologies concerned with agriculture and food are especially important. It is also worthwhile to mention that in the fields of health, pollution control, energy, and chemical products, Mexico has important biotechnology needs that could be met by industrial development in those areas. In the field of health, human insulin and interferon already are being produced, and the production of vaccines, antibodies, antibiotics, and enzymes is also on the horizon. In energy, despite the nation's abundant endowment in hydrocarbons, the use of biomass energy in the rural sector is also an attractive possibility. For efforts to combat pollution, the treatment of waste water is a technological possibility. Finally, in the area of chemical engineering, industrial inputs and ingredients for the food and medical industries can be produced.

In agriculture and forestry, virtually all activities would benefit markedly from biotechnology. Through seed production, plant improvement, and the manufacture of enzymes and pesticides, biotechnology offers Mexico the exciting possibility of raising productivity and production levels in agriculture as well as in cattle raising.

Tremendous potential exists not only for the genetic manipulation of tissue culture, but also for spectacular increases in the yield of

Table 2. Some Products and Processes Whose Development in Mexico is Considered Feasible: Diverse Estimates

Products and Processes	Diverse Estimates of Timing of Technical (T) and/or Economic (E) Feasibility:		
	1984	1990	2000
Utilization of marine algae spirulina	T,E	T,E	
Reutilization of excretions	T,E		
Increased digestibility of farm produce and agro-industrial byproducts	T,E	T	
Vitamins	T,E	T,E	T,E
Foliar protein and other concentrates	T	T,E	T,E
Single-cell proteins:			
Agro-industrial byproducts (solids and liquids)	T,E	T,E	T
Molasses	T,E	T,E	T
Methanol	T,E	T,E	T
Others	T,E	T,E	T
Mushroom and fungus production	T,E		
Bone meal and dried blood, meat and/ or fish	T,E		
Enzymes (a-amylases, gluco-amylase, lactose, invertase, proteases, pertinase, glucose isomerase, penicillinase, cellulases)	T,E	T,E	T
Proteolytic enzymes of plant origin	T,E		T
Amino acids (lysine, glutamic acid, methionine, tryptopan, and all other essential amino acids)	T,E	T,E	T,E
Protein enrichment of various substances	T		
Biopolymers	T,E		
Production of micro-algae	T		
Production of essential oils		T,E	
Mononucleotides (6MP, 5MP)		T	
Processes based on improved and/or genetically constructed rootstalks		T	

Products and Processes	Diverse Estimates of Timing of Technical (T) and/or Economic (E) Feasibility:		
	1984	**1990**	**2000**
Improved production of vitamins, single-cell proteins, biopolymers, fungi, powders, protein concentrates		T,E	
Pigment production		T,E	
Production of alternative feedstock (fermentation of solid base)	T,E	T,E	
Lactic acid		T,E	
Sweeteners (fructose)		E	
Microbe oil		E	
Unconventional new food sources		E	
Immobilized enzymes		T,E	
Synthetic protein			E
Anaerobic digestors for biogas production	T,E		
Biogas reactors (UASB)		T,E	
Methane production from:			
Sanitary landfills		T,E	
Industrial waste		T,E	
Animal waste	T,E		
Hydrogen production			E
Ethanol production from:			
Sucrose	T,E		
Starch and other unconventional bases		T,E	
Cellulose and agricultural byproducts			T,E
Hydrocarbon production from:			
Rapid-growth plant species		E	T,E
Biochemical combustible cells		E	T

Source: Rodolfo Quintero Ramírez, ed., *Perspectiva de la biotecnología en México* (Mexico: Javier Barros Sierra Foundation and CONACYT, 1985), pp. 474–75. Table prepared for the Javier Barros Sierra Foundation from responses obtained from energy experts (Quintero and Solórzano, 1984).

Table 3. Priority Areas for Biotechnology Development in Mexico

Food and Feed Development

Food conservation
Unconventional food sources from single-cell proteins
Protein enrichment of materials
Fermented regional foods

Farming Productivity

Biological fertilizers
Bioinsecticides

Agricultural and Livestock Productivity

Improvement of animal and plant species

Pollution Limitation

Biodegradation of agricultural, animal, and municipal waste
Biodegradation of organic, synthetic, and chemical by-products
Water purification

Energy

Production of biogas, enzymes, and fuel alcohol

Health

Production of vaccines, biologically active substances in natural
    sources, antibiotics, and amino acids and vitamins

Minerals

Mineral leaching through microbe use

Petroleum

Production of genetically engineered microbes to help extract
    petroleum
Bioconversions

Source: *Perspectiva de la biotecnología en México*, op. cit.

cereals, legumes, vegetables, and oil-producing and fruit-bearing plants. Such advances would be accomplished through the genetic incorporation of qualities resistant to pests, drought, and salinity, and through the enhancement of nitrogen fixation, to reduce the need for fertilizers and agrochemicals.

In addition, through related techniques, biotechnology would reduce the amount of time needed to develop new strains—significantly accelerating the research, selection, and development of different crops. In the case of sugar cane, for example, the cycle would be cut from fourteen to seven years; for coffee, from fifteen or twenty years to only seven or eight years; and for the tomato, from seven or eight years to three or four years. In animal husbandry, biotechnology would have an impact on major as well as minor species by rapidly improving breeds, by creating new breeds, by controlling disease through vaccines, and by inducing growth with additives. The breeding and maturation period of an animal could thus be considerably reduced, allowing for the improvement of a herd in just one life cycle.

In summary, biotechnology offers at least three important, potential avenues for the betterment of plant and animal species: (a) increasing resistance to adverse climatic, nutritional, and ecological conditions; (b) raising yields—whether by plant, worker, or machine; and (c) reducing losses in the post-harvest and industrial-processing phases. The following list includes potential products and techniques anticipated from some probable biotechnological advances:

• New nutrients, especially enzymes and essential amino acids;

• Tissue culture through new developments in plant biology (Mexico itself, because of its resource endowment and present technical capabilities, has good prospects for the rapid development and application of this technology);

• Nitrogen fixation in cereals and legumes; and

• Animal feed alternatives, particularly single-cell proteins and the utilization of organic wastes.

Equally important potential biotechnological advances in the food industry include:

• Development of vegetable proteins in basic foodstuffs, especially in corn, rice, other cereals, and legumes;

• Amino acids for use as nutritional supplements and "extenders";

• Biopolymers and polysaccharides (chemical components with multiple uses in the food and chemical industries);

• Utilization of recyclable wastes; and

• Exploitation of unconventional edible plants.

The Policy Dimension of Biotechnology

A Mexican national strategy for biotechnological development should certainly address Mexico's most fundamental food and agriculture problems. The predominant mode of production in the Mexican countryside unfortunately continues to be one of very small productive units, or *minifundio* land tenure patterns, and extensive rural poverty in agricultural regions. Biotechnology alone of course cannot solve these grave problems, but it *can* contribute to their alleviation. In the first place, many biotechnologies are relatively neutral to scale and require a low ratio of capital per unit of labor once the technology is developed, permitting their application in conditions of very small-scale exploitation. Since empirical research in this area is still lacking, however, the application of biotechnology to the *minifundio* remains an interesting hypothetical field to explore through field research.

Other potential applications of biotechnology involve increasing the productivity of technologies that are native to Mexico—for example, the *chinampas* (small garden tracts in ponds and lakes). Thus the most traditional agricultural practices can be linked to the cutting edge of technology. Using biotechnology, Gustavo Viniegra[6] has made a valuable contribution to the concept of rural development strategies in impoverished areas; this approach involves the *integration of agricultural cycles* to enhance the production of essential grains such as corn. After the produce has been harvested, the stalks, cobs, and the rest of the plant are used as an energy source and as feed for a small number of livestock. These strategies, similar to those used on integrated agro-ecological farms, demonstrate the advantages of the new biotechnology techniques to a complete ecosystem in zones characterized by poverty and seasonal crops.

Furthermore, this kind of technology can help preserve Mexico's diverse genetic wealth and conserve its soil. The Mexican germ plasm, among the richest in the world, is being threatened with partial extinction by widespread resort to "modern" agricultural practices that use improved seeds and agrochemicals intensively—as well as by urbanization. The germ plasm must be preserved. One way to do so would be by developing self-sustaining agro-ecosystems in zones of wide-ranging genetic variety—in anticipation of a transition from agriculture dominated by agrochemicals and mechanization to an agriculture of biological and cultivation practices that are in harmony with the ecosystems.

The problem of seeds—the fundamental phytogenetic resource—merits special attention. It is important to reinforce the view that access to basic natural resources should be assured to every nation and not only to a small group of multinational corporations. Mexico has defended this position before the FAO and other multilateral forums, and this principle should form an integral part of its agricultural policy. For instance, patents should not be granted only for the decoding of the genetic structure of an already existing plant. In any case, a transition from one era to another in agricultural technology can be made possible by biotechnology. A complex and multifaceted country like Mexico must be able to discriminate among policy options in this field in order to foster certain types of products; it must be able to put differentiated policies such as those advocated here into action and to make them work to advance its development.

Conclusion: Biotechnology and the U.S.-Mexican Relationship

If the developing countries of the South are unable to develop their own biotechnology with a degree of autonomy, they will be obliged to pay for the right to use products and technologies that are already being developed by the large multinational biotechnology firms. Moreover, they will have to rely upon technology packages that frequently do not correspond to national needs and local resources. For Mexico and other Third World countries, it is therefore imperative to confront the challenge and not attempt to evade the menacing aspects of developments in the field.

In this setting, what should be the character of the U.S.-Mexican relationship in this field? A cooperative biotechnology policy would benefit both Mexico and the United States and could offer an example of the creative management of interdependence. It is irrefutable that the United States leads—by a wide margin—in all areas of biotechnology. It is also true that Mexico is in turn a country with great promise for development in this field. Above all, the application of biotechnology presents Mexico with the possibility of addressing some of its most pressing social and economic needs. The fact that biotechnology is making highly dynamic and important advances at the production level of many different goods and processes makes it one of the most exciting areas for cooperation in the near future.

While biotechnology offers much promise, it also presents great risks. Among these is the danger that the external dependence of developing countries—including Mexico—will increase to an even greater degree if the industrial countries of the North master biotechnology and sell "packages" that complement the factor endowments of rich countries and frequently do not correspond to the local resources and national needs of poor countries. If the most advanced industrial nations are able to impose their own technological affinities and to enjoy a virtual monopoly on patents and commercialization, the countries of the Third World will remain disadvantaged trading partners. Biotechnology presents risks similar to past experience with international trade in the products of the famous "green revolution" and other agrochemical and agricultural advances that were dominated by certain countries and a small number of those countries' multinational corporations. This scenario may not yet have transpired in the case of biotechnology—and there still may be time to take steps to ensure that technological developments in this field are more equitably distributed among the nations of the world and suited to the needs and characteristics of poor countries.

The substitution of new products coming from biotechnological innovation for certain traditional Third World exports has lowered—and will continue to lower—some commodity prices. At times, the result has been the total displacement of a product from the market. One of the most notable examples of this is sugar cane, which formerly was critical to the balance of payments of many Latin American and other developing countries. Sugar cane has been dramatically squeezed out by corn syrup and other sweeteners. The African palm oil industry has suffered a similar fate. Through a monopoly on new technologies, the multinational firm Unilever has acquired an enormous advantage in productivity in the African palm oil industry that may displace many competing countries. Similar risks also exist with cereals and other food staples—given astonishing productivity increases due to biotechnological improvements in seeds and tissue culture techniques.

Another critical area relates to seeds. Genetic engineering plays a major role in seed development and its importance in this field will continue to increase further. Almost all seed development proceeds under the auspices of a virtual oligopoly from a small number of developed countries. The struggle for markets, as well as technological development—and even the jurisdiction of patents in seed products—are all of crucial interest to Mexico and other developing countries.

Again, Mexico has the potential to generate a very important comparative advantage in the field of biotechnology because it is endowed with a unique and huge pool of germ plasm—a formidable genetic arsenal that can provide the basis for many biotechnological experiments. The value of this key resource should not be underestimated in the formulation of any biotechnology development strategy. The genetic material should be conserved, studied, and eventually patented once research and development facilities have been incorporated. One of the biggest agricultural problems today—one that makes agriculture extremely vulnerable—is the growing dependence on a limited number of strains that require the use of a wide range of agrochemicals and artificial products. Therefore, the conservation, production, and development of this priceless germ plasm should be fundamental to Mexico's future strategy. In concrete terms, the high rate of extinction of species must be halted, and the number of mutations and the creation of new species should be maintained at levels and rates consistent with the occurrence of such changes in nature so that the germ plasm of the country is not reduced.

In the case of trade, relations between the United States and Mexico in agriculture and livestock are intense and increasingly unfavorable to Mexico.[7] Meanwhile, trade has both increased and changed in composition. The United States produces a surplus of industrial inputs, technology, machinery, and finished products—as well as of basic grains. Mexico, on the other hand, has maintained an advantage only in fresh produce. Mexico needs to reverse this situation, as its level of development dictates that it be a net importer of many other goods and services. A discussion of the viability of such a strategy will not be attempted here, but the concept of transforming the trade structure to reflect better the comparative advantages of both economies is worthy of further examination.

Mexico should be able to continue to sell the United States increasing amounts of vegetables, fruit, meat products, and processed foods, and it should be able to reduce its basic grain purchases. It is possible to conceive of a strategy of net transfer of technology to Mexico that coincides with and facilitates the transition from agrochemicals to biotechnology. Such a strategy will require from Mexico a coordinated and well-implemented policy for agriculture and for food—and, from the United States, an attitude of cooperation and goodwill.

The Mexican strategy should give definition to a specific biotechnology policy that anticipates the underlying tendencies of this process and permits the creation of a regulatory framework for Mexico. In doing so, a capacity should emerge to adapt and adopt technology. The policy should also have other elements—among them the education of highly trained personnel—keeping in mind that biotechnology will be developed through improvements in many disciplines, not just in biology. Programs to promote biotechnology should include appropriate financial instruments, provide for the sharing of investment risks, and strengthen and sustain needed links among the academic, governmental, and productive sectors. Institutional innovation and strengthening are as essential as providing a new set of rules and norms to regulate and promote biotechnology.

Mexico likewise needs to have a clear understanding of the capital goods and scientific instruments required by the field and only partly available from native manufacturers. It must also improve upon the regulatory framework for foreign investment, technology transfer, and the operation of multinational firms in the Mexican economy. Suffice it to say that given the U.S. primacy in the field, the regulatory apparatus should include joint investments and enterprises only when there is truly a transfer of useful and appropriate technology.

The United States, on the other hand, may well have no interest in creating a specific industrial biotechnology policy. Even so, it can provide assistance so that Mexico can better anticipate and accelerate key areas of the technological revolution in biology in order to alleviate some of Mexico's grave developmental deficiencies. For example, assistance from U.S. universities and companies could greatly improve human resources in some crucial fields such as the production of one-celled proteins, alternatives to pasture grazing, vaccines, and grafting.

Mexican regulatory legislation of U.S. investment in these areas need not be understood within the narrow parameters of the limitation of activities, but rather in terms of the optimization of mutual benefits from activities concentrating on the provision of essential goods and services. Given the open nature of the U.S. economy and the proximity of the United States and Mexico, an underexplored avenue that warrants serious consideration is the possibility of Mexican capital and technicians participating in U.S. biotechnology companies. Mexican participation in the capital and management of biotechnology enterprises in the United States could offer an element of equity and transfer—in management expertise as well as in technology.

For Mexico, it will be essential to develop biotechnology to function also within the needs of the peasant or *campesino* economy of the impoverished *minifundio*. While methods to augment the production of exports should clearly be sought, this must not be to the exclusion of the development of nutrients and improvements in foods for mass consumption. The new biotechnology strategy should utilize biomass potential to its fullest, reduce the consumption of energy (especially in the rural sector), and improve agricultural and industrial productivity. To reap the benefits of the genetic revolution and to develop comparative advantages in international trade, Mexico must differentiate among specific food chains of strategic significance (nutritional, export potential, etc.) according to its own socioeconomic priorities. For instance, wastes such as stalks and other agro-industrial sub-products should be recycled, creating alternatives for, among other things, feeding livestock without using basic nutritional grains for this purpose and providing rural energy sources. Biotechnology should also be used to resolve the frequent contradictions between cattle raising and agriculture by producing feed alternatives so that the grains now used to feed livestock can be used to provide food for people. This would be accomplished principally by developing fermentations and single-celled proteins for livestock consumption.

Finally, in biotechnology perhaps as in no other field, cooperation among Latin American countries—given their level of development,

abundance of natural resources, and relative industrial maturity—
would allow them to reach the "cutting edge" in some strategic areas.
Certainly Mexico, Brazil, and Argentina—and to a lesser extent Co-
lombia, Peru, and Chile—possess the institutions, and valuable
human capital, as well as sufficient complementarities among them, to
make it desirable to seek mutual benefits through cooperation in this
field. A networking program should be initiated and might usefully
start by defining the more promising and strategic areas for the region.
A priority task certainly should be to evaluate, and launch policies to
conserve and enhance, the germ plasm of Latin America.

Herein lies the challenge for Mexico in this field: It can take
advantage of the benefits offered by the level of development and
proximity of the United States only to the extent that it has itself
developed in this pivotal area. In conclusion, biotechnology offers great
opportunities, but not without significant risks. It is not too late for
Mexico to develop a coherent and articulate biotechnology strategy and
avoid a retreat into backwardness and dependence. Far from shutting
out exchange and cooperation with the United States, Mexico needs to
weight its policies according to its actual needs and resources and
make biotechnology a mechanism to accelerate progress and equity.

Notes

Note: The translation of this chapter from Spanish was prepared by Vanessa Cano.

[1] Biotechnologies such as fermentation and some other medical and agricultural
practices have of course existed since ancient times.

[2] See Economic Commission for Latin America (ECLA; or CEPAL in Spanish)
*Reunión de expertos CEPAL/UNESCO sobre las consecuencias para América Latina y el
Caribe de los adelantos de la biotecnología incluida la ingeniería genética*, Montevideo,
Uruguay, November 21-25, 1983 (ECLA Document LC/G.1315, August 27, 1984).

[3] Rodolfo Quintero has created an interesting model that illustrates this point. See
Rodolfo Quintero Ramírez, ed., *Perspectiva de la biotecnología en México* (Mexico: Javier
Barros Sierra Foundation and CONACYT, 1985).

[4] Ibid.

[5] Ibid.

[6] G. Gustavo Viniegra, "Más alimento pero, para quién?," *Cuadernos de Nutrición*,
No. 5/6, 1982, pp. 25-40.

[7] Cassio Luiselli, *The Mexican Road to Food Self-Sufficiency: A Normative View*,
(unpublished research paper, Center for U.S.-Mexican Studies, University of California,
San Diego, 1985).

Chapter 8

The Mexican Pharmochemical and Pharmaceutical Industries

Joan Brodovsky

The development of the Mexican pharmochemical and pharmaceutical industries illustrates some of the issues and differences that intrude on relations between Mexico and the United States and need to be addressed in the public policy of both countries. This chapter describes the Mexican pharmaceutical and pharmochemical industries, examines their advances and problems, and suggests how events in these industries impinge on U.S.-Mexican relations.

The Mexican government's industrial policies and legislation have contributed abundantly to the growth and development of the pharmaceutical and pharmochemical industries in Mexico. After at least forty years of protection directed toward giving Mexican industry a head start (especially through import restrictions, tax incentives, and cheap loans) and about twenty years of legislation (relating to technology transfer, foreign investment, and patents) enacted to reduce the financial advantages that large international companies could have over domestic companies, Mexico has indeed succeeded in establishing a remarkably diverse industrial base. Moreover, citizens who previously remained outside the money economy are rapidly being incorporated into the consumer market. In the pharmochemical area, Mexico manufactures a variety of basic drugs not produced in any other country south of the Río Grande. In finished pharmaceuticals, Mexico is equal to any developed nation in traditional technology. In short, the Mexican policies worked.

Recently, however, these same policies, or their extensions, are weakening these industries. The decapitalization of the pharmaceutical sector began some years ago. Its effects are seen in the large number of laboratories that have merged, closed, or been sold; in the number of pharmaceuticals that have been discontinued; and in the increasingly frequent experience of discovering that previously obtainable medicines are not available when needed. The tendency of the pharmaceutical companies in Mexico is to eliminate their older, cheaper products and to substitute new, more expensive—and more profitable—drugs, or even cosmetics. The source of this problem of unavailability lies in the administration of Mexico's price control policy. The result has been a scarcity of drugs.

In the pharmochemical industry, after about fifteen years without patent protection for health products and with restrictions on the licensing of technology, many companies manufacture with their own technology the bulk pharmochemicals that were commercially important twenty to thirty years ago. Mexican expertise in this area has grown remarkably. This growth, however, has been in technological areas now being discarded in the developed world, and Mexico's ability to "license-in" new technologies is now hampered.

The technological advances of the 1980s in the health area have been quite as amazing as those in electronics, and Mexico has not been acquiring the new know-how. Today—to cite just a few examples—Brazil and Argentina manufacture kidney dialysis filters, but Mexico does not; Argentina has technology for Transderm® patches, but Mexico does not; and menopausal gonadotropins (the only fertility drug effective for many childless couples) are available throughout Latin America, but not sold in Mexico.

Mexico today is seen as a source of certain basic pharmaceuticals (aspirin and penicillins, for example) that are considered in the developed world to have unacceptably low profit margins or unacceptably high risks (poisonous effluents, for example) in their manufacture.

Moreover, Mexico itself now imports not only all the new pharmochemicals coming onto the world market that are raw materials for the finished pharmaceuticals made in Mexico, but also many finished high-tech medical products, such as dermal patches, surgical adhesive, special sutures, and intravenous pumps. What is alarming is not the fact that it is importing these finished goods at present, but that companies in Mexico—both Mexican and international firms—appear to have no plans to acquire the important new technologies from abroad or to develop them domestically.

Mexican legislation and policies of the past forty years attempted to promote the development of the country's industrial sector so as to attain international norms, but now many of these same policies and laws are an impediment to Mexico's pharmaceutical and pharmochemical industries. Both of these industries are today losing ground. Their technological expertise is behind that of the developed countries, and both they and their consumers are experiencing the impact of this retardation.

Global Technological Change in the Pharmaceutical and Pharmochemical Industries

The pharmaceutical and pharmochemical industries together cover the manufacture of finished drugs—from the synthesis of a chemical substance (or pharmochemical) with curative properties to the formulation of this drug into a tablet, suppository, or other pharmaceutical form that can be administered to a patient. As will be discussed later, the manufacture of active chemical substances (also referred to here as pharmochemicals, bulk drugs, or bulk pharmaceuticals) by the pharmochemical industry and the manufacture of finished pharmaceuticals (also referred to here as finished drugs or medicines) by the pharmaceutical industry involve the use of quite different technologies.

Pharmaceuticals

The manufacture of finished pharmaceuticals involves specialized mixing operations to produce, for example, a tablet that will not disintegrate in the bottle or dissolve in the mouth as it is swallowed, but that will quickly dissolve in the stomach, permitting the active chemical it contains to be rapidly absorbed into the bloodstream and carried by it to all the body tissues. The precision of pharmaceutical technologies must be strictly controlled during the manufacturing process by qualitative and quantitative assays to ensure that the finished drug contains what it claims, in the amounts stated, and that it will cause the medical effect desired.

All of the common pharmaceutical forms—tablets, suppositories, injectable solutions, creams, and intravenous solutions—have existed since the early years of this century. Until the 1970s, developments in pharmaceutical technology concentrated on production efficiency, speed, and safety rather than on basic changes in products. The more recent advances in pharmaceuticals, however, involve technologies ranging in complexity from a simple skin patch to a dialysis machine, and innovations are being introduced continually. For decades, drugs have been delivered to their sites of action in the body via tablets, creams, syrups, injectable solutions, and the like. Their action is generally systemic: The drug reaches all parts of the body, regardless of the particular organ or area needing treatment. In the last ten years, however, products have been developed that completely change the manner of delivery. Progestasert®, for example, is an intrauterine device impregnated with a contraceptive hormone that is released directly into the uterus, the target organ; the amount of hormone that penetrates to farther parts of the body is a fraction of that received by a woman who takes oral contraceptive tablets, yet the uterus itself receives a therapeutic dose. Microcapsules—tiny beads made of a mixture of polymer and drug—have been developed to control the dose of the medication they carry; the beads, enclosed in capsules, are formulated to fix their dissolution rate, reducing the frequency of medication by allowing slower or longer release. And Transderm®, a skin patch that transmits a drug through the skin at a constant rate, can feed a nearby target organ or area just the right amount of medication; a Transderm® nitroglycerine chest patch, for example, can keep an angina pectoris patient free of cardiac pain for a specific period, and a Transderm® scopalamine patch behind the ear can prevent seasickness symptoms for twenty-four hours.

Pharmochemicals

The production of pharmochemicals involves chemical synthesis on a massive scale; large quantities of raw materials are processed at a time, with quality control mainly limited to assays of the final product.

Chemical research to develop new compounds with pharmacological effects was fruitful in the 1950s and early 1960s, but the rate at which new compounds appeared on the market decreased considerably in the 1970s. The introduction a few years ago of cimetidine (Tagamet) marked a resurgence of drug development. At about the same time, recombinant genetic techniques for modifying bacterial metabolism opened new possibilities—already being realized today in the cases of insulin and growth hormone—for manufacturing by fermentation many substances previously obtained from natural, and therefore finite, sources.

Thus the technologies that are transforming these health-related industries include innovative systems for drug "delivery" to target sites in the body, new chemical substances with pharmacological effects, and the use of recombinant genetic techniques to modify bacteria for use in the synthesis of complex molecules for therapeutic use. Mexico's capacity to absorb these technologies is limited in part by its inadequate scientific infrastructure and further hampered by its laws and public policies.

Mexico's Pharmaceutical Industry

Early Development

In Mexico, the pharmaceutical industry was launched and reached maturity between 1920 and 1950—the period during which most foreign firms established subsidiaries in the country. In the 1940s, the wartime interruption of shipments of finished drugs from Europe, and, on the positive side, the medical services offered by the newly created Mexican Social Security Institute (IMSS), both fostered local pharmaceutical manufacturing operations. Indeed, the growth of the industry in the 1940s and 1950s was nearly exponential. By the 1960s, the pharmaceutical industry supplied virtually the entire Mexican market and was exporting to Central and South America.

The number of pharmaceutical firms grew from 60 in 1940 to over 1,000 in 1965. Of these establishments, however, only about 60 foreign and perhaps 40 Mexican firms could be considered truly professional pharmaceutical manufacturers. Most of the remainder were distributors, packaging and labeling operations run by persons with contacts in government purchasing offices, or rudimentary establishments that operated cost-cutting manufacturing activities located in facilities that for the most part lacked adequate supervision and quality control by professional pharmacists. In 1978, legislation enacted to control pharmaceutical and pharmochemical manufacturing reduced the number of laboratories to about 300; by 1986, there were 220.[1]

Mexican laboratories manufacture all the traditional pharmaceutical dosage forms, such as tablets, coated tablets, freeze-dried powders, soft and hard capsules, suppositories, creams, syrups, and oral, opthalmic, and injectable solutions. Related industries are appearing: There are now sixty-five companies that manufacture hospital supplies and thirty-eight that make diagnostic reagents for clinical laboratories.[2]

The Industry's Domestic Market

The dominant characteristic of the Mexican domestic pharmaceutical market is official price control over all finished drugs. The Ministry of Commerce and Industrial Development establishes the maximum price permitted for every drug sold on the private market. It also determines a price above which bids are not accepted for each generic drug open to competitive bidding in the government sector. As a result, the prices of common medicines in Mexico are as low as one-tenth the price of equivalent drugs in developed countries, and the prices of most drugs are one-third to one-half the U.S. price.

Nearly all of the finished drugs sold in Mexico are made in Mexico. For years, sales of imported finished pharmaceuticals represented less than 1 per cent of the total, but since 1980 they have reached nearly 2 per cent.[3] Exports of Mexican drugs—representing about 2 per cent of total sales—traditionally have gone to Central and South America. Since 1980, the value of exports, which reflects both the devaluation of the peso and an increase in the unit sales of products leaving the country, has been above 4 per cent, amounting to some $U.S. 40–60 million per year. New markets have been found in Africa, the Caribbean, and Asia.

For many years the domestic market for drugs held at about $1 billion. Recent devaluations of the peso, which have not been accompanied by compensating increases in official drug prices, have caused that value to drop to less than $500 million. International companies in Mexico supply a little more than half the value of this market.

The finished pharmaceuticals sold to the Mexican government are distributed through the various national social security systems, especially the Mexican Social Security Institute (IMSS), which has thirty-five million members, and the State Workers Institute for Social Security and Services (ISSSTE). The remainder is sold to private pharmacies, hospitals, physicians, and distributors. Although 15–25 per cent of the *value* of the market is attributed to government sales, nearly 40 per cent of the sales *units* is destined for the public sector, as the unit prices of products sold to the government are lower. Also, the government directs its purchases toward older, and therefore largely cheaper, drugs. The average unit price of drugs to the private consumer is about twice that of drugs purchased by the government for its social security programs.

Sales to the government are handled through an annual open bidding competition that favors those companies with majority Mexican capital. Awards are not exclusive; as many as three laboratories may win contracts for each particular item. The government accepts bids only for those drugs listed on the *Cuadro Básico de Medicamentos del Sector Salud,* (National Health List), which includes about 500 presentations of 330 generics.[4]

In the past decade, Mexican-owned companies sold about 35 per cent of their output to the government; in 1983, however, as a result of the national economic crisis, that proportion rose to over 60 per cent. Before 1983, the international firms in Mexico—which limit their sales to the government because they are less profitable—directed about 15 per cent of their sales to the government. In 1983, that proportion suddenly rose to 23 per cent. This increase in government purchases in 1983 and later reflects the greater use of the social security systems by a public receiving a reduced real income as a result of the sharp economic downturn.

Table 1. Sales of Finished Pharmaceuticals, Mexico (millions of pesos)

	1979	1980	1981	1982	1983	1984	1985
Total Sales[a]:	23,300	27,600	33,500	48,100	106,000	173,000	383,000
Imports	138	529	529	540	1,050	1,100	2,870
% of total sales	(0.6)	(1.9)	(1.6)	(1.1)	(1.0)	(0.6)	(0.7)
Exports	600	805	1,380	3,420	6,300	7,730	14,700
% of total sales	(2.6)	(2.9)	(4.1)	(7.1)	(5.9)	(4.5)	(3.8)
Average Exchange Rate (pesos/dollar)	23	23	23	60	150	184	319

[a] Domestic sales, imports, and exports.

Source: National Registry of the Pharmaceutical Industry, SECOFI, Mexico City.

Table 2. Sales of Finished Pharmaceuticals by Sector, Mexico (millions of pesos)

	1979	1980	1981	1982	1983	1984	1985
Total Sales[a]	23,300	27,600	33,500	48,100	106,000	173,000	383,000
to government	3,400	4,700	5,600	8,600	26,000	39,000	72,000
to private sector	19,900	22,900	27,900	39,500	79,600	133,000	311,000
Mexican Firms	6,300	8,000	10,400	13,600	31,600	52,000	100,000
to government	1,600	2,100	2,600	3,600	12,400	22,700	38,200
to private sector	4,700	5,900	7,800	10,000	19,200	29,300	62,000
International Firms	17,000	19,600	23,100	34,500	74,000	121,000	283,000
to government	1,700	2,600	3,000	5,000	13,800	16,600	34,000
to private sector	15,300	17,000	20,100	29,500	60,200	104,000	249,000
Average Exchange Rate (pesos/dollar)	23	23	23	60	150	184	319

[a] Domestic sales, imports, and exports.
Source: National Registry of the Pharmaceutical Industry, SECOFI, Mexico City.

Although the private market is dominated by the international firms, Mexican-owned companies find niches in some specialty areas, for example, in direct sales to physicians—especially those in the provinces, who sell the drugs they prescribe directly to their patients—and in sales to private hospitals, which purchase generics.

In the past, virtually all of the drugs available in the advanced countries have been available and manufactured as finished pharmaceuticals in Mexico. In recent years, however, the number of specific drugs available in Mexico has declined, due to the elimination by the health authorities of ineffective or unsafe products on the one hand, and to the elimination of unprofitable products by the drug companies on the other. During the last three years, residents of Mexico frequently have discovered that a drug prescribed by their doctor is not on the pharmacy shelves, or that a drug they have been using regularly suddenly is not available. Sometimes the drug has been discontinued, and sometimes production or distribution has been temporarily suspended due to the lack of raw materials or due to the manufacturer's deliberate response to official limitation on the price of the product. In 1985, for example, products that could not be obtained (some temporarily and some indefinitely) included: codeine tablets, chorionic gonadotropins, chlorodiazepoxide (Librium), chloroquin or equivalent, and epinephrine; phenobarbital in infant formulation; and menopausal gonadotropins, Transderm®, scopalamine, and influenza vaccine.

Product Development

The sources of manufacturing technology for finished pharmaceuticals are largely internal. Some of the foreign firms receive formulations for new products from their home offices, but most have autonomy both to select new products and to develop the formulations with Mexican excipients.

The Mexican laboratories either develop their own formulations of a generic drug or they contract the work with a Mexican consultant who specializes in pharmaceutical product development. The laboratory that seeks development abroad for generic drugs is the exception.

The larger Mexican firms purchase "dossiers" from foreign pharmaceutical enterprises that have developed novel active chemicals. The dossier gives the medical and pharmacological data needed by the laboratory to register the product with the health authorities. The foreign firm, normally a unique manufacturer, then sells the raw material to the Mexican company, licensing out to the Mexican company the right to commercialize the drug in Mexico. The Mexican company then normally develops in-house the formulation for the finished product.

Mexican pharmacists are trained in new product development. Both the National Autonomous University of Mexico (UNAM) and the National Polytechnical Institute (IPN) have for decades offered degrees in industrial pharmaceutical sciences. Today the younger Metropolitan Autonomous University and at least a dozen provincial universities also graduate industrial pharmacists.

In the case of traditional pharmaceuticals, production technology in Mexican firms can be as advanced as in others elsewhere in the world, although some laboratories still use outdated equipment when a newer technology does not represent a cost advantage. Thanks to government regulations and pressure from the Mexican Social Security Institute (IMSS), the laboratories generally adhere to "good manufacturing practices" similar to those promulgated by the U.S. Food and Drug Administration (FDA). Although as recently as 1974 a United Nations consultant lamented the "lack of appreciation for in-process quality control and good manufacturing practices,"[5] in the last ten years plants have been paying attention to such matters as the inviolability of sterile areas, the danger of cross-contamination, and the need for in-process quality control.

The quality-control technology of both Mexican domestic and foreign pharmaceutical companies in Mexico tends to be a few years behind that of U.S. and European companies. Since production volumes in a Mexican pharmaceutical company are usually low by international standards, the purchase of expensive equipment can be prohibitive. Nevertheless, the latest analytical techniques are usually available in the country in the IMSS, in private analytical service laboratories, or in universities.

Obstacles to Future Development

As long as the advances in world pharmaceutical technology remained in the areas of production efficiency, speed, and safety, and not in any intrinsic change in the products, Mexican companies were able to keep up with global technological changes by purchasing new tablet-making or packaging equipment or by instituting routine quality-assurance procedures in production.

But with the appearance of new drug delivery systems, which can represent great therapeutic advantages, Mexico's ability to provide its population with the most effective available drugs has declined. Both Mexican and foreign-owned companies seek new products and their technologies abroad; they want novelty both in the active ingredient and in the delivery system.

As earlier indicated, the technologies for many novel drug delivery systems have not been acquired in Mexico. Since the techniques cannot be protected by Mexican patents, their inventors are reluctant to license the know-how. For example, some micro-encapsulation technologies, used for slow or regulated dosage forms, are not available locally. Soft capsule manufacture is controlled by three companies that have equipment for large volume production; other companies subcontract their soft capsules with one of these. The manufacturing technologies for the new products based on constant velocity release systems such as Ocusert® and Transderm® have not appeared in Mexico. Products such as these, if they are offered on the local market, are imported in finished form to be packaged and sold domestically.

The factors that impede Mexican companies' acquisition of the new pharmaceutical technologies include their cost relative to the income they could produce, the reluctance of foreign licensors due to what they perceive to be inadequate protection of intellectual property and restrictive regulations, and the lack of professionals with training and practical experience in these latest developments.

Price control and profits. The Mexican pharmaceutical industry in general has been decapitalizing due to its inability to obtain official prices that permit an adequate profit. In a 1986 series of in-depth interviews with twenty-two pharmaceutical and pharmochemical companies, the average profit margin reported was less than 4 per cent—a figure representing a real loss in light of the 60-per-cent annual inflation rate of 1985. The cost of developing a new technology or licensing it cannot be entertained today by many companies in this industry.

As a result of industry-government confrontations in late 1986 and early 1987, significant increases in the prices of private market pharmaceuticals have been permitted. There is now a tacit understanding that prices may be adjusted according to a formula based on *Banco de México* (the central bank) indices of consumer and production prices. In return, the industry is selling a number of basic pharmaceuticals as generics, in government outlets, with only marginal profit.

Legal and regulatory factors that discourage foreign licensing. Most sophisticated technologies in the pharmaceutical area have been developed by international companies with years of experience working in developing countries. These companies consider the Mexican technology transfer laws and regulations very unfavorable to product and process innovators and prefer not to license in Mexico. Most international companies today even refuse to grant their own Mexican subsidiaries licenses for their newest technologies. Some of the Mexican companies perceive the technology transfer laws as a bureaucratic impediment and for that reason are reluctant to consider newly offered technology or to initiate a search for foreign technology.

In this two-sided reluctance are involved a) the lack of patent protection for new products on the market[6], b) the traditional lack of enforcement in Mexico of the existing patent laws, c) the time—and consequent cost—of dealing with the National Registry for Technology Transfer even when patents are not involved (they usually are not), and d) the limitations placed by the law on both the licensor and licensee in the technology transfer process.

Lack of professional access to latest developments in field. Mexico's scientific and technical professionals have no experience with the novel pharmaceutical technologies. Even so, the industry has an excess of capable people who have the basic technical knowledge needed to assimilate the new concepts and techniques. Thus the lack of specific knowledge in Mexico presents no more than a temporary hindrance to acquiring new technologies.

Mexico's Pharmochemical Industry

In the case of many of the bulk pharmochemicals it produces, Mexico is making substances that have passed their market prime and is competing with other advanced developing countries to sell them on the world market. The drug companies in the United States, Europe, and Japan are shifting their own pharmochemical manufacturing from the older and now highly competitive to the innovative, high risk, and high profit drugs. This situation did not always prevail.

The pharmochemical industry began in Mexico in the 1940s, when different Mexican companies, led by Syntex, S.A., developed technologies to produce steroid hormones from the diosgenin obtained from barbasco, a native plant. By the late 1960s, there were six steroid manufacturers, all foreign-owned. In 1975, steroids were ranked tenth in importance among Mexico's exports. Although Mexico had enjoyed a monopoly position in the supply of steroids to the world market, many foreign firms were developing alternative technologies that became economically feasible after the Mexican government company, Proquivemex, took over the harvest and sale of barbasco in 1975, multiplying by 35 the price of that raw material. Mexico's four remaining manufacturers now supply less than 10 per cent of the world's steroids.[7]

In the meantime, both the private sector and the Mexican government became interested in manufacturing bulk pharmaceuticals in Mexico, especially since overpricing by the importers was evident. In the 1960s, a few extraction or "last-step" processes were developed to obtain products such as caffeine, aspirin, phenylbutazone, and a few inorganic salts. By 1975, sixty-eight companies were making sixty-seven products, accounting for 40 per cent of the value of the market. By 1986, eighty companies were manufacturing over 300 distinct chemically active principals, or pharmochemicals, many of which are themselves produced from Mexican raw materials. In value, about half of the pharmaceutical industry's raw materials (pharmochemicals) are now produced in Mexico.

Although twenty-three of the pharmochemical companies also produce finished pharmaceuticals, most are not associated with the laboratories that make medicines. A few produce bulk drugs for their own use, but most sell all or part of their production on the open market. While seventeen of the pharmochemical producers are subsidiaries of international firms, sixty-three are Mexican-owned.

In value terms, a little over half the bulk pharmaceuticals used by the pharmaceutical laboratories are produced in Mexico. The self-sufficiency of the Mexican pharmochemical industry has increased from 35 per cent in 1977 to 57 per cent in 1983.[8] Futhermore, the industry exports 10–20 per cent of its production, representing about $U.S. 60 million a year.

Although the government is empowered to set prices for pharmochemicals, in practice it controls only those for acetyl salicylic acid (aspirin) and antibiotics. For this reason alone, the relationship between the government authorities and the pharmochemical manufacturers is somewhat less antagonistic than is that between the same authorities and the pharmaceutical laboratories. Pharmochemical purchases for use as raw materials by the manufacturers of finished pharmaceuticals in Mexico reached $U.S. 330 million in 1983, of which nearly $U.S. 200 million were for locally manufactured material. Mexican-owned companies have dominated this market, producing about 60 per cent of the total (in value terms) in the early 1980s.

Even though the Mexican Social Security Institute (IMSS) has a program to promote Mexican manufacture of the generics on the *Cuadro Básico*, and the government-owned pharmaceutical laboratory, Proquivemex, purchases pharmochemicals, the government does not exert the direct influence over these markets that it does over those of finished pharmaceuticals.

Technologies in Use in Mexico

Most traditional chemical and biological methods are employed to produce pharmochemicals. Organic synthesis is the process used for the majority of the chemical substances, and fermentation is used especially for antibiotics. Nearly 70 per cent of the technologies presently in use in Mexican pharmochemical plants were developed locally. The remainder represent both the technologies licensed by foreign firms to Mexican subsidiaries and those licensed by Mexican firms from foreign manufacturers or patent holders. Licensed technologies are subject to constant development and improvement by the Mexican

Table 3. Sales of Bulk Pharmochemicals, Mexico (millions of pesos)

	1979	1980	1981	1982	1983	1984	1985
Total domestic consumption of pharmochemicals	8,270	8,510	11,900	20,800	49,800	65,700	130,000
Domestic sales of Mexican-made pharmochemicals	3,680	3,870	5,660	8,930	28,600	39,400	67,900
Imports	4,590	4,650	6,280	11,900	21,200	26,300	62,500
Exports	900	1,360	1,520	2,400	9,600	9,200	18,200

Source: National Registry of the Pharmaceutical Industry, SECOFI, Mexico City.

Table 4. Sales of Bulk Pharmochemicals by Manufacturer, Mexico (millions of pesos)

	1979	1980	1981	1982	1983	1984	1985
Total sales of Mexican-made pharmochemicals (including exports)	4,570	5,060	7,290	11,200	36,300	48,600	86,100
by Mexican-owned firms	2,880	2,930	4,960	6,650	23,500	26,200	70,800
by International firms	1,690	2,130	2,330	4,550	12,800	22,400	15,300

Source: National Registry of the Pharmaceutical Industry, SECOFI, Mexico City.

licensee. Often after a few years they are unrecognizable to the original licensor, who nevertheless continues to receive a royalty.

The steroid technologies developed in the country made Mexico the world leader from the 1940s until the mid-1960s, when Syntex moved its research group to Palo Alto. Since then, chemical research in steroids has shifted to the United States and to Europe, and the Mexican chemists trained in that specialty have found other work. Even the universities and research institutions have in effect eliminated steroid research.

Using traditional synthetic procedures, the Mexican pharmochemical industry can develop manufacturing technology for nearly any chemical structure that requires raw materials available on the free market. In the near future, however, the development of fermentation technology for the economical manufacture of some presently expensive drugs will be limited by the country's genetic research capabilities. Theoretically, a Mexican company or institute could develop the strain of microorganisms it needs for a desired product, or it could obtain it and its attendant know-how through licensing. In practice, however, Mexico's research in recombinant genetics is directed toward a few specific projects. The country does not have the capacity to handle all the biogenetic pharmaceutical projects it could use. Because of increasing wariness on the part of foreign investors of Mexico's restrictive laws on technology transfer and its lack of patent protection, the possibilities of obtaining licenses in this area are limited.

The technological levels of other areas of the pharmochemical industry range from the crude, as in the case of some extractive procedures, to the sophisticated, as in the case of antibiotic fermentation reactions that require precise control of many reaction parameters. The quality of Mexican bulk pharmaceuticals is improving constantly—now propelled by a policy of granting import permits for materials when those made in Mexico do not meet the specifications required by the buyer.

As Mexico—now a full member of the General Agreement on Tariffs and Trade (GATT)—lowers trade barriers on its previously protected pharmochemicals, the number of bulk drugs produced domestically will surely diminish.

Obstacles to Future Development

The factors that impede acqusition of new pharmochemical technologies by Mexican companies include the following:

Lack of patent protection. Mexican chemical companies frequently search for existing foreign technology to license, for acquiring a license can represent a large savings in cost, in terms of the time required for start-up. But the international companies that have know-how in the pharmochemical field prefer to block potential competitors to ensure recovery of R & D costs by preventing unlicensed competition. Mexico's lack of patent protection has made it nearly impossible to obtain technology for the synthesis of new pharmochemicals. Know-how for older drugs can be got, but often what is offered is obsolete.

Cost factors. The cost of a license for know-how is not the severe impediment for most pharmochemical manufacturers that it is for pharmaceutical laboratories, for they do not suffer the same pressure of price controls. Even so, one manufacturer of bulk antibiotics (which are price-controlled) complains bitterly that his allowed prices are based on his costs—thus he is rewarded for inefficiency. When he has reduced costs, his official price also has been reduced. This manufacturer does not seek licenses.

Relations Between the Mexican Government and the Industries

The relationship between the Mexican government and the phar-mochemical and pharmaceutical industries is—as in most countries—frequently antagonistic. The government is charged with protecting the health and well-being of the population. To carry out its responsibility, it uses measures such as licenses, permits, registrations, price controls, and inspections—all of which are unpalatable to the industry. At the same time, the government promotes industrial development through measures such as financial incentives, tax breaks, loans, import restrictions, and export rebates—actions that naturally are applauded by the companies. The industries, for their part, must show a profit to their stockholders. They thus find the government's regulatory actions inhibiting and irritating.

There should be only two sides to the relationship: government and companies. In reality, however, the relationship is three-sided, since the government grants those companies with more than 50-percent Mexican ownership certain advantages, for example permits to manufacture bulk pharmochemical substances such as cimetidine (which Smith-Kline, its original patentor, has been prohibited from making in Mexico). The large companies with majority international capital vigorously protest this discrimination. Even so, they sometimes obtain special concessions or advantageous positions simply because they—unlike the smaller Mexican companies—can afford investments, legal actions, and costly marketing techniques.

The large number of government agencies that affect the phar-mochemical and pharmaceutical industries demonstrates the complexity of the interaction between private enterprise and the government and is indicative of the influence and the degree of regulation exerted on these industries. The companies consider the cost of compliance to be not only in pesos, but in the inordinate amount of time taken by employees, staff, and executives to deal with this bureaucracy.

The Mexican government regulates the pharmaceutical and pharmochemical industries through the obvious channels, including the tax authorities and the health ministry, but other official organizations also influence or control the industry. The most important entities are the ministries of finance, health, commerce and industrial development, and agriculture.

- *Ministry of Finance and Public Credit (SHCP).* The SHCP collects taxes on income and value added. It administers tax incentive plans for such activities as technological development, production of bulk drugs of special interest to the Mexican government, exporting, and moving operations away from the Mexico City metropolitan area.

- *Ministry of Health (SSA).* The SSA exercises sanitary control over the processing, import, and export of finished pharmaceuticals and the registration of new products. It receives applications for new pharmochemicals under investigation and new pharmaceutical products. The sanitary authorities limit the registration of new pharmaceuticals to those that clinical tests in Mexico have proved to be effective. In addition, the SSA has been reviewing previously registered products and requiring definitive proof of their efficacy and safety. This activity has removed some useless or dangerous products from the list of available drugs. Furthermore, the SSA officials have considerable discretionary powers when reviewing applications for new drug registration. The SSA also inspects pharmaceutical manufacturing installations on a regular basis. It can and does fine or suspend operations of laboratories that have violated safety regulations in manufacturing or have put unsafe products on the market.

- *Ministry of Commerce and Industrial Development (SECOFI).* SECOFI sets the maximum permitted prices for finished pharmaceuticals, bulk antibiotics, and bulk aspirin. It has the legal faculty to set prices for all bulk pharmochemicals, but has not yet exercised it. In the 1960s and 1970s, when inflation was minimal, the original maximum allowed price of a finished pharmaceutical product rarely was changed. Until 1987, drug prices were reviewed on an irregular basis. Today there is a tacit arrangement to review prices every three months.

SECOFI also grants import and export permits and sets duties for imported products. For forty years the importation of finished pharmaceuticals has required a (rarely granted) permit. The pharmochemicals manufactured in Mexico have been similarly protected, although imported products are allowed when the petitioner can show that the Mexican-produced material does not meet his quality control standards.

In 1987, in a move that the Mexican-owned pharmaceutical firms view as a threat, SECOFI lifted the requirement for a permit to import finished pharmaceuticals that contain antibiotics, vitamins, or antacids. The reasons for this government action are not clear to these firms, which have responded with newspaper advertisements protesting the move.

Through the National Registry of the Pharmaceutical Industry (the *Padrón*), SECOFI controls the companies that are permitted to produce bulk pharmochemicals and finished pharmaceuticals, as well as other health products. Registration in the *Padrón* is granted for one to three years; renewal depends on an inspection of the facilities and a review of the products manufactured.

The pharmaceutical laboratories—whose number was reduced from more than 1,000 (including distributors) to 200 when the *Padrón* was instituted in 1979—must demonstrate effective in-plant quality control and assurance and the use of good manufacturing practices.

The pharmochemical manufacturers must show a pattern of progressive integration of Mexican raw materials into their manufacturing processes. Their registrations specify the products they are allowed to manufacture. The products they manufacture by simple, last-step transformations of chemical substances nearly identical to the active pharmochemical may be denied registration on the *Padrón*—effectively revoking the permission to manufacture.

- *Ministry of Agriculture and Hydraulic Resources (SARH).* The SARH regulates veterinary drugs. It must approve all applications for drugs intended for use on animals.

- *Ministry of Energy, Mines, and Parastate Industries (SEMIP).* The SEMIP directs Vitrium, the umbrella company for the government's pharmaceutical enterprises, which include Proquivemex (collection and sale of barbasco for steroids), Proquivemex Pharmaceuticals (finished pharmaceutical manufacture), and Vitrium (projects for bulk pharmochemicals). Another state enterprise is PRONABIVE, which makes veterinary vaccines and serums.

Other government organizations that affect the pharmaceutical and pharmochemical industries are part of the government's efforts to promote industrial development. These agencies, which primarily offer financial incentives and technological support, include the following:

- *The National Council of Science and Technology (CONACYT),* the organism through which the government channels funds for research and post-graduate education, has a shared risk program for new product research. A few pharmochemical companies have taken advantage of the program, mostly to develop technological improvements to existing manufacturing processes.

- *Innovation-Information-Technology (INFOTEC),* a service-oriented industrial library, has the most complete collection of pharmaceutical and industrial chemical publications in Mexico. A yearly membership fee permits use of the library and services.

- *Nacional Financiera, S.A. (NAFINSA),* the national finance bank, offers low-interest loans for consulting services, plant expansion, and moving away from the Mexico City metropolitan area.

- *Banco de México,* Mexico's central bank, offers low-interest loans to finance export costs, new equipment, technological development, and pollution control.

- *The Mexican Center for Pharmaceutical Research (CEMIFAR),* links Mexican university researchers who do drug formulation development or clinical testing with pharmaceutical and pharmochemical companies that need these services.

The Mexican pharmaceutical and pharmochemical industries are of course affected by legislation, beginning with Mexico's post-revolution constitution. A few of the decrees and laws important to these industries are:

The Political Constitution of the United Mexican States assures all persons the right to health protection. A 1984 amendment guaranteed this right, theoretically bringing the entire population of 80 million under state health care and thus at least doubling the market for drugs. In practice, this amendment simply makes explicit the task begun seventy years ago, of bringing medical care to all. In the past ten years the Mexican government has made special efforts, primarily through the social security system, to place additional segments of the population under state protection. The pharmaceutical industry perceives the effort as an approximately 12 per cent yearly increase in the consumption of pharmaceuticals.

The General Health Law charges the SSA with regulation of the sale of all drugs, the manufacture of finished pharmaceuticals, their import and export, and their publicity—both advertising and labeling.[9] This law is fundamental in the regulatory relationship between the government and the industries.

Foreign investment laws require that pharmaceutical and pharmochemical manufacturing enterprises in Mexico must be at least 51-per-cent Mexican owned. Companies that were in foreign hands when the original law was enacted are exempted, but they may not enter new manufacturing activities. These laws have enabled the government to favor Mexican companies, especially in awarding incentives for producing new pharmochemicals. The fact that the pharmochemical industry has had strong representation from Mexican-owned companies is due primarily to these laws.

Foreign trade regulations have protected Mexico's entire industrial plant for more than 40 years. Since the 1940s, Mexico has required— and rarely granted—import permits for foreign-finished pharmaceuticals. In 1987, certain finished pharmaceuticals (antibiotics, antacids, vitamins) were liberated from this restriction. Although it is too soon to know how this policy will affect the industry, it is doubtful that any imported medicine can compete with Mexico's very low-priced products.

As the bulk pharmaceutical industry grew, protection was also granted to pharmaceutical raw materials. Until late 1985, bulk drugs made in Mexico could be imported only if the Mexican products did not meet standards in quality. Today many drugs may be imported without permits, for the local industry is being protected instead with high import tariffs. These will be lowered gradually now that Mexico is a full member of the General Agreement on Tariffs and Trade (GATT).

The Mexican Social Security Law. IMSS, the institute administering the law, is a major drug purchaser that has long stimulated the industry to produce the drugs it needs. The IMSS restricts its purchases to those items included in the *Cuadro Básico*. It has imposed and enforced high standards of quality for the drugs it receives and for their manufacturing processes. Close informal ties with the U.S. Food and Drug Administration have fostered these actions.

Mexico's patent laws, through amendments adopted some fifteen years ago to exclude product patents for health products, sought to strengthen the Mexican companies and to break monopoly positions of the international firms. Although patents had never been an important mode of protection for domestic industrial know-how, these measures gave impetus to the local practice of formulating drugs that were elsewhere protected by patents. For example, diazepam tablets could be produced and sold even when the trademark product, Valium, was still enjoying exclusive patent rights in most countries in the world. Mexican firms today are manufacturing bulk cimetidine, although Tagamet patents still apply elsewhere.

These patent amendments have kept the international firms from monopolies only in certain selected products, and it is doubtful that they have in fact strengthened Mexican companies. Few of the Mexican companies compete significantly with the international firms on the Mexican market; none of these firms has developed a new pharmochemical; and none has established itself in the international market. The improved marketing and technological position of the leading Mexican-owned companies is due to their excellent administrative and financial management, not to any special advantage they have in the Mexican market.

Technology transfer laws require any Mexican licensee of technology to register its contract with the National Registry for Technology Transfer. Excessive royalties are prohibited, as are exclusive raw material or machinery purchase agreements. The objective is to prevent an unreasonable outflow of foreign exchange and to stimulate Mexican industrial innovation. In the early 1970s, the Registry could point to savings in foreign exchange due to the non-renewal of many old contracts. By the mid-1980s, most Mexican companies regarded the restrictions as irritants that could be circumvented if necessary. However, foreign potential licensors regard the laws as serious impediments to their licensing out to Mexican companies.

The Pharmaceutical Decree of February 23, 1984 amplified price controls and stipulated low profit margins on pharmacy sales of some 500 basic drugs that are included in the government's *Cuadro Básico.* When sold to private pharmacies, these drugs must display their generic names as prominently as their trade names. The use of trade names on the drug packages sold to the government was originally prohibited, but a later modification of the decree now permits such use. Bulk drug prices will be controlled, and special incentives are offered to companies willing to manufacture any of a list of sixty pharmochemicals.[10] The final regulations, published in 1985, permit the inventor of a new chemical substance with pharmacological effect ten years' exemption from the generic labeling requirement and reduce the required prominence of the generic name on a drug package.[11]

The Pharmaceutical Decree attempted to give Mexican consumers a chance to choose between brands of the same drug by requiring the prominent display of the generic name on the label. At the same time, the decree limits profit margins on basic drugs. Mexican laboratories are thus encouraged to compete with transnational companies that sell basic drugs under well-known brands—for example, cimetidine (Tagamet), diazepam (Valium), or furosemide (Lasix). However, since on just these drugs they must reduce their profits, this encouragement is effectively negated.

Three years after the Decree was promulgated, many pharmaceutical laboratories have refused to comply with the generic name provisions of the law. Apparently the government has chosen to ignore this defiance, for no legal actions have yet been filed against the companies.

Through these diverse programs, the Mexican government has had a great deal of success in upgrading the quality of both pharmaceuticals and their manufacturing processes, in increasing the number of

bulk pharmochemicals made in Mexico, in increasing exports of pharmochemicals and finished drugs, in increasing the Mexican component
in the manufacturing processes for pharmochemicals, and in promoting Mexican pharmaceutical research. It has also kept drug prices to a
minimum and reduced what it considered to be excess profits in the
pharmaceutical industry. Mexico is a competent copier and manufacturer of existing pharmochemicals and pharmaceuticals, but it develops neither new products nor novel pharmaceutical forms.

Although the expressed aim of the Mexican government is to
promote and further the development of the pharmaceutical and pharmochemical industries, and the aim of the industries is to contribute to
the development and growth of the health sector in Mexico, relations
between the government and the private firms are contentious. Government officials who deal with these firms tend to view them—
especially the pharmaceutical laboratories—primarily in terms of
what they consider to be excessive profits. There is a pervasive attitude,
based on the history of overpricing and cover-up in the industry, that
the pharmaceutical firms become rich at the expense of patients. The
executives of the pharmaceutical laboratories, for their part, feel un-
justly judged by the government functionaries with whom they deal.
Further, they feel that their industry, which, in contrast to some industries, must invest constantly to meet quality manufacturing standards,
is being penalized by regulations that interfere with their ability to
make a profit.

The principal point of conflict between the two sides is price control of finished drugs. The government has tried to compensate for its
need to keep the costs of medicines low by offering the industries
incentives such as low-interest loans for research and export development, but the price increases it granted in the past have been too small
and too infrequent to satisfy the industry.

The pharmaceutical industry has responded by developing strategies for obtaining financial relief. Of thirty-one companies interviewed in 1985 (both those with majority Mexican and majority foreign
capital), twelve planned to shift their product mix to concentrate on
cosmetics or non-essential popular drugs (cosmetics have no price controls, and drugs considered palliatives are not regulated as strictly);
nine were seeking foreign licenses specifically for high-priced novel
pharmaceuticals; one was curtailing sales to the government; two had
withheld new drugs from the market; and four were shifting to pharmochemicals. Only five companies had no specific plans for dealing
with a situation they saw as threatening to their profits and, in some
cases, their very survival.

In 1985 the pharmaceutical industry complained that the government, in not granting promised regular price increases, had violated a
verbal agreement. In early 1986, after having received price increases

that were months delayed and considerably below those necessary to compensate for their cost increases, over thirty companies—both Mexican and international—raised their drug prices in open violation of the law. This action reflects the desperation of the pharmaceutical industry, which has complained of price controls for years, but has previously maintained a policy of strict adherence to the government regulations. In 1987, however, after a final confrontation on the price issue during which many companies were temporarily closed by the government, a formula was agreed upon for regular increases in the prices of finished products. Although the industry has been satisfied with the accord, it feels that the recent opening to imports of finished pharmaceuticals could be the government's response to the aggressive stance taken by the industry on prices in the winter of 1986–87.

U.S.-Mexican Relations and the Mexican Pharmaceutical Industry

Although in Mexico the assumption on the part of the Mexican press, government, and industry has been that the United States government has a long history of pressuring the Mexican government and its pharmaceutical industry with the object of protecting U.S. interests and the subsidiaries of U.S.-based firms, neither Mexican government officials, nor industrial chamber representatives, nor businessmen in the industry could report any specific incidents of such pressure until 1984. Even in 1970, when the government prohibited the six foreign steroid companies from collecting barbasco and raised the price of that raw material from 2 to 70 pesos per kilo, the U.S. government apparently did not protest. The six foreign companies (three of them U.S. firms) fought that Mexican government action alone—and they lost.

Nevertheless, the Mexicans feel beleaguered, and the case of the 1984 Pharmaceutical Decree illustrates some of the reasons. The pharmaceutical and pharmochemical industries were not, in themselves, a focus for open discussion or disagreement between the United States and Mexico until the promulgation of the Pharmaceutical Decree of 1984, which, among other goals, sought to provide the public at large with the 500 products mentioned on the *Cuadro Básico* at low official prices, at the same time requiring trademark drugs from that list to carry the generic name prominently displayed when sold in pharmacies.

The U.S.-owned companies established in Mexico felt pressured by Mexico's foreign investment laws limiting their expansion into pharmochemicals; by the patent laws, which removed protection from new compounds; by import restrictions that forced some of them to buy from

Mexican manufacturers products that they themselves produce elsewhere; and by price controls. They sought through the Pharmaceutical Manufacturers Association, an organization of U.S. companies, the support of the U.S. government, which was apparently sympathetic.

When the original 1984 Decree was slightly amended in April 1985 to permit the "innovator" of a new drug substance freedom from the requirement of generic labeling for ten years as well as to reduce the required prominence of the generic name on a drug package, many industry-watchers felt that the Mexican government had conceded to pressure from the Reagan administration, perhaps in exchange for favorable treatment on some other issue. Other concessions were included in that amendment; for example, brand names on products sold to the government—originally prohibited—are now allowed.

In the relationship between Mexico and the United States, the principal motivation on each side is of course economic. That is, each country acts and reacts according to its perception of its own economic benefits. But the observer who seeks only an economic explanation of the U.S.-Mexican difficulties can neither predict nor understand the events he sees, for the assumptions on which the politics of each country rest are quite different.

The discussions and comments on this case by both industry and government representatives illustrate fundamental differences in the postures of the two countries in their views of themselves and in their outlook toward the world around them. This difference in perspective underlies nearly every complaint of lack of understanding and cooperation by the other party.

The Mexican position on this issue—as on others involving international relations—derives from the principles of its 1910–20 revolution. Mexico's internal politics, in keeping with these principles, generally support measures that favor the underprivileged. In its dealings with other nations, Mexico attempts to apply this same approach. When dealing with the United States, however, Mexico sees itself as the underdog, not as an equal. What Mexico expects from the United States is respect for its rights as a sovereign nation and tolerance and sympathy for its efforts to develop; it does not expect its neighbor to hinder or oppose the measures it might take to increase its industrial strength.

The U.S. approach, on the other hand, appears to derive from its own revolution—from the statement in the Declaration of Independence that says that all men are created equal. U.S. law is grounded in the precepts that protect individual, as opposed to class, rights. The United States, even in its bilateral relations, does not easily admit to differences in status between two discussants, and it follows that it tends to give concessions only in return for those offered by its counterpart. It considers fair play to be treatment under the law for its companies on a basis equal to that of the sovereign nation's companies. Although these almost unconscious assumptions may be fortified or diluted by the political philosophies in vogue in either country at any given moment (Democrats versus Republicans, government management versus free enterprise, free government spending versus tight budget, etc.), the basic outlook of each side is constant.

From this suggested perspective, the emotions aroused by the promulgation of the Mexican Pharmaceutical Decree can be understood. Mexico saw itself defending its local industry against the greater power of its Northern neighbor and the developed nations in general. As a lesser power, it felt completely within its sovereign rights to do so; it had no reason—either from its experience with foreign reaction to previous Mexican protectionist legislation, or from its own view of the world—to foresee an aggressive response from the U.S. government. This view underestimated the depth of feeling in the international industry, and in the United States in particular, with regard to the treatment of foreign investors in this industry.

The United States, on the other hand, basing its global view on its own political principles—and on what it saw as an erosion of its international competitiveness—felt completely within its rights to insist on equal treatment for U.S. companies in Mexico. It countered with an aggressive rejoinder—pressure on the Mexican government to change the Decree—to what it saw as discrimination that the U.S. government does not apply to foreign companies operating in the United States.

Neither side will soon forget the landmark controversy surrounding the Pharmaceutical Decree. The United States has received a clear warning that the advanced developing nations intend to promote their technological development in any way they can, including favoring local industries; licensing, copying, or developing technology; and adopting legislation that is in accord with their own economic interests and political principles.

Mexico, in turn, was subjected to an affront over a key piece of social legislation. By exerting such pressure, its stronger neighbor has sent the message that Mexico's considerable development is now seen as important and potentially threatening to the United States, which will seek a reciprocal negotiation to resolve problems posed by Mexican actions that affect U.S. interests.

Many of the conflicts that divide our countries are deeply rooted in differences in political philosophy. We can only hope to keep these differences from interfering with our collaboration on matters of mutual interest. Legislators and officials in both countries must be alert to the effects their actions will have on their neighbor nation. Even more important, they must measure the consequences of their actions in terms of their final effect—after their neighbor's reaction—on their own country.

If U.S. policymakers take into account Mexico's history, and especially the revolutionary basis of its present-day politics, they can understand Mexico's viewpoint and can thus predict the possible results of a particular gesture on their part. Conversely, Mexican policymakers can foresee U.S. reactions and behavior if they include in their evaluation of the circumstances an awareness of the traditional U.S. emphasis on individual, as opposed to class, interests. A constructive working relationship is necessary to both Mexico and the United States. Diplomatic disputes can be minimized if policymakers on each side see their own country's interests clearly, recognize and understand the viewpoint of the other country, and evaluate the potential results of their statements or actions in those terms.

Notes

[1] National Registry of the Pharmaceutical Industry, Ministry of Commerce and Industrial Development (SECOFI), Mexico City.

[2] Ibid.

[3] SECOFI.

[4] The General Health Council (Consejo de Salubridad General), *Cuadro básico de medicamentos del sector salud* (Mexico, D.F., 1984).

[5] John J. Sciarra, *The State of the Pharmaceutical Industry in Mexico* (unpublished paper, U.N. Industrial Development Organization, 1974).

[6] Although the patent law has been changed recently to provide broader protection for intellectual property, the changes will not apply to pharmaceuticals and some other items of social importance until 1997. *Diario Oficial,* January 16, 1987.

[7] Gary Gereffi, *The Pharmaceutical Industry and Dependency in the Third World* (Princeton, N.J.: Princeton University Press, 1983).

[8] National Registry of the Pharmaceutical Industry, op. cit.

[9] *Diario Oficial,* February 7, 1984.

[10] Ibid., February 23, 1984.

[11] Ibid., April 2, 1985.

[12] Ibid., February 23, 1984.

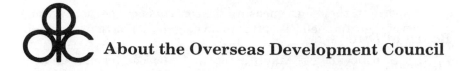 **About the Overseas Development Council**

The Overseas Development Council is a private, non-profit organization established in 1969 for the purpose of increasing American understanding of the economic and social problems confronting the developing countries and of how their development progress is related to U.S. interests. Toward this end, the Council functions as a center for policy research and analysis, a forum for the exchange of ideas, and a resource for public education. The Council's current program of work encompasses four major issue areas: trade and industrial policy, international finance and investment, development strategies and development cooperation, and U.S. foreign policy and the developing countries. ODC's work is used by policy makers in the Executive Branch and the Congress, journalists, and those concerned about U.S.-Third World relations in corporate and bank management, international and non-governmental organizations, universities, and educational and action groups focusing on specific development issues. ODC's program is funded by foundations, corporations, and private individuals; its policies are determined by a governing Board and Council. In selecting issues and shaping its work program, ODC is also assisted by a standing Program Advisory Committee.

Victor H. Palmieri is Chairman of the ODC, and J. Wayne Fredericks is Vice Chairman. The Council's President is John W. Sewell.

Overseas Development Council
1717 Massachusetts Ave., N.W.
Washington, D.C. 20036
Tel. (202) 234-8701

Board of Directors

ODC Program Advisory Committee

The Editors

The United States and Mexico: Face to Face With New Technology is the eighth volume in the Overseas Development Council's series of policy books, U.S.-Third World Policy Perspectives. The co-editors of this series—often collaborating with guest editors contributing to the series—are Richard E. Feinberg and Valeriana Kallab. Cathryn L. Thorup is guest editor of this volume.

Cathryn L. Thorup is the director of the U.S.-Mexico Project of the Overseas Development Council. Prior to joining ODC in 1980, she spent six years in Mexico, studying and working as a journalist for the Mexican news magazine *Razones*. She has written extensively on U.S. policymaking toward Mexico, conflict management in U.S.-Mexican relations, regional security, and Mexican economic and political reform. Ms. Thorup is a member of the Board of Directors of the Consortium for U.S. Research Programs for Mexico (PROFMEX).

Valeriana Kallab is vice president and director of publications of the Overseas Development Council and series co-editor of the ODC's U.S.-Third World Policy Perspectives series. She has been responsible for ODC's published output since 1972. Before joining ODC, she was a research editor and writer on international economic issues at the Carnegie Endowment for International Peace in New York.

Richard E. Feinberg, vice president of the Overseas Development Council, is co-editor of and a frequent contributing author in the Policy Perspectives series. Before joining ODC in 1981, Dr. Feinberg served as the Latin American specialist on the Policy Planning Staff of the U.S. Department of State, and as an international economist in the Treasury Department and with the House Banking Committee. Dr. Feinberg is the author of numerous books as well as journal and newspaper articles on U.S. foreign policy, Latin American politics, and international economic and financial issues.

Contributing Authors

Alan Madian, an economist, is managing director of Erb & Madian Inc., an economic and financial consulting firm, and of Lafayatte Capital Corporation, an investment banking firm that specializes in transnational acquisitions and divestitures. He formerly served as principal associate of Robert R. Nathan Associates, and as economic advisor to the Governor of New York and to the U.S. Senate Antitrust Subcommittee. He has been a consultant to the World Bank, the Asian Development Bank, the United Nations, and to governments in the Middle East, East Asia, Latin America, and the Caribbean. Dr. Madian was on the faculties of the London School of Economics, Oxford University, New York University, the University of Rochester, Columbia University, and the University of Calfornia, Berkeley. He is the author of articles and monographs on international investment, employment, and trade.

James K. Galbraith is associate professor at the Lyndon B. Johnson School of Public Affairs, University of Texas at Austin. He served as executive director of the Joint Economic Committee, Congress of the United States, from 1981-83. He is the author of articles on economic policy in such journals as *The Journal of Post-Keynesian Economics, The Journal of Economic Education, Challenge, Working Papers Magazine*, and elsewhere. He is a member of the Program Advisory Committee of the Overseas Development Council.

Mauricio de Maria y Campos is Mexican Under Secretary for Industrial Development in the Ministry of Commerce and Industrial Development. He has also held the post of Director-General of Foreign Investment in the Ministry of Commerce and Industrial Development, Executive Secretary of the National Commission for Foreign Investment, and Director-General of Fiscal Promotion in the Ministry of Finance and Public Credit. Recently, he was nominated to be a member of the special group of advisors to the director-general of UNIDO. He is an associate member of the Center for Survey Studies of the Javier Barros Sierra Foundation. In addition, he has served as Coordinator of Industrial Development of the Institute for Social, Economic, and Political Studies of the Institutional Revolutionary Party (PRI). He has published articles in Mexico and abroad on foreign trade, industrial policy, transfer of technology, foreign investment, the pharmaceutical industry, and fiscal incentives.

James P. Womack is the research director of the International Motor Vehicle Program at the Massachusetts Institute of Technology. This four-year, fourteen-country study of the world motor vehicle industry includes government and industry participants from the United States and Mexico. Dr. Womack was the co-author of *The Future of the Automobile* (MIT Press, 1984), the final report of a previous MIT program on the international motor industry.

Susan Walsh Sanderson is associate professor at the School of Management of Rensselaer Polytechnic Institute. Prior to this appointment, she was a senior research associate at the Conference Board, and a faculty member of the School of Urban and Public Affairs at Carnegie-Mellon University. Her published work covers a wide variety of topics related to social policy, trade, and technology. She has carried out research on social and economic policy at El Colegio de México in Mexico City. Dr. Sanderson's related publications include: "Impacts of Flexible Assembly Systems on Offshore Assembly and Future Manufacturing Locations," (with Timothy Ballenger, Gregory Williams, and Brian J.L. Berry) in *Regional Studies*, 1987; "American Industry Can Go Home Again," in *Across the Board*, 1986. She is author of *Land Reform in Mexico: 1919-1980*, published by Academic Press in its Series on Social Discontinuity, 1984.

M. Patricia Fernández Kelly is a research scientist at the Institute for Policy Studies and an associate professor, on a part-time basis, at the Department of Sociology at the Johns Hopkins University. She is the author of *For We Are Sold, I and My People: Women and Industry in Mexico's Frontier* (Albany: State University of New York Press, 1983). With filmmaker Lorraine Gray, she co-produced "The Global Assembly Line," an award-winning documentary exploring the effects of economic internationalization in the Philippines, along the U.S.-Mexico border, and in the United States.

Cassio Luiselli Fernández, an agricultural economist, is currently deputy director of the Interamerican Institute for Cooperation on Agriculture (IICA) in Costa Rica. He has served as Advisor to the President (1976-1980), General Coordinator of the Mexican food system (SAM) (1980-1982), and Deputy Director of the Economic Commission for Latin America (ECLA/CEPAL). He has taught at the Centro de Investigación y Docencia Económica (CIDE) and the National Autonomous University of Mexico (UNAM). The author of several publications on agricultural economics and food policy, Dr. Luiselli's most recent book (co-edited with Bruce F. Johnston) is *U.S.-Mexico Agricultural Relations* (1987).

Joan Brodovsky is an independent consultant in Mexico. She specializes in market research, technology transfer, and information searches relating to the pharmaceutical and pharmochemical industries. Her clients include Mexican government institutions and both Mexican and international manufacturing firms. Before becoming an independent consultant in 1982, she held the post of program manager for the pharmaceutical industry at INFOTEC, a Mexican government institution dedicated to providing technical information for industry.

A New Series from the Overseas Development Council

U.S.-THIRD WORLD POLICY PERSPECTIVES

Richard E. Feinberg and Valeriana Kallab, Series Editors

"These volumes have the virtue of combining cogent and comprehensive analysis with constructive and practical policy recommendations."

—Lawrence A. Veit
Brown Brothers Harriman & Co.

In this series, the Overseas Development Council singles out for policy analysis and action recommendation issues that merit priority attention on the U.S.-Third World policy agenda. Each volume offers a variety of perspectives, by prominent policy analysts in the United States as well as other countries, on different facets of a selected policy theme. The series addresses itself to all who take an interest in U.S.-Third World relations and U.S. participation in international development cooperation—in the U.S. government, Congress, international institutions, U.S. corporations and banks, private U.S. education and action organizations, and academic institutions.

Richard E. Feinberg is vice president of the Overseas Development Council. He previously served as the Latin American specialist on the Policy Planning Staff of the U.S. Department of State, and as an international economist in the Treasury Department and with the House Banking Committee. His most recent book is *The Intemperate Zone: The Third World Challenge to U.S. Foreign Policy* (1983).

Valeriana Kallab is vice president and director of publications of the Overseas Development Council. Before joining ODC in 1972, she was a research editor and writer on international economic issues with the Carnegie Endowment for International Peace in New York.

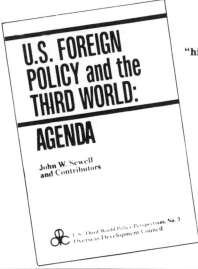

U.S. FOREIGN POLICY and the THIRD WORLD:

AGENDA

John W. Sewell
and Contributors

U.S.-Third World Policy Perspectives, No. 3
Overseas Development Council

"high-quality analysis has made ODC's *Agenda* necessary reading for anyone interested in American foreign policy or development issues"

—Joseph S. Nye
John F. Kennedy School of Government
Harvard University

ODC's Agenda— now part of this series

U.S. POLICY AND THE THIRD WORLD: AGENDA 1988

John W. Sewell and contributors

The Overseas Development Council's 1988 *Agenda*—the eleventh of its well-known annual assessments of U.S. policy toward the developing countries—contributes uniquely to the ongoing debate on U.S. jobs and trade competition with other nations. The study highlights important aspects of these issues that bear on Third World development and U.S. relations with developing countries. Is it possible to enhance U.S. competitiveness and to increase U.S. exports and jobs so that growth and progress in the developing countries are also promoted rather than damaged?

Economic relations between industrial and developing countries may be undergoing fundamental shifts as a result of changes in industrial technology and organization. These changes may affect different parts of the developing world in different ways. The contributors to this volume assess how technological advances and changes in the organization of production are affecting international markets. Have commodity markets shifted against producers? Will the new technologies and methods of production erode the labor-cost advantage of developing countries? Are patterns of demand within the developed world changing as populations stabilize and age, and if so, with what impact on developing-country exports? The authors explore the implications of these and other trends for U.S.-Third World interdependence and U.S. policy.

Contents:

Overview: The Competitiveness Crisis in U.S.-Third World Relations

Manuel Castells and Laura Tyson—High Technology, North-South Relationships, and Economic Policy: The Strategic Choices Ahead

Ray Marshall—The Shifting Structure of Global Employment

Raymond F. Mikesell—The Changing Demand for Raw Materials

Robert L. Paarlberg—U.S. Agricultural Trade with the Developing World: A Formula for Joint Gains

Jonathan D. Aronson—Trade in Services and Development

Stephanie Y. Wilson—Poverty and Protectionism

Stuart K. Tucker—Statistical Annexes: U.S.-Third World Interdependence, 1988

John W. Sewell has been president of the Overseas Development Council since January, 1980. From 1977 to 1979, as the Council's executive vice president, he directed ODC's programs of research and public education. Prior to joining the Council in 1971, Mr. Sewell directed the communications program of the Brookings Institution. He also served in the Foreign Service of the United States.

A contributor to past *Agenda* assessments, he is co-author of *Rich Country Interests and Third World Development* and *The Ties That Bind: U.S. Interests in Third World Development.* He is a frequent author and lecturer on U.S. relations with the developing countries.

U.S.-Third World Policy Perspectives No. 9
ISBN: 0-88738-196-0 (cloth) $19.95
ISBN: 0-88738-718-7 (paper) $12.95
January 1988   **256 pp.**

BETWEEN TWO WORLDS:
THE WORLD BANK'S NEXT DECADE

Richard E. Feinberg and contributors

In the midst of the global debt and adjustment crises, the World Bank has been challenged to become the leading agency in North-South finance and development. The many dimensions of this challenge—which must be comprehensively addressed by the Bank's new president assuming office in mid-1986—are the subject of this important volume.

As mediator between international capital markets and developing countries, the World Bank will be searching for ways to renew the flow of private credit and investment to Latin America and Africa. And as the world's premier development agency, the Bank can help formulate growth strategies appropriate to the 1990s.

The Bank's ability to design and implement a comprehensive response to these global needs is threatened by competing objectives and uncertain priorities. Can the Bank design programs attractive to private investors that also serve the very poor? Can it emphasize efficiency while transferring technologies that maximize labor absorption? Can it more aggressively condition loans on policy reforms without attracting the criticism that has accompanied IMF programs?

The contributors to this volume assess the role that the World Bank can play in the period ahead. They argue for new financial and policy initiatives and for new conceptual approaches to development, as well as for a restructuring of the Bank, as it takes on new, systemic responsibilities in the next decade.

Contents:

Richard E. Feinberg—Overview: The Future of the World Bank
Gerald K. Helleiner—The Changing Content of Conditionality
Joan M. Nelson—The Diplomacy of the Policy-Based Lending:
    Leverage or Dialogue?
Sheldon Annis—The Shifting Ground of Poverty Lending
Howard Pack—Employment Generation Through Changing Technology
John F. H. Purcell and Michelle B. Miller—The World Bank and Private International
    Capital
Charles R. Blitzer—Financing the IBRD and IDA

Richard E. Feinberg is vice president of the Overseas Development Council and co-editor of the U.S.-Third World Policy Perspectives series. From 1977 to 1979, Feinberg was Latin American specialist on the policy planning staff of the U.S. Department of State. He has also served as an international economist in the U.S. Treasury Department and with the House Banking Committee. He is currently also adjunct professor of international finance at the Georgetown University School of Foreign Service. Feinberg is the author of numerous books as well as journal and newspaper articles on U.S. foreign policy, Latin American politics, and international economics. His most recent book is *The Intemperate Zone: The Third World Challenge to U.S. Foreign Policy* (1983).

ISBN: 0-88738-123-5 (cloth)   **$19.95**
ISBN: 0-88738-665-2 (paper)   **$12.95**
June 1986   **208 pp.**

INVESTING IN DEVELOPMENT:
NEW ROLES FOR PRIVATE CAPITAL?

Theodore H. Moran and contributors

The tone of the debate about foreign direct investment in Third World development has changed dramatically since the 1970s. There are expectations in both North and South that multinational corporations can play a key role in restoring growth, replacing aid, providing capital to relieve the burden on commercial bank lending, and (together with the private sectors in the local economies) lead to an era of healthier and more balanced growth.

To what extent are these expectations justified? This volume provides a reassessment of the impact of multinational corporate operations on Third World development. It covers not only direct equity investment in natural resources and manufacturing, but non-equity arrangements extending to agriculture and other sectors as well. It examines whether the efforts of less developed countries to attract and control multinational corporations have constituted a serious "distortion" of trade that threatens jobs in the home nations. It analyzes the link between international companies and the "umbrella" of World Bank co-financing as a mechanism to reduce risk. Finally, it attempts to estimate how much of the "gap" in commercial bank lending might plausibly be filled by direct corporate investment over the next decade.

In each case, it draws policy conclusions for host governments, for home governments (focused particularly on the United States), for multilateral institutions such as the World Bank and the agencies of the United Nations, and for the multinational firms themselves.

Contents

Theodore H. Moran—Overview: The Future of Foreign Direct Investment in the Third World
Dennis J. Encarnation and Louis T. Wells, Jr.—Evaluating Foreign Investment
Vincent Cable and Bishakha Mukheriee—Foreign Investment in Low-Income Developing Countries
David J. Glover—Multinational Corporations and Third World Agriculture
Charles P. Oman—New Forms of Investment in Developing Countries
Stephen Guisinger—Host-Country Policies to Attract and Control Foreign Investment
David J. Goldsbrough—Investment Trends and Prospects: The Link with Bank Lending

Theodore H. Moran is director of Georgetown University's Landegger Program in International Business Diplomacy as well as professor and member of the Executive Council of the Georgetown University School of Business Administration. A former member of the Policy Planning Staff of the Department of State with responsibilities including investment issues, Dr. Moran has since 1971 been a consultant to corporations, governments, and multilateral agencies on investment strategy, international negotiations, and political risk assessment. His publications include many articles and five major books on the issues explored in this new volume. He is a member of the ODC Program Advisory Committee.

ISBN: 0-88738-044-3 (cloth)   **$19.95**
ISBN: 0-88738-644-X (paper)   **$12.95**

DEVELOPMENT STRATEGIES RECONSIDERED

John P. Lewis and Valeriana Kallab, editors

> "First-rate, comprehensive analysis—presented in a manner that makes it extremely valuable to policy makers."
> —Robert R. Nathan
> Robert Nathan Associates

Important differences of opinion are emerging about the national strategies best suited for advancing economic growth and equity in the difficult global adjustment climate of the late 1980s.

Proponents of the "new orthodoxy"—the perspective headquartered at the World Bank and favored by the Reagan administration as well as by a number of other bilateral donor governments—are "carrying forward with redoubled vigor the liberalizing, pro-market strains of the thinking of the 1960s and 1970s. They are very mindful of the limits of government." And they are "emphatic in advocating export-oriented growth to virtually all comers."

Other prominent experts question whether a standardized prescription of export-led growth can meet the needs of big low-income countries in the latter 1980s as well as it did those of small and medium-size middle-income countries in the 1960s and 1970s. They are concerned about the special needs of low-income Africa. And they see a great deal of unfinished business under the heading of poverty and equity.

In this volume, policy syntheses are proposed to reconcile the goals of growth, equity, and adjustment; to strike fresh balances between agricultural and industrial promotion and between capital and other inputs; and to reflect the interplay of democracy and development.

Contents:
John P. Lewis—Development Promotion: A Time for Regrouping
Irma Adelman—A Poverty-Focused Approach to Development Policy
John W. Mellor—Agriculture on the Road to Industrialization
Jagdish N. Bhagwati—Rethinking Trade Strategy
Leopoldo Solis and Aurelio Montemayor—A Mexican View of the Choice Between Inward and Outward Orientation
Colin I. Bradford, Jr.—East Asian "Models": Myths and Lessons
Alex Duncan—Aid Effectiveness in Raising Adaptive Capacity in the Low-Income countries
Atul Kohli—Democracy and Development

John P. Lewis, guest editor of this volume, is professor of economics and international affairs at Princeton University's Woodrow Wilson School of Public and International Affairs. He is simultaneously senior advisor to the Overseas Development Council and chairman of its Program Advisory Committee. From 1979 to 1981, Mr. Lewis was chairman of the OECD's Development Assistance Committee. He has served as a member of the U.N. Committee for Development Planning. For many years, he has alternated between academia and government posts, with collateral periods of association with The Brookings Institution and The Ford Foundation.

ISBN: 0-88738-044-1 (cloth)   **$19.95**
ISBN: 0-87855-991-4 (paper)   **$12.95**
1986   **208 pp.**

HARD BARGAINING AHEAD: U.S. TRADE POLICY AND DEVELOPING COUNTRIES

Ernest H. Preeg and contributors

U.S.-Third World trade relations are at a critical juncture. Trade conflicts are exploding as subsidies, import quotas, and "voluntary" export restraints have become commonplace. The United States is struggling with record trade and budget deficits. Developing countries, faced with unprecedented debt problems, continue to restrain imports and stimulate exports.

For both national policies and future multilateral negotiations, the current state of the North-South trade relationship presents a profound dilemma. Existing problems of debt and unemployment cannot be solved without growth in world trade. While many developing countries would prefer an export-oriented development strategy, access to industrialized-country markets will be in serious doubt if adjustment policies are not implemented. Consequently, there is an urgent need for more clearly defined mutual objectives and a strengthened policy framework for trade between the industrialized and the developing countries.

In this volume, distinguished practitioners and academics identify specific policy objectives for the United States on issues that will be prominent in the new round of GATT negotiations.

Contents:

Ernest H. Preeg—Overview: An Agenda for U.S. Trade Policy Toward Developing Countries
William E. Brock—Statement: U.S. Trade Policy Toward Developing Countries
Anne O. Krueger and Constantine Michalopoulos—Developing-Country Trade Policies and the International Economic System
Henry R. Nau—The NICs in a New Trade Round
C. Michael Aho—U.S. Labor-Market Adjustment and Import Restrictions
John D. A. Cuddy—Commodity Trade
Adebayo Adedeji—Special Measures for the Least Developed and Other Low-Income Countries
Sidney Weintraub—Selective Trade Liberalization and Restriction
Stuart K. Tucker—Statistical Annexes

Ernest H. Preeg, a career foreign service officer and recent visiting fellow at the Overseas Development Council, has had long experience in trade policy and North-South economic relations. He was a member of the U.S. delegation to the GATT Kennedy Round of negotiations and later wrote a history and analysis of those negotiations, *Traders and Diplomats* (The Brookings Institution, 1969). Prior to serving as American ambassador to Haiti (1981-82), he was deputy chief of mission in Lima, Peru (1977-80), and deputy secretary of state for international finance and development (1976-77).

ISBN: 0-88738-043-3 (cloth)
ISBN: 0-87855-987-6 (paper)
1985

$19.95
$12.95
220 pp.

ADJUSTMENT CRISIS IN THE THIRD WORLD

Richard E. Feinberg and Valeriana Kallab, editors

"major contribution to the literature on the adjustment crisis"
—B. T. G. Chidzero
  Minister of Finance, Economic Planning
    and Development Government of Zimbabwe

"The adjustment crisis book has really stirred up some excitement here"
—Peter P. Waller
  German Development Institute (Berlin)

Contents:

Richard E. Feinberg—The Adjustment Imperative and U.S. Policy
Albert Fishlow—The Debt Crisis: Round Two Ahead?
Tony Killick, Graham Bird, Jennifer Sharpley, and Mary Sutton—
  The IMF: Case for a Change in Emphasis
Stanley Please—The World Bank: Lending for Structural Adjustment
Joan M. Nelson—The Politics of Stabilization
Colin I. Bradford, Jr.—The NICs: Confronting U.S. "Autonomy"
Riordan Roett—Brazil's Debt Crisis
Lance Taylor—Mexico's Adjustment in the 1980's: Look Back Before Leaping Ahead
DeLisle Worrell—Central America and the Caribbean: Adjustment in Small, Open
  Economies

ISBN: 0-88738-040-9 (cloth)	**$19.95**
ISBN: 0-87855-988-4 (paper)	**$12.95**
1984	**220 pp.**

UNCERTAIN FUTURE: COMMERCIAL BANKS AND THE THIRD WORLD

Richard E. Feinberg and Valeriana Kallab, editors

"useful short papers by people of differing backgrounds who make quite different kinds of suggestions about how banks, governments and international bodies ought to behave in the face of the continuing debt difficulties"
—*Foreign Affairs*

Contents:

Richard E. Feinberg—Overview: Restoring Confidence in International Credit Markets
Lawrence J. Brainard—More Lending to the Third World? A Banker's View
Karin Lissakers—Bank Regulation and International Debt
Christine A. Bogdanowicz-Bindert and Paul M. Sacks—The Role of Information:
  Closing the Barn Door?
George J. Clark—Foreign Banks in the Domestic Markets of Developing Countries
Catherine Gwin—The IMF and the World Bank: Measures to Improve the System
Benjamin J. Cohen—High Finance, High Politics

ISBN: 0-88738-041-7 (cloth)	**$19.95**
ISBN: 0-87855-989-2 (paper)	**$12.95**
1984	**144 pp.**